ECONOMIC
GROWTH AND DEVELOPMENT:
THE LESS DEVELOPED
COUNTRIES

ECONOMIC GROWTH AND DEVELOPMENT: THE LESS DEVELOPED COUNTRIES

By

EVA GARZOUZI

Associate Professor of Economics
Ithaca College

VANTAGE PRESS

NEW YORK   WASHINGTON   HOLLYWOOD

FIRST EDITION

*All rights reserved, including the right of
reproduction in whole or in part in any form.*

Published by Vantage Press, Inc.
516 West 34th Street, New York, New York 10001

Manufactured in the United States of America

Standard Book No. 533-00508-6

Introduction

As it became obvious that structural change and
accelerated sustained growth - the basic ingredients of
economic development - in tradition-bound societies could
not be achieved as fast as the promotors of the "Revolution of Rising Expectations" wished, the zeal for economic
development of the immediate post-World War II period re-
ceded.   In the wake of a certain disillusionment, reports
on the results and prospects of economic development have
been critical of much that had been considered elementary
in formulating and implementing development policies.
But neither the thesis of the vicious circle of poverty
and stagnation, nor the concept of the widening gap between the rich and the poor countries provide a satisfac-
tory explanation of the disappointing results of "induced
economic development" in most of the Third World.   New
approaches are indicated and a reexamination of basic
ideas and theories are in order.   The present study of
development economics offers new approaches.   Based on
almost a generation's experience in development economics,
Professor Garzouzi's book provides the adequate measure
of balance and perspective required to approach the
intricate and multifaceted aspects of that field.

Federal Reserve Bank of New York   J. O. Ronall

Foreword

During many years of teaching the course on Economic Growth and Development, I have always been pleasantly surprised by the interest shown by students in the developing countries of this world: they bring to the study of the subject a refreshing sense of purpose, a questioning mind and a desire to understand the fundamental reasons at the root of the problems involved.

The most important aspect of the study of Economic Development, in the view of this author, is how to find the best way that the less developed countries can help themselves to a better standard of living. One way to this end is to formulate their problems in practical terms and to use yardsticks and tools of analysis readily available to them and easy to handle by their policy makers. An attempt to describe the conditions of underdevelopment and to find practical means of treating them is what this book is trying to achieve. For students and readers with a basic knowledge of economics it is a work they can understand; for researchers it provides basic data they can use.

The manuscript of the book was used in the classroom for three years and my appreciation goes to the many students whose genuine interest in my work was a challenge to me. I am particularly thankful to my good friend Jo Ronall who also put the first part to the test of the classroom, to my colleague Ira Brous for reading the manuscript and making suggestions, and to Doreen and Geoff Scanlan who with unrelenting effort marshalled the final copy to the Publishers.

Ithaca, New York   Eva Garzouzi
April 1972

ECONOMIC GROWTH AND DEVELOPMENT:

THE LESS DEVELOPED COUNTRIES

Table of Contents

Table of Contents (cont'd)

List of Tables

List of Tables (cont'd)

Maps

ECONOMIC GROWTH AND DEVELOPMENT: THE LESS DEVELOPED COUNTRIES

PART I

BASIC CONCEPTS AND PRACTICAL ASPECTS

Part I includes an introduction to the subject of economic development, defining its basic concepts, and a study of its practical aspects from both the domestic and the international points of view.

Chapters one through three define economic development and study the various ways of achieving it, by comparing the past growth patterns of the presently developed nations with the conditions and future prospects of the developing ones. Then, chapters four and five set forth the basic growth theories and development models which provide the framework for the treatment of the subject of economic development in general and more particularly for its application in the forthcoming regional studies.

Domestic aspects are covered by chapters six through eight which study respectively the role of agriculture, the problems of industrialization and the mix of monetary and fiscal policies required for development. The international aspects include the contribution which can be made by foreign trade and the impact of foreign investments, technical assistance as well as foreign economic aid; these are covered by chapters nine and ten.

The coverage is basic and by no means exhaustive: it is meant, rather, to acquaint the reader with the subject and to induce further investigation and research, for which a large choice of references is given at the end of every chapter.

CHAPTER I

THE MEANING OF ECONOMIC DEVELOPMENT

It has become usual in modern textbooks to use
the words economic growth in connection with developed
countries, and economic development in connection with
underdeveloped nations.   The distinction which may have
been one of semantics at the beginning, is now not only
condoned by usage but has acquired real significance.
A brief explanation appears, therefore, to be called for.
First, both terms are meant to refer to an increase in a
country's yearly production of goods and services - an increase which occurs at a rate higher than the rate of population growth.   So that if total output is divided by
total population, the result, which is the per capita
gross national product, should show an increase from one
year to another.   If there is no increase in output, then
there is neither development nor growth.   Secondly, the
specific use of the two terms stems from differentials in
economic structure and potential for development between
nations.   For instance, at any point of time, the degree
of economic maturity may greatly differ between one economy and another.   This latter point will be easier to understand when the two terms are defined.

Growth and Development Defined

Economic Growth.   The increase in either total
or per capita gross national product[1], taken by itself,
is what is meant by economic growth.   Almost by definition, the term applies to countries which have already
reached a stage in the development of their capital stock

---

[1] total national output of goods and services, inclusive of
depreciation, valued at market price.

of productive capacity which enables them to increase their output, merely by expanding production of capital equipment. In such countries, capital formation has been taking place over a number of decades, or centuries, endowing them with capital equipment such as factories and plants, as well as social overhead capital (S.O.C.). The latter term includes the infrastructure for development, e.g. power stations, means of transport and communications, bridges and dams, etc...as well as social services such as schools, training centers, hospitals and the like.

In other words, these countries are ready for production on a gradually increasing scale: they have reached or are about to reach the stage of economies of scale in production which make sustained growth possible. Economic growth in developed countries is, therefore, a phenomenon of the twentieth century; it is one on which economists, statesmen and businessmen in such countries keep a close watch in order to make sure that levels of production, employment and income are such that they not only provide the yearly increasing population with all its needs in goods and services, but with employment for its growing labor force; thus gradually leading to an improvement in its standard of living. To realize this objective, output must grow at a rate higher than that of the increase in population. Hence the emphasis on economic growth involves primarily a concern for a high level of employment of both capital and labor, so that the nation may realize its full potential.

Economic Development. In its present connotation and use, development includes all of what has been said about growth plus a change in the economic structure of a country. In order to increase its output, a nation must have the productive capacity to do so; if its economic structure is such that its capacity for output is limited, for instance, if it is an agrarian economy still in the early stages of industrialization, it has to start by building up its productive capacity before it can sizably increase its output of goods and services. This means that it will be allocating more of its natural resources and factors of production to the manufacturing of capital goods and to the building up of its social capital. In actual practice, this would amount to a transfer of labor and capital inputs from the agricultural to the industrial sector and a consequent change in resource allocation and output.

This process of change or "transformation" is reflected on the one hand in the pattern of income-elasticities of demand for goods - both in consumers markets and in factor markets - and, on the other hand, in the marginal saving propensities of the various strata of the population. These two points are very important and should be fully taken into consideration in any study of developing countries. They mark the transition of an economy from the primary stage (agricultural and pastoral), to the secondary (manufacturing, mining and construction) and tertiary (transport and communications, trade, government, personal and domestic services) stages. This transition paves the way to economic growth - i.e. to an increase in output at a rate higher than that of population increase - while providing the means to achieve such growth. It can be said, therefore, that economic development involves a change in economic structure first and then an increase in output. It is a dual process, more comprehensive than simply that of economic growth.

Relative and Absolute Degrees of Development

Because underdevelopment results in poverty, the
two terms are often mistakingly considered to be synonymous. A country may be rich in resources, but until such
resources are adequately developed, its inhabitants will
have a low standard of living. However, this does not
mean that the country is poor; it is just underdeveloped.
For example, before the discovery of large oil reserves in
their soil, both Libya and Kuwait were considered poor
countries: Libya was a vast expanse of pasture land
sparsely inhabited except for a few coastal towns, and
Kuwait, just a barren desert roamed by nomadic tribes.
In both countries the population was formerly poor but the
countries were not; now both have thriving economies and
their per capita share of national output is among the
highest in the world. However, while the lack of resources does aggravate the extent of underdevelopment,
there are examples in the history of mankind of nations
which have achieved a high level of civilization and material well-being while almost completely lacking in natural resources. The best example of such countries is
Switzerland which has reached its present state of development by means of the industry of its people and by chan-
nelling the snow on its mountain tops into a source of
cheap energy.

The degree of economic development is a relative
concept in more than one sense; it is also an absolute
one. First, we judge a country's progress by comparison
with the degree of achievement of another country. Second, a brief glance at the underdeveloped countries of the
world will reveal that the degree of underdevelopment
greatly differs between one country and another.

Consequently, a conventional line of demarcation - based
on certain specific yardsticks - has been established in
order to distinguish the developed from the developing
nations of the world.   So that, if the degree of development as such is relative, its quantitative measurement in
absolute terms is carried out according to certain criteria or economic indicators.   It is a case in which ordinal
measurement is based on cardinal magnitudes.

The Measurement of Development

To gauge a nation's ability to satisfy its people's needs in goods and services and to go on increasing
the supply, we take a look at its national income accounts.   The gross national product is the classification
in these accounts which is the most commonly used yardstick for measuring progress: "real" gross national product, which is output measured in "constant" dollars is
divided by the population to get per capita real g.n.p.[2]
This latter result will show whether average share (per
inhabitant) of actual goods and services produced has increased from one period of time to another.   By relating
total product to population it stresses the normative as
well as the positive aspects of economic development.
This means that the extent of economic progress is judged
by welfare criteria.   National income is the gross
national product viewed from the income side: it excludes
capital consumption allowance and indirect business taxes.
Calculated on a per capita basis, it is a relatively meaningful yardstick for comparing the standard of living of
one country with that of another.

----

[2] or $y = Y_r/P$ where Y_r is real g.n.p., P is population and y
is per capita real g.n.p.

Although the above mentioned yardsticks are
those most currently used, some reservations should be expressed regarding their adequacy. It should be recalled
that for purposes of comparison the national incomes of
all countries are converted into one currency, usually the
dollar. A first reservation is concerned with the great
differentials in purchasing power between nations: what
one dollar buys in the United States is generally far less
than what the equivalent of a dollar in local currency
would buy in a less affluent, or poorer society. That is
because rich countries have a higher standard of living
and hence higher wages and prices. To judge, therefore,
a nation whose per capita income is, say $300 or $400 a
year on what this amount would purchase in the United
States in rent, food, clothes, etc. would be greatly misleading. The second reservation is concerned with the
conversion factor used: most developing countries have
more than one rate of exchange and the question arises as
to which rate would be nearer the reality of the market
place; very often not the official one. Finally, there
is the fact that in an agrarian economy much of the produce is consumed on the farm and does not even enter into
the calculation of the national product.

Other yardsticks for measuring development which
are less currently used, or applied only to specific studies, include the ratio of labor output per man-hour to
total output, changes in per capita disposable income, and
per capita consumption of electricity. They all have
their limitations. In the first instance, the ratio of
labor productivity would be meaningful only if the working
hour week remains constant over time. Similarly,
changes in per capita disposable income over time, though
a normative measure of the increase in well-being of

individuals and families does not show the share of the
g.n.p. which is allocated through the public sector to
social overhead capital projects.   It also assumes no
change in the tax structure.   Finally, changes in per
capita consumption of electric energy are useful within
the context of the industrialization effort.

The Need for Structural Change

It was mentioned earlier that the process of
economic development involves the transition of the economy from the primary stage to the secondary and tertiary
stages, with a consequent re-allocation of resources.
Before analyzing the transition itself, a point should be
noted about what is called the tertiary stage, or services
sector.   The usual assumption in economics is that the
increase in employment in that sector is synonymous with
development: although this is usually the case, one must
also remember that in poor countries where job opportunities are scarce, employment as household servants and
in other menial chores accompanies backwardness.[3]

Determinants.   During the transition, there are
two stimuli behind the re-allocation of resources: a) the
change in demand consequent upon the growth of income, and
b) the better functioning of factor markets.   In the
first instance, as income increases new goods have to be
produced in order to stimulate demand and promote growth.
For this to happen, new entrepreneurial initiative is required to effect the transfer of capital and labor to the

---

[3] see Bauer and Yamey, "Economic Progress and Occupational
Distribution," The Economic Journal, Dec. 1951, reprinted
in Morgan, Betz and Choudhry (eds.) Readings in Economic
Development, 1963, Selection 26.

production of new goods. The implication here is that with higher incomes the demand for new or higher quality goods increases more than proportionately to the rise in income, while that for food or other goods increases less than proportionately to the rise in income.[4] However, in the less-developed countries the mobility of productive factors and more especially labor, shows a great degree of stickiness; this is generally due to imperfect knowledge and poor organization of markets.

Intersectoral trade-off. If capital and labor do not move readily they may have to be re-allocated: redundant labor will be transferred from the agricultural sector where its marginal product is very low, but positive (even if labor is only sharing in the communal diet, its marginal product is equal to the opportunity cost of the food it consumes) to the new industrial sector, at relatively low wages. This will lead to high profits[5] in the industrial sector because of the low production costs and the increased demand from the transferred workers. When this profit is re-invested it will lead to an increase in the marginal productivity of labor in the industrial sector. On the other hand, as more and more workers are moved away from the farm, the marginal productivity of the remaining workers in agriculture will increase and, with the gradual improvement in agricultural methods resulting from rationalization, will come to

----

[4]Engel's law and the pattern of the income-elasticity of demand.

[5]sometimes also called the "capitalist's surplus"; see Lewis, W.A., "Economic Development with Unlimited Supplies of Labour," Manchester School, May 1954; reprinted in Morgan, Betz and Choudhry, op. cit. Selection 20.

equal that in industry at the beginning of the transfer process.[6]   Hence, the effect of the re-allocation of productive factors will eventually be reflected in the improved performance of factor markets - even if such re-allocation has to be planned, at least in the initial stage and if it does not happen naturally.

The foregoing simplified model is based on the assumption of an unlimited supply of labor, with capital being the scarce factor; it makes no allowance for depreciation or the time lag in production. It constitutes a basic framework which will be expanded and further developed in the forthcoming pages. As it stands, it agrees with conditions prevailing in developing nations; however, if we substitute labor for capital as the scarce factor, then the model can be applied to developed countries with the qualification that in such a case the absence of allowance for capital consumption and for the production period will cause a greater distortion than in the case of the developing countries.

The Stages of Development

The study of the various stages that an economy goes through on its path to development, seems to have held some fascination for many authors, at various points of the economic history of mankind, each stressing a particular aspect of this evolution. To Friedrich List, a leading writer of the German historical school, the main transition was in occupational terms: his five stages go gradually from the savage, or primitive, stage to the

---

[6]the assumption here is that with the re-investment of the capitalist's surplus, productivity in the industrial sector will also have been moving.

agricultural, industrial and commercial.[7]   To Bruno
Hildebrand, for whom the distinction was mainly between
an exchange economy, a money economy, and a credit economy, the emphasis in explaining evolution was in the process of distribution.[8]   Although this distinction is
still prevalent nowadays for purposes of comparison between developed and underdeveloped nations, or even different sectors within the same economy, Hildebrand does
not seem to have provided the benchmarks for marking the
transition between his three stages.   Coordinating the
ideas of his predecessors, Karl Bucher put the emphasis on
the evolution of the production process according to its
ultimate distribution.   He thus made the distinction between a) the household economy where goods are produced
and consumed within the household; b) the town economy
where goods are produced and bartered between economic
units within the town, and c) the national economy, a
stage which involves trade and the existence of middlemen.[9]

A more modern version of the stages of economic
development is that of W. W. Rostow[10] who distinguishes
five stages, namely: 1) the traditional society which is
static, economic change, if any, coming in spurts due to
some exogenous factor, such as an armed invasion; 2) the
preconditions for take-off which include changes motivated

---

[7]List, Friedrich, National System of Political Economy,
Philadelphia, 1856.

[8]Hildebrand, Bruno, Die Nationalökonomie der Gegenwart und
Zukunft, 1848, new ed. by Gehrig, 1922.

[9]Bucher, Karl, Die Enstehung der Volkswirtschaft, 1893.

[10]Rostow, W. W., The Stages of Economic Growth: An Anti-
Communist Manifesto. New York: Cambridge University
Press, 1960.

12

in most instances by non-economic factors such as a revolution which marks the end of feudalism, or of foreign
occupation, the Reformation which changed people's outlook regarding certain economic criteria, etc.; 3) the
take-off stage which breaks with the past, overcoming all
obstacles to development and putting the country on a new
path where the rate of investment rises from 5 to 10 per
cent with a concomitant accelerated increase in the rate
of growth.   Beside the increase in investment, the take-
off requires the existence of one or two important manufacturing centers as well as the institutional framework
for expansion; 4) the drive to maturity naturally follows
the take-off and is spurred by new technology and increased efficiency in production spreading from the leading sectors to the rest of the economy; maturity is
reached when every sector is able to grow on its own;
5) finally, the economy achieves the stage of mass consumption: this is the actual state of the countries of
Western Europe, North America and Japan.   Mass production of consumers durables for consumption denotes a relatively high personal as well as per capita income.

Overview

The foregoing description seems to be too much
of a compartmentalization of development; although the
events and factors mentioned are generally part of the
development process, they do not always happen to coincide together, or in the same sequence; also, a country
can take off and then crash, because the process of development is not linear.   Moreover, it should be remembered that these patterns are based on empirical evidence,
essentially taken from the past history of the already

13

developed nations and may not necessarily apply to developing economies under present-day conditions.

REFERENCES

1. Enke, S., Economics for Development. Englewood Cliffs, N. J.: Prentice-Hall, 1963.

2. Kindleberger, C. P., Economic Development. New York: McGraw-Hill Book Company, 2nd edition, 1965.

3. Morgan, Betz and Choudhry (eds.), Readings in Economic Development. Belmont, Cal.: Wadworth Publishing Co., Inc., 1963, selections 20 and 26.

4. Rostow, W. W., The Stages of Economic Growth: An Anti-Communist Manifesto. New York: Cambridge University Press, 1960.

5. Schumpeter, J., History of Economic Analysis. New York: Oxford University Press, 1954.

REVIEW QUESTIONS

Most of the terms used in this chapter are familiar to you from your previous courses in Economics. However, your full understanding of them will facilitate your assimilation of the chapters which follow.

Terms

social overhead capital

infrastructure for development

labor and capital inputs

factor markets

primary, secondary & tertiary sectors

positive and normative economics

economies of scale

productive capacity

income-elasticity of demand

marginal propensity to save

"constant" dollars

marginal labor productivity

14

Questions

1. What is the main difference in theory and in practice between economic development and economic growth?

2. Why is it said that economic development is a relative as well as an absolute concept? What is the most effective yardstick for measuring it?

3. What is the difference from the point of view of measurement between per capita gross national product and per capita national income?

4. Explain the process of structural change or "transformation"; name its determinants.

5. What is the purpose of any study of the "stages" of development?

MATHEMATICAL APPENDIX

At any point of time, a country possesses a stock of capital which constitutes its productive capacity, i.e. the means which contribute to produce its yearly output. We shall represent this stock of capital by (K). The flow which this stock of capital produces every year is a country's output of goods or services in real terms, i.e. after abstraction is made of price increases. We shall represent this flow by (Y). The greater part of this flow of goods and services is made for consumption (C) and a smaller part constitutes new capital equipment (I) which is an addition to the stock of capital, or produced means of production. The investment made in producing this capital equipment is obtained by saving (S), i.e. foregoing present consumption, but the new capital equipment will help increase production of consumers goods in the future.

The following is a simplified model which does not take into account depreciation, i.e. the new capital equipment which goes to replace worn-out equipment and does not, therefore, add to the stock of capital. The model does not also take into account the gestation lag, i.e. the time it takes for the goods to be produced, which may be longer than one year.

Given a level of aggregate demand high enough to keep all capital equipment working at full capacity, then net investment (I) will represent an increase in the real stock of capital, which we shall represent by (ΔK)

1) $I = \Delta K$

this increase in real capital, given the productivity of investment (σ), will lead to an increase in real output (ΔY):

2) $\sigma I = \sigma \Delta K = \Delta Y$

Given the state of technology, industrial development, the rate of interest, the average and marginal propensities to save, then net investment is a ratio of present income (δY):

3) $I/Y = \delta$

It is also a determinant of future income, inasmuch as it increases the stock of capital. Then the rate of increase in the productive capacity of the economy over time (dK/dt) depends on both the investment ratio (δ) and the productivity of investment (σ):

4) $\qquad (dK/dt) = (\sigma\delta)$

Given a constant capital/output ratio, then both capital and output will grow at the same rate and exponentially:[1]

5) $\qquad\qquad Y_t = Y_{t-1} e^{\sigma\delta t}$

6) $\qquad\qquad K_t = K_{t-1} e^{\sigma\delta t}$

---

[1] the capital/output ratio is the reciprocal of the productivity of capital; it is a measure of the amount of capital investment needed to produce one unit of output. See Ch. V.

Substituting figures, let us assume that an economy invests 10 per cent (σ = .10) of its current national income, of say \$400 million (Y_{t-1} = 400), that the productivity of investment is 3 per cent (σ = 0.03) then the addition to its stock of capital is 40 x 0.03 = \$1.2 million.

CHAPTER II

HISTORICAL PATTERNS OF ECONOMIC DEVELOPMENT

In the last chapter the point was made that
economic development is a relative process in terms of
both time and space and that a nation's development can
be measured only in comparison with that of another
nation's, or in comparison with its development at an
earlier period of time. The various yardsticks for
measuring development were assessed and compared and the
reasons given for the preference accorded the two most
commonly used, namely, total and per capita national income and total and per capita gross national product.
The distinction was made between economic growth and development to the effect that the latter process involves
a transformation in the nation's economic structure, so
that a nation has to build up its productive capacity in
order to be able to realize its potential output.

In this chapter, we will look back through time
at the developed nations of the world to find out how they
have realized their development, whether the pattern and
the timing were the same for all of them and, if not, if
the differences were due to conditions inherent in these
countries' own structure, or to the motivations for development. This will not be an economic history of these
countries, but rather a brief study of the factors and
conditions which promoted their development and the measurement of their growth by means of prevalent yardsticks.
However, before doing so a brief review of the major objectives, motivations and prerequisites which accompany
a nation's expansion would help explain the historical
facts which will be assessed later.

Objectives, Motivations and Prerequisites

Objectives. The major objective of any nation
is the full utilization of all its human and material resources in order to increase its real output and thus improve its standard of living. As both productive capacity and the volume of production are increased, there
follow the improvement in social conditions and the material well-being which usually accompany the rise in income. As explained in the last chapter, this implies
the process of growth plus change. The monetary measurement of such a transition is the per capita income.

However, a nation is made of people, individuals
who go about their everyday business without giving much
thought to such facts as capital formation and economic
growth, particularly if they are poor and have difficulty
in keeping body and soul together. Moreover, when they
are still in their primitive condition, the needs of human
beings are small and they are willing to sacrifice their
leisure and go to work - i.e. submit to the disutility of
labor - only to the extent of satisfying their modest
needs; in other words, there is no incentive for them to
work harder or longer than is absolutely necessary.
What is it, then, that makes a nation suddenly aspire to
a better standard of living and strive for it? What is
the impulse which triggers the initial take-off?

Motivations. The motivations behind people's
behavior - or their propensities to do one thing or another, as W. W. Rostow calls them[1] - may be prompted by one
or more of several impulses. The first and most legit-
imate such motivation is the need felt by people living
under subsistence standards to free themselves from their

---

[1]Rostow, W. W., Process of Economic Growth, 1962.

economic shackles and achieve a better life for themselves
and their offsprings.   This urge provides the incentive
for working longer hours, for learning and improving one's
skill and ability and thus gradually bridging the gap between primitive conditions of production and more advanced
ones.

Nationalism is another such motivation: in this
case the initiative is usually taken by an ambitious lead-
er - not necessarily a ruler, at least at the beginning -
who emerges from the people and, by speaking a language
which is better understood by them, manages to awaken
their civic pride and to overcome their natural aversion
to the disutility of labor for a higher cause which is the
advancement of their country.   Starting from this point,
the success which results from their efforts and gives
them the taste of a better standard of living acts as an
incentive by itself in sustaining their desire for better
conditions.

The emergence from tribal rule to nationhood,
or from colonialism to self-rule, is another motivation:
allegiance is no longer to a person, the tribal chief, or
to a disliked colonial ruler, but to a nation.   With this
realization, individuals acquire the feeling of being now
part of a big whole and they develop a sense of purpose in
contributing to expand this bigger entity to which they
now belong.   However, for this kind of motivation to develop a certain amount of civic awareness or maturity is
required.

The motivation takes on a different allure when
it comes from the government and not from the people.
The reasons which prompt a government to initiate expansion are generally connected with the need to achieve

self-sufficiency and thus to become independent from re-
sorting to other nations for help.

Prerequisites. A number of factors are essential to the realization of economic progress or development. Some, such as population and resources, are part
of the country's natural endowment and others, such as
capital accumulation and technological progress have to
be fostered through effort and incentive.

Population growth is a strong factor in economic development, although it is a double-edged tool:
the expansion of the labor supply certainly made an important contribution to the development of the Western
European nations in the 1800's; on the other hand, many
an emerging nation of today finds that its high rate of
population growth saps away any increase in production
leaving it no better off than it was before its efforts
at economic growth. In this connection, improved health
and medical facilities and the lowering of the infant mortality rate, though positive achievements in themselves,
have further complicated the task of the emerging nations
in increasing per capita share of output.

Natural resources are not evenly distributed between nations: land, the major natural resource, is fixed
in supply and the availability of vast areas of fertile
land has become a rare thing. However, technology and
trade are two ways by means of which a country's land supply can be increased. The former by bringing more dry
land under cultivation through additional means of irrigation and the latter by facilitating access to the products
of other lands through trade and exchange. It should not
be forgotten, though, that the initial start of most countries' progress was fuelled by agricultural production.

Capital formation is the saving out of current national output to increase future output; it can take the form of factories and equipment for these factories, power projects, highways, bridges, dams, schools, hospitals, etc. This saving out of current income is harder when the level of income is already low.

Technological progress has become recently a very important ingredient in any economic advance; however, although it has gained recognition and been stimulated by research in modern times, technology has always been at the root of any advance and there is no better proof of that than the Industrial Revolution in Europe of which more will be said in the coming pages. The developing nations of today find technological progress available for the asking; their main problem is to adapt the new technology to their local conditions so that massive unemployment is not the price they have to pay for the increase in production. There was a time when the proper use of any technological innovation was in the hands of the entrepreneur, but the age of the managerial revolution and of mass production, has replaced the original adventure-seeking, risk-taking entrepreneur by droves of anonymous stockholders and a group of salaried technical experts.

Concomitant with technological improvement is the theory of economies of scale which refers to the reduction in the cost of production per unit of output which can be achieved by increasing the scale of production. This is based on the principle of the division of labor which leads to specialization in tasks performed, and sometimes to the development of new techniques by workers through experience gained in their jobs. The introduc-

tion of new techniques, either by workers or by scientists and researchers, accounts to a great extent for the
economies in scale.

Patterns of Development

The developed nations of today have obviously
followed the path of development along different lines
and under the prompting of different motivations. Paul
Alpert[2] qualifies the various patterns of development
followed by these nations as 'spontaneous', 'induced' and
'forced'. The first is identified with the development
of the countries of Western Europe and North America: it
took a longer period of time than the other two, was not
planned, but was realized on a private enterprise basis,
within the operation of a market economy. As such, it
was dictated by self-interest and influenced by ruling
conditions; hence its qualification of 'spontaneous'.

'Induced' economic development which is identified with that of Japan, was government-sponsored and pow-
er-motivated: it was "undertaken in order to modernize
and strengthen the country's military, political, and
economic organization, the objective being the preservation of Japan's independence from Western encroachment."[3]
It was entirely planned and carried out by the Government
who later transferred the many projects which it had initiated to individuals of the feudal class who thus became, with government assistance, the new class of entrepreneurs.

'Forced' economic development is identified with
that of the Soviet Union; it differs from the other two

---

[2] Alpert, Paul, Economic Development, 1963, Ch. 1.
[3] Ibid., p. 21.

in that it had no room for private enterprise: it was
based exclusively on collective ownership and total government control. More amazing still, this rapid development was achieved, particularly in its beginning, in
the complete absence of a price system. The motivation
in this case was to bridge the gap separating the Soviet
Union from the other industrialized nations; the objectives were self- sufficiency in capital equipment and the
build-up of an adequate military potential.

Having stated the objectives and motivations of
the various patterns of economic development, let us now
take a brief look at how such development took place.

The Western World

Chronologically, the countries of the western
world were the first to become industrialized and if their
development took longer, it must not be forgotten that
they created the apparatus which the others had only to
develop further. The economic development of the western
world during the 19th century was a reflection of the impact of several factors, some economic and others non-
economic, but strictly interrelated. The Renaissance
and the Reformation; the agricultural revolution of the
17th century and the emergence of a middle class of entrepreneurs and merchants; the industrial revolution of
the 18th century and the consequent rise in productivity;
the building of means of transportation; the discovery of
new lands, and the opening of new foreign outlets which
led to the development of foreign trade; the coming to
power of strong central governments; all these factors
contributed in their various ways to the evolution of the
western world to 19th and 20th century capitalism.

Not only was economic development 'per se' not planned, but it took place in spite of the general gloomy belief, inherited from the Middle Ages, that human affairs were in "steady retrogression"[4] from some "golden age (which) was variously placed in time..." and the retrogression was expected to go on. This outlook gradually changed under the impact of the Renaissance which, by stimulating people to think and read, revived their hope in the future and conditioned their mind for progress. The Reformation, in turn, led to the gradual abandonment of the long established taboos against capital accumulation and interest-bearing loans and brought about the confiscation of the rich estates owned by the churches. The latter action had two effects: the availability of more funds for development and the more rational exploitation of the confiscated agricultural land. Finally, with the new spirit of enterprise fostered by the Protestant ethic, "material success became a proof of righteousness and the manifestation of divine blessing".[5]

England was the first of the western countries to achieve its development and to set an example for the others. The main factors which contributed to its emergence were the agricultural expansion made possible by the enclosures, new and improved means of transport and communications, the industrial revolution and the expansion of foreign trade and investment.

The large inflow of gold from the new world into Europe had led to a severe inflation which hurt most those feudal landlords whose income consisted mainly of fixed

---

[4] Buchanan and Ellis, Approaches to Economic Development, 1955, p. 120.

[5] Alpert, op. cit., p. 15.

rents or dues. To make up their losses they decided to
increase the income from their estates by enclosing them,
expelling their tenants and putting the land to more productive use. The enclosures system achieved two purposes: the first was the consolidation of fragmented
plots through more intensive land utilization and the disappearance of an obsolete system of crop rotation called
the "three-field system" which allowed one third of the
land to remain fallow every year. Secondly, it brought
some of the land previously used for pasture under cultivation.

There were more far-reaching consequences of
the enclosures: the availability of additional land made
possible the application of the newly discovered techniques. This resulted in a doubling of yields and increased food production for the consumption of the urban
areas as well as for the additional workers employed in
the new industrial projects. The new techniques were
also labor-saving, so that additional cheap manpower from
agriculture was made available for industry. The improvements in agriculture attracted a new market-oriented
group of entrepreneurs and this marked the transition of
English agriculture to commercial farming (cash crop).
It also gave it a superior position in Europe: other
countries came to copy English methods and adapt them to
their soil.[6]

European countries thus followed England's lead
in improving their agricultural methods. Modernization
had two ultimate effects, the breaking up of the large
feudal estates and the transition to commercial farming.
The latter was facilitated by the introduction of new

---

[6]Buchanan, op. cit., p. 130.

crops, and the opening of new markets.

An increase in the output to be marketed usually leads eventually to an improvement in the means of transport and communications leading to markets, whether it is steamers to overseas markets, or highways, canals or railroads to local ones. The additional volume of goods carried, also lowers the cost of freight. The development of means of transportation is considered to be the largest single factor in the growth of the economies of Western Europe during that period. It made possible mobility of labor, increased the availability of markets and permitted rapid access to raw materials. A point of interest to be made in this connection is that although the highways and railroads which were then build had a most favorable impact on economic development, they did not benefit the capitalists who had borne the initial cost of building them. As many public utilities, their usefulness was to the community as a whole[7] over a long period of time, but the immediate returns did not carry adequate compensation to the investors.

Taking the terms "industrial revolution in their broader concept, economic historians are now more inclined to see in it the connotation of a blossoming of a whole group of new industries, rather than earth-shattering inventions in textiles and iron manufacture. So that the so-called "revolution" is now more likely to be considered an "evolution" as far as England is

---

[7] this situation is somewhat similar to what is referred to in Public Finance as "quasi-private" (or "quasi-public") goods, which are derived from a mixture of public and private wants and allocated by either the public or the private sector (see Bernard, P. Herber, Modern Public Finance, pp. 23-24).

concerned - in view of the developments which came before
it: apart from the improvements in agriculture discussed
earlier in this chapter, there had been scientific discoveries in the 17th century in which, an Englishman, Sir
Isaac Newton had a leading position.[8]

Up to the middle of the 19th century, industrial
development in England was concentrated mainly in textiles, coal and iron (coal production rose from 6.2 million tons in 1770 to 65 million tons in 1856)[9]; growth
and diversification of manufacturing came after 1870 and
it was concentrated in four European countries and America, namely, 31.8 per cent in England, 23.3 per cent in
the United States, 13.2 per cent in Germany and 10.3 per
cent in France.[10] The funds for investment came from
the merchant class who had amassed large fortunes from
foreign trade especially under the policies prevailing at
the time of the Mercantilists. The new factories had
their forerunners in earlier days under the "merchant-
employer" system used in connection with textiles and
whereby the actual work of weaving and spinning was "put-
out" to large groups of workers, often as many as 1,000,
residing in the countryside.[11] Now, production was concentrated in one spot, the modern factory, which made
possible a better division of labor but where working
conditions were still unhealthy and unsafe, and wages
often at the subsistence level. The latter situation
was to continue for quite some time before improvement

---

[8]see Gill, Richard T., Economic Development: Past and
Present, 2nd. ed., 1967, p. 42.
[9]Alpert, op. cit., p. 17.
[10]Buchanan, op. cit., p. 142.
[11]see Gill, op. cit., p. 43.

came by means of reform.[12]

As in agriculture, the new industrial methods spread from England to other European countries, but there the state played a greater role. Buchanan and Ellis[13] give three reasons for this role. The first was the close connection in these countries between the new industrial expansion and politics, whether it was to gain prominence by means of better production, or to help the creation of new industries by weakening foreign ones. The second reason was that the European countries tried to benefit from England's example by avoiding the social unrest and the decline in agricultural production which England had suffered. This was achieved by a collaboration of the state with private initiative. The third reason and one which the authors themselves question, was that there existed in the other European countries a certain dearth of entrepreneurs and capitalists to undertake the new industrial ventures, so the government had to fill the gap.

Starting later, the United States, not only benefited from the European experience in development and carried it further, but had certain advantages which were its own. Some of these were natural advantages, such as the size of the country, its large resources and its rich soil, but others were the result of early wise management. The first of these was the population expansion, through both natural growth and an early immigration policy which brought to the country valuable labor, primarily from Europe, during the 19th century. For example, the inflow

---

[12] it was this situation which led Ricardo to formulate the "iron law of wages."

[13] Buchanan, op. cit., p. 161.

increased from 600,000 immigrants in the decade of the
1830's, to 1.7 million during the 1840's and 2.6 million
in the 1850's.[14]   The second factor was the rapid capital accumulation which took place at a rate even faster
than that of population growth: the stock of capital
grew from less than $1 billion at the beginning of the
19th century to over $400 billion in 1948,[15] with a con-
comitant increase in the ratio of capital to labor.   A
great extent of this increase was fuelled during the 19th
century by public investments, more particularly at the
state level, and by foreign investments.   As regards domestic private investments, these consisted mainly of retained earnings by enterprises developed in the second
half of the century; the growth of these had been helped
by the external economies provided by the social overhead
capital built earlier (mostly from public funds), such as
canals, highways and railroads.   Between 1820 and 1838,
the states borrowed $60 million for canal construction,
$53 million to capitalize state banks, $43 million for
railroads, $7 million for turnpikes.   Most of the borrow-
ing was from Europeans, mainly the British, who were attracted by the wide opportunities for investment and by
the efficient management of American enterprises.
British investments increased from an estimated $20 mil-
lion in 1805 to $175 million in 1838.   The discovery of
gold in California further stimulated European investments
in American securities which amounted to $225 million by
1853.

A third factor was the abolition of economic
boundaries between the states which created a large free

---

[14]Studensky and Kroos, The Financial History of the
United States, 2nd. ed., 1963, p. 124.
[15]Gill, op. cit., p. 70.

trade area, thus stimulating production.   (By comparison, Europe did not follow this example until 1950 when
the Treaty of Rome signalled the creation of the European
Economic Community.)   At the same time, geographical expansion, the "move westward" provided ever new resources
and thus set back the law of diminishing returns.   Not
least, certainly, was the discovery of gold in California
which provided, between 1848 and 1853, a total of $128.4
million in gold.   Half of this output was exported and
the other half went to swell bank reserves.[16]   As in
Europe, the development of communications across the vast
American continent, first prompted by geographical expansion and later by the creation of big industrial projects,
was the single factor which contributed most to American
economic development.   During the 1890's new means of
communications made up between 10 and 15% of GNP and by
1900 total investment in railroads alone was greater than
that in all manufacturing industries.   A final and non-
economic factor, is that the country has enjoyed great
political stability after Independence, except for the
years of the Civil War.

Modern Japan

The arrival of the American Commodore Matthew
Perry at Tokyo Bay in 1853 forced Japan to open its doors
to Western civilization.   It also stimulated a claim
from the Japanese people for a reorientation of power and
the end of the stagnating feudal system.   Supreme power
was restored to Emperor Meiji in 1868.   This date also
marks the beginning of Japan's economic development: its
rulers had realized that they had no choice but to

---

[16]Studensky, op. cit., p. 124.

industrialize if they wished to maintain the country's independence.

The government introduced several reforms to realize its objectives: it abolished the feudal system in agriculture, appropriated land not officially registered, instituted a land tax based on a fixed assessment of the land's potential irrespective of the volume of production, thus helping to increase output. Public investments were channelled to three different sectors: social overhead capital, industry, and banking. These ventures which were handed over eventually to private capitalists in the nobility, were financed initially by income derived from the land tax which by 1880 constituted about 80 per cent of public revenue.[17] Expansion of silk production provided, through increased exports, the foreign exchange needed for imports of equipment goods. During the period 1868 to 1920, exports increased 152 times and imports 56 times. Various village industries were created to provide employment to rural workers. Finally, great emphasis was placed on education and vocational training.

The first of the large industrial enterprises in Japan were textile mills equipped with British machinery (1859). The government then took the lead in building model factories with a view of encouraging private investors to follow suit. Financial assistance was made available to those wishing to launch new enterprises. The state also initiated postal and telegraphic services and simultaneously started construction of railroads.

---

[17]Alpert, op. cit., p. 23.

Further government legislation lifted the ban on the sale
of land in 1872 enabling private ownership by the people.[18]

Japan had no surplus population problem when
it started its economic development; it had then less
than a third of its present population of about 103 million (1970 est.). The rate of population growth which
was of 1.10 per cent in 1888, fell gradually reaching
.79 per cent in 1897 and, with very few setbacks, has
climbed slowly since, reaching its peak of 2.5 per cent
in the early 1930's. The industrial labor force increased from 4.9 million in 1888, to 14.9 million in
1930. More important still, the ratio of industrial
capital stock to labor declined gradually from over 4 per
cent in 1888 - i.e. the initial stage of industrialization - to less than 3 per cent in the late 1920's.
This was still higher than the rate of population growth,
but low enough to indicate the emphasis on labor-intensive rather than capital-intensive investment, up to the
early 1930's.[19]

The rapidity of Japan's economic transformation
can be seen in a comparison of the production of 1873
with that of 1900. The index of primary production rose
from 15.7 to 52.1 while the index of mineral production
increased from 1.03 to 28.15 (with the years 1921-1925
taken as a base). The rice output increased from 119.1
million bushels to 205.6 million bushels. However, the
rise in rice output was accompanied by such a rise in
population growth that there was barely enough to meet

---

[18]Buchanan, op. cit., p. 23.

[19]see Ranis, G., Allocation Criteria and Population
Growth. American Economic Review, May 1963, p. 631,
Table 1.

demand.   Silk output increased sixfold while the output of cotton yarn in 1900 was 430 times greater than it had been in 1873.[20]   The total number of industries was 24 at the beginning of the Meiji restoration.   By the turn of the century this figure had reached 662.   The major emphasis of the government was centered on heavy industry to prepare the nation for possible war.   Other industries came second to this objective; they were developed with state aid to help pay for the imports of raw materials necessary for war production.

The transition to the Taisho era after the death of Emperor Meiji witnessed some disturbances: during the rice riots of 1918 rice stores were looted in Tokyo in protest of rising prices.   As a result of the riots, measures were taken to increase food supplies by expanding rice imports from other parts of the Japanese empire. This was a revolt of workers and consumers rather than farmers, and probably the inevitable result of rapid industrialization.   The government had neglected agricultural development to concentrate on industry.   Just as the country was recovering from the rice shortage the disastrous Kanto earthquake destroyed old Tokyo killing over 100,000 Japanese citizens.   Japan's national debt mounted greatly due to loans of over $250 million from Western powers needed to rebuild Japan's largest port, Tokyo.

The government's financial difficulties became evident with the beginning of the great depression in 1929.   In 1931, the depression brought with it a depreciation of the yen.   Also, Japan had geared her machinery

---

[20]Buchanan, op. cit., p. 176.

of production to external trade.   Problems arose when
Japan, at the expense of the workers' wages, cut the cost
of goods only to be met by higher tariffs or stiffer
quotas from other nations.   This checked Japanese merchandise trade and greatly harmed her economy.   Between
1931 and 1937 payments on imports rose twice as fast as
the proceeds from exports.

During Japan's period of early development
there was little or no concern with improving the conditions of a vast majority of the population.   Like England, the cost of economic development was paid by the
peasants and factory workers in the form of taxation and
low wages.   Not until after World War II did the wages
of the workers rise much above the minimum subsistence
level.   Meanwhile, the increase in taxes, when wages were
so low, led the combined Japanese labor unions to establish a Joint Labor Union Council.

The Japanese experience.   In terms of capital
stock, Japan was a poor country in 1868 before it started
on the path of development.   Capital formation was rapid
since in 1914 it had become an emerging industrialized
nation.   Its development was entirely planned by the government and it was adequately planned: heavy taxation,
mainly of the land, and inflationary spending were used
to obtain the capital necessary to finance development.
Both capital accumulation and resource allocation were determined by the government, and consumption by the masses
of the people was kept at a minimum level - even after
the initial stages of development - in order to ensure
continued saving.   Without underestimating the Japanese
accomplishment, one can surmise that it would not have
been possible were the present international regulations

concerning labor rights in force at the time, and Japan a member, as it is now, of all the international organizations, and more particularly the International Labor Organization (I.L.O.).

According to a Japanese economic historian, "the chief factor which aroused the (Japanese) industry out of inaction, was not any favourable turn in the marginal efficiency of capital".[21]   It was rather the tireless efforts of the Japanese government, motivated by the same desire for self-sufficiency rather than by profit; the government imported the capital equipment and then induced the firms to use it by various means.   Thus, in providing the capital the state dominated the scene: directly or indirectly, it financed practically all the conspicuous expansion at the time.

The Soviet Union

As in the case of Japan, the Soviet leaders decided to concentrate their investments on industry rather than agriculture, and more particularly on heavy industry.   However, while the Japanese government was creating projects which were eventually to become private undertakings, the Russian government meant to keep all the new projects under its control.   In this respect the Soviet experience is unique in that it did entirely away, especially at the beginning, with the market mechanism, and was successful in achieving a high rate of growth.

The Soviets started on the path of development later than the other industrialized nations, but they had some headstart;   they did not start from scratch.

---

[21] Shigeto Tsuru, "Economic Fluctuations in Japan 1868-93" The Review of Economic Statistics, Vol. XXIII, 1941.

Before the Revolution of 1917 they already had a substantial network of railroads serving the industrial centers, especially in the European part of Russia; their heavy industry was established, their coal production was sixth in importance in world output, their pig iron was fifth, and petroleum was second. Finally, Russia had had a higher rate of industrial growth between 1870 and 1913 than any of the Western European nations. However, its agriculture was backward, in marked contrast to its industry which had received the benefit of foreign technical and financial assistance, as well as foreign investments.

In 1917, after the revolution, the Communist government seized all foreign enterprises and nationalized foreign capital. These seizures yielded, in addition to the cancellation of all foreign debts, about $10 billion. Moreover, within the country all land was nationalized and so was the banking and credit system. Industrial establishments were subjected to a system of workers' control; at the same time, the need for labor discipline and skilled management were strongly emphasized. Between 1918 and 1920, all enterprises which employed more than ten workers - and more than five, if motor power was used - were brought under the control of the state. Meanwhile, foreign trade had also been nationalized and private domestic trade was forbidden. The former move isolated Russia from the new techniques which were being developed in the outside world, a mistake which was to be partly corrected later by heavy purchases of both consumers and capital goods from Western European nations, especially Great Britain. The stringent measures introduced had a damaging effect upon industrial production which by 1920 had dwindled to a small percentage of its

pre-war output: 18 per cent for the large scale industries and 43 per cent for the smaller enterprises. Both
productivity and wages also dropped to below pre-war levels, and workers started migrating from the cities to the
rural areas in search of food.

To remedy the situation, the New Economic Policy
(N.E.P.) was introduced in 1921. It was based on the
proposal that a tax in kind of approximately one tenth of
the peasants' produce should be substituted for the former
arbitrary requisitioning of all agricultural surplus output. Concomittantly, small scale private trade brought
foodstuffs to parts of the country which had been previously deprived of them, and also provided an incentive
for the peasants and the Kulak farmers to produce above
their subsistence needs. Individual ownership of small
shops and businesses and limited free enterprise in manufacturing, were also allowed, but the government maintained control of the major industries such as iron, coal
and transportation, as well as the regulation and management of the credit system and foreign trade. At the same
time, reforms were carried out to improve the government
machine: accounting methods were improved, budgets were
made to balance and the large industrial enterprises were
asked to show a surplus in order to provide the funds
badly needed for development. Socially, the payment of
rent for land and housing and of taxes and charges for
public services were once more put into effect and signalled, at least partly, the disappearance of the welfare
state. The ruble was stabilized at its former rate of
51.2 U.S. cents and this semblance of limited capitalism
provided both farmers and industrial workers with an incentive to increase production.

The New Economic Policy lasted 7 years: the death of Lenin and his succession by Stalin brought a different and harsher policy to the fore. Meanwhile, those seven years had given the Soviet planners a sort of respite during which they learned from their mistakes and had time to prepare themselves for the more intensive socialization which was to follow. Under the first Five-Year Plan (1927) agricultural land was collectivized, emphasis was put on heavy industry and almost no social overhead capital was provided. The plan provided for less than 9 per cent of investments into housing.[22] Transportation became a major bottleneck. Investments during the period of the plan amounted to about 30 per cent of the Gross National Product, but less than 20 per cent of the amounts invested went into the development of agriculture. Production of capital goods was intensified.

Cost of development. While production of pig iron increased 345 per cent from 1913 to 1937, agricultural production increased only from 25 to 30 per cent i.e. by 5 per cent only in 24 years. This led to rationing, low levels of consumption and restrictions on employment in agriculture. Financing of the step-up in industrial production was obtained from a high sales tax on foodstuffs, mainly bread. This tax which provided two thirds of government revenue, amounted to 64 per cent of gross personal income. The cost of development, therefore, was the sacrifice in consumption and well-being of the majority of the people.

---

[22] Baldwin, and Meier, Economic Development: Theory, History, Policy, 1957, p. 87.

Overview

None of the three different types of economic
development which have been studied in this chapter appears entirely relevant or suitable to the underdeveloped
countries of today, though they are of interest at least
as a base of reference.   The pattern followed by the
Western countries is slow and requires resources in capital and technical knowledge not available to them.
That of Japan, while speedier and animated by a nation-
alist spirit in many respects similar to that of the
presently developing nations, used methods of exploitation
of the low-income groups which are generally rejected in
our times.   The tremendous speed of development and industrialization of the Soviet Union and the results
achieved would command admiration if they were not offset
by the heavy cost in hardships of the present generation,
as well as by the establishment of an economic and political totalitarian pattern of government.[23]

REFERENCES

1.   Alpert, Paul, Economic Development.   New York: The
     Free Press of Glencoe, 1963, Ch. 1.

2.   Baldwin and Meier, Economic Development: Theory,
     History, Policy.   New York: John Wiley & Sons,
     Inc., 1957.

3.   Buchanan and Ellis, Approaches to Economic Develop-
     ment.   New York: The Twentieth Century Fund, 1955,
     Chs. 6-10.

4.   Gill, Richard T., Economic Development: Past and
     Present.   Foundations of Modern Economics Series.
     Englewood Cliffs, New Jersey: Prentice-Hall, Inc.
     2nd. ed., 1967.

---

[23]see Alpert, op. cit., pp. 35-36.

40

5. Ranis, G., "Allocation Criteria and Population Growth." American Economic Review, Papers and Proceedings of the 75th Annual Meeting. May 1963.

6. Rostow, W. W., Process of Economic Growth. Homewood, Illinois: Dorsey Press, 1962.

7. Shaffer, Harry G., ed., The Soviet Economy. New York: Appleton-Century-Crofts, 1963.

8. Studensky and Kroos, The Financial History of the United States, 2nd. edition. New York: McGraw-Hill Book Company, 1963.

9. Tsuru, Shigeto, "Economic Fluctuations in Japan, 1868-93," The Review of Economic Statistics, Vol. XXIII, 1941.

REVIEW QUESTIONS

Terms

subsistence economy

take-off stage

the entrepreneur

age of mass production

the Reformation

the industrial revolution

a feudal agricultural system

land tax

disutility of labor

capital formation

the managerial revolution

the Renaissance

the enclosures system

the Mercantilists

a collective farm

nationalization of industry

Questions

1. Describe in a few words each of the three different patterns of development and their respective characteristics.

2. Was the motivation the same in all three patterns? Main difference?

3. Why is it said that the progress in health conditions and in wages has made the achievement of development harder?

4. What was the rate of capital accumulation in the U.S. during the period of development? and the effect of

the abolition of boundaries between the states of
the Union?   and the greatest single investment?

5. What was the significance of the Japanese land tax
    for development and its percentage of total public
    revenues?   and the trend of the capital/labor
    ratio?   the main initiative in Japanese develop-
    ment?   and the pattern of consumption and wages?

6. What was the main emphasis in Russian development?
    main source of financing?   purpose of the New
    Economic Policy?   of the first Five-Year Plan?
    the cost of development?

7. Is there one important phenomenon which is common
    to all three patterns of development?

CHAPTER III

THE CASE OF THE PRESENTLY DEVELOPING NATIONS

Certain symptoms are common to all countries
which have not yet achieved their economic maturity, but
the basis of them all is the absence, or low rate of
economic growth. A review of these symptoms follows.

The Facts about Underdeveloped Countries

The various aspects of underdevelopment can be
summed up under three headings, namely, a) a low per capita income; b) low productivity of the factors of production, and c) inadequate productive capacity. The
three aspects are closely interrelated.

Low per capita income. This is the result of
the low level of employment and productivity and is very
often due to the fact that the economy is predominantly a
primary producing one where industrial activity is still
in the growth process. Associated with this condition
sometimes is the existence of a barter economy and the
complete absence of a developed credit system.[1] Food
constitutes the larger percentage of output and there is
a strong pressure of population on resources. A usual
corollary to this situation, is the unequal distribution
of income between the low-income majority and a rich
elite of landowners, or a few industrialists, whose members often prefer to invest their savings outside the
country. Finally, a non-economic though strong factor

---

[1]with the exception of one or two cities where the
presence of a money, market-oriented economy alongside
a modern industry creates a state of dual economy.

contributing to the low level of earnings is the disutility of labor: in a society which has not yet started
on the path of progress and has not been exposed to the
so-called demonstration effect (or to Madison Avenue-type
of demand-creating publicity), needs are modest and
leisure is a highly-priced commodity. People are not
disposed, therefore, to exert more effort than is necessary for their essential needs.[2] Thus, the extent of a
given society's choice between work and leisure will determine the ratio between a country's population and its
economically active manpower. This ratio, together with
that of labor productivity, gives us the "real income 'per
breadwinner'".[3] In conclusion, with income low, saving
is limited by the size of income and the rate of capital
formation is equally limited.

Low productivity. Here the distinction will
be made between the productivity of labor and that of
capital equipment. Low productivity of labor may be
due to poor health conditions, lack of educational and
training opportunities, and insufficient or inadequate
capital equipment. In poor farming communities, the
problem is aggravated by the presence of large families
living on fragmented holdings and sharing in an income
which could have been obtained with a lesser number of
workers - a phenomenon sometimes called "disguised unemployment".[4] In such farming areas capital equipment

---

[2] this phenomenon has often been a cause of frustration to
Western planners and experts trying to get a poor country
to increase its production.

[3] Kurihara, K. K., The Keynesian Theory of Economic
Development, 1959, p. 43.

[4] see Nurkse, Ragnar, Problems of Capital Formation in
Underdeveloped Countries, 1953, see also Chapter VI.

is scarce and even where the yield per acre of land is high, output per worker is low.[5]   In the industrial sector, apart from a few modern industries, probably owned and managed by foreign interests, production is usually at the handicraft stage, or made up of small-scale industries for food-processing or the production of light consumers goods.   The non-agricultural population is crowded in the few large cities where, apart from the comparatively small proportion of employment in industry, government jobs and services for the wealthy, constitute the opportunities for employment.

The picture, then is that of a large supply of (unskilled) labor input, and a low capital/labor ratio compared to that in richer countries - a result of the low saving capacity of the economy.   Moreover, the quality and quantity of entrepreneurship is such that the demand for capital is limited.   The implication is either that the economy does not generate enough investment opportunities, or that if it does, the existing entrepreneurs fail to recognize and exploit such opportunities. This may also be due to the fact that the social and financial atmosphere which lends itself to investment does not exist.   One economic school of thought would have development plans deliberately create imbalance, in order to "induce" decision-making by entrepreneurs.[6]

The low productivity of capital equipment is measured in the high ratio of capital to output and is

------

[5]output per worker, rather than per capita, is a better measure of productivity.

[6]Hirschman, Albert O., The Strategy of Economic Development, 1958, pp. 62-64.

due to the inadequate rate of capital formation[7] and to
poor technology.   At any point of time, a country's
stock of capital is the result of past saving and investment so that if saving has been low and the investment which follows has not been carried out according to the least-cost techniques and/or the latest technology, the resulting additions to the stock of capital
will not be as productive as similar investments in
industrialized countries.   Coupled with the unskilled
labor force, it is not difficult to see how the productivity of capital could be low.   Measured in ex-post
terms, the net addition to the stock of capital, given
the level of total output, is relatively smaller and less
productive than in developed economies.   The meaning of
less productive in this connection is that with the same
quantity of inputs, output would be less than it would
have been under similar circumstances in other countries.

 Inadequate productive capacity.   From the
foregoing it follows that the productive capacity of an
economy at any point of time, given the state of technology, is the result of past saving and capital formation.
If we assume that the ratio of the labor force to the
population is given, then the rate of increase in productive capacity becomes a function of the rate of capital
formation.   The latter will depend on the ratio of saving (average and marginal) to net national income,[8] or

1) $s = S/Y$

and on the measure of such saving which is invested,

---

[7] capital formation is the creation of produced means of
production, put differently, it is the foregoing of present consumption for larger future aggregate consumption.

[8] leaving out allowance for depreciation and for time-lag
in production.

i.e. the investment ratio

2) $\qquad \delta = I/Y$

and on the productivity of the addition to the stock of capital constituted by such investment

3) $\qquad \sigma \Delta K = \Delta Y = \sigma I$

where (K) stands for the stock of real capital and (σ) for productivity of investment - or the reciprocal of the capital/output ratio. In the short-run this relationship is a constant. The rate of increase of output (G) then will be equal to the investment ratio times the productivity of investment, or

4) $\qquad \delta \sigma = G$

The cornerstone of the above argument is the rate of saving or capital accumulation: if that is low, as in the case of the type of economy which is being studied, then productive capacity will increase at a low rate.

Moreover, there is still another aspect to the problem: capital formation means the construction of specific physical items for use in further production. This process implies the existence of an apparatus producing capital goods; in the absence of such an apparatus, the investment ratio gives us the capacity of the economy to produce capital goods, only on the condition that output is homogeneous, i.e. that factors of production and resources can be easily transferred from the consumers goods sector to the capital goods one.

Inadequate productive capacity, when reflected in a lower rate of growth of capital relative to labor often results in labor unemployment due to lack of capital equipment. This type of unemployment which is peculiar to underdeveloped countries should be distinguished from the unemployment resulting from lack of effective demand.

Finally, some mention should be made of the availability - or lack of it - of natural resources which, necessarily play a role in capital formation. The usual assumption is that underdeveloped countries are deficient in natural resources and that development is synonymous with their easy availability. However, examples exist of the contrary in both cases. Kuwait, Venezuela, Nigeria and Chile on the one hand, though they are considered to have less developed economies, are comparatively rich in resources, while highly developed countries such as Switzerland and Japan have scarcely any resources to speak of. Though there is no doubt that endowment in natural resources would make it much easier for a country to attain economic development, it is not impossible to do so even without resources.

In comparing the conditions of the presently developing countries with those of today's industrialized nations during their stages of development, several differences are immediately apparent, and most of them are related to the major one that the industrialized countries were not hampered during their period of development by the problem of excess population. For instance, the presently developing nations have started at a lower level of per capita national output, a lower land/man ratio, a lower level of agricultural productivity, more inequality in income distribution but less possibility for capital formation, and no opportunity to greener and more spacious lands. Anachronistic social and political structures resulting from a background of colonial rule accentuate the differences further.[9]

If intensive capital formation is needed to
break out of the circle of poverty, then consumption must
be curbed in spite of its very low level, in order to
stimulate investment.   Under feudal systems and totalitarian economies, this can be achieved by coercion,
but under an even relatively democratic society, this is
only possible by means of progressive taxation.   To obtain progressive taxation in underdeveloped countries, a
comprehensive reform of what is usually an obsolete and
ineffective taxation system is needed.

Dual Economy Pattern and Leading Sector Role

By the beginning of World War I the industrialized countries of the West had extended their influence
over most of the underdeveloped areas of the world: most
of Africa, Asia - with the exception of Japan which, as
seen earlier, had developed by its own efforts - and most
of Latin America.   The scope of their influence reflected
the long road covered by the Western nations which though
at first were behind some of the older civilizations -
especially those of South Asia - had caught up with them
mainly through trade and conquest.   The growth of industrialization in Europe was accompanied by an increase in
the needs of its countries for raw materials and, in some
instances, foodstuffs.   The nations of the outer world,
whether colonized or just under protective mandate,
offered an ample supply of both cheap labor and raw materials.   European capital in search of profitable

---

[9] see Kuznets, Simon, Economic Growth and Structure:
Selected Essays, 1965, and Higgins, Benjamin, Economic
Development, revised edition.

ventures was channelled to the underdeveloped countries
into investments requiring large capital outlays and
advanced technology and producing for the export market,
such, for instance, as mineral production and commercial
plantations. The commodities they exported gradually
made up an ever increasing proportion of the host countries' national output.

The outcome of these developments had two
different aspects: the first was reflected in the direction and composition of international trade which consisted of manufactured goods from the Western countries
to the rest of the world, and primary products from the
latter to the former.[10] The second aspect appeared in
the imbalance in the economic structure of the underdeveloped countries where the concentration of foreign
investments producing for the competitive international
markets, was in marked contrast with the industries producing for the local market. The latter, consisting
mainly of agricultural products, village industries and
handicrafts, were still in the primitive stage. This
is the phenomenon known as the "dual economy" and the
particular industry, or sector, which has benefitted
from a higher degree of development is sometimes called
a "leading sector." However, there is usually more than
one cause at the root of the development of a leading
sector: the initial impulse does not necessarily have
to come from a foreign investment; it may be triggered
by the initiative of domestic producers who, with the
help of the government, may shift from subsistence agriculture to the production of cash crops for export.

---

[10]this pattern is discussed more fully in Chapter IX.

Or, it may be initiated by immigrant settlers coming
from areas more advanced economically, who apply their
skills to produce for export.[11]   In all instances, the
new pattern of production draws workers away from the
traditional sector and though it may signal the beginning of the transition to an exchange economy, it tends
to create an imbalance in the economic structure of the
developing country.   Such imbalance can and has been
made to help in the development process.   To understand
this point, let us first define what a leading sector is.

Leading sectors.   The definition of a leading
sector is one which has grown and is growing at a rate
above the average for the other sectors in a given economy and its growth has been autonomous, i.e. independent from that of the economy.   The reasons behind this
phenomenon are usually that the sector has advantages in
either supply or demand.   Advantages in supply can be
because of better technology - probably acquired through
a foreign investment in a local industry and this is
usually connected with some natural endowments, e.g. oil
and other natural deposits, or primary products such as
cocoa, coffee, cotton, etc.   Advantages in demand come
from the need for the final good and the resulting incentive to expand production.

Thus the leading sectors tend to provide the
necessary stimuli to the other less developed sectors to
grow because of the intersectoral technological linkages
via input-output exchanges.   The possibility of using

---

[11] see Meier, Gerald M., Leading Issues in Economic
Development, 1970, III.A.   Examples of Dual
Economies.

more efficient (least-cost) techniques of production is
created.

The type of leading sector with which this
study is concerned is that which exists in some countries
as a result of natural endowments, geographical position,
or just past history.[12]   For example, the agricultural
sector in Egypt is highly developed and this is due to
an efficient irrigation network installed by the British
when the country was under their mandate.   This was in
order to provide cotton for the mills of Lancashire.
This sector is still providing the input to the most developed Egyptian industry, textiles, apart from the foreign exchange receipts from exports of raw cotton which
still constitute about 70 to 80 per cent of total exports.   Another example is that of Lebanon which by its
own choice and geographical position, is one of the few
free exchange centers in the world and certainly the only
one in its area.   Its exchange and banking activities, in
relation to the size of the country and its population,
are highly developed and provide the funds for investment
in housing and industrial expansion.   Finally, it was
seen in Chapter II that the economic development of
Japan was financed to a great extent by the proceeds
from its exports, mainly pure silk.

Recent Growth Trends

According to the World Bank, the combined gross
national product of the developing countries during the

---

[12]though this nomenclature is broader than that mentioned
under the 'dual economy' description, the basic causes
behind the relatively higher degree of development are
the same.

fifteen years prior to 1967 had increased by over 100 per
cent. (In appraising this figure, one should keep in
mind the small base from which such expansion started.)
This rate of growth was due mainly to the structural
change in these countries' economies from agricultural
to industrial, so that the expansion has been fuelled to
a large extent by industrial production. However, because of the high rate of population growth, the corresponding average increase in per capita income has been
of less than three per cent annually. The latter rate
was higher during the decade of the fifties but has been
dwindling recently, reaching in some countries as low a
level as one per cent.

The recent decline in the rate of growth seems
to have been due to two main causes. One was the slowdown in the pace of economic activity in the industrialized countries which manifested itself during the first
quarter of 1966 but was due to phenomena dating from earlier years. This slowdown had a strong adverse impact
on the economies of the developing nations and was reflected in a decline in their export receipts as well as
in their share of international aid. The second cause
of decline was a slackening in the rate of their agricultural output which failed to keep up with the population
increase. For these countries as a group, the decline
in per capita agricultrual output was as high as five per
cent in 1965 and 1966. However, in Latin America, the
1966 crops registered a sizable improvement over 1965.

International Aid

According to a study published by the United
Nations in June 1967, on the "International Flow of Long-
term Capital and Official Donations, 1961-66" the total

net flow of long-term capital from developed to underdeveloped countries for the five-year period which marks
the first half of the Development Decade,[13] was $39.9
billion, spread out as follows: (in billion U. S. $'s)

1961	1962	1963	1964	1965
8,013	7,478	7,474	7,828	9,129

A breakdown of the total outflow according to sources
gives the following (in billion U. S. $'s)

	Amount	% of total
Public grants and other contributions	18.6	47%
Government capital	7.-	17.5%
Transactions with multilateral agencies	3.6	9%
Total private invest-ment (of which $8.5 bn of direct investments including reinvested profits, and $2.2 bn of portfolio invest-ments)	10.7	26.5%
	39.9	100%

This aid was either sent direct to the receiving
nations, or it was channelled through international agencies.   In 1961, it represented about 0.88 per cent of
the combined gross national product of the industrialized
nations and approximately 3 per cent of their gross domestic fixed capital formation, but the latter percentage
declined in the following years and by 1965 and 1966
amounted to only 2.4 per cent.   To the beneficiaries,
the above flow of capital contributed about 20 per cent
of their gross domestic capital formation, although this

---

[13]United Nations, Development Decade, 1962-1972.

figure might be misleading because of the unequal distribution of aid and investments.

    The contribution of the United States in-
creased from 52 per cent of the total in 1961 to 58 per
cent in 1965 but those of France and West Germany declined from 17 and 9 per cent in 1961 to 13 and 6 per
cent respectively in 1965. The contribution of the
United Kingdom remained unchanged at 9 per cent during
the whole period.

    In assessing the measure in which such aid has
been able to finance development, one problem which
should be kept in mind is the servicing of past debts,
including both interest and repayment. It is considered
at present that this item already absorbs two thirds of
the flow of capital to developing countries, more especially when it consists of the settlement of bills due
for the purchase of capital equipment which has not yet
become productive.

    The flow of credits from the Soviet bloc to
developing countries averaged $600 million a year for
the period 1954-1966, most of it from the U.S.S.R.
The latter pledged an overall amount of $4.9 billion
for the period mentioned, although the actual allocation
of the credit for each individual project is usually the
subject of a separate agreement.

Overview

    The newly emerging countries have come to
realize that political freedom can be meaningless if it
is not accompanied by an improvement in their standard
of living. They need capital resources, technological
know-how, managerial enterprise, skilled labor and expanding markets. While the availability of foreign aid

55

is desirable, the terms of such assistance have generally
been hard: the cost of repayment involves either a depletion of their scarce foreign exchange, or, when payment is made in kind, a loss of natural resources. Experience has proved that the essential stimulus to development as well as to sustained economic growth, must come
from internal sources. In their efforts to develop,
they accumulate the knowledge of how best to achieve their
own progress.

REFERENCES

1. Enke, Stephen, _Economics for Development_. Englewood
    Cliffs: Prentice-Hall, Inc., 1963.

2. Higgins, Benjamin, _Economic Development_, Revised
    edition. New York: W. W. Norton & Company, Inc.

3. Hirschman, Albert O., _The Strategy of Economic
    Development_. New Haven: Yale University Press,
    1958.

4. Kurihara, K. K., _The Keynesian Theory of Economic
    Development_. New York: Columbia University Press,
    1959.

5. Kuznets, Simon, _Economic Growth and Structure:
    Selected Essays_. New York: W. W. Norton &
    Company, Inc., 1965.

6. Nurkse, Ragnar, _Problems of Capital Formation in
    Underdeveloped Countries_. Oxford: Basil Blackwell,
    1953.

7. Staley, Eugene, _The Future of Underdeveloped Coun-
    tries_. New York: Harper & Row Publishers, Inc.
    1957.

8. United Nations, _International Flow of Long-Term
    Capital and Official Donations_. 1961-66
    (E/4371) U.N., New York, June 1967.

9. United Nations, _The External Financing of Economic
    Development_. New York: 1968 Report of the
    Secretary General, Sales No.: E.68.II.D.10.

10. United Nations, _The United Nations Development
    Decade_. New York: Proposals for Action, 1962,
    Sales No.: 62.II.B.2.

REVIEW QUESTIONS

Terms

a barter economy

the demonstration effect

disguised unemployment

imbalance in development

ex ante and ex post

the saving ratio

capital accumulation

effective demand

dual economy

input-output exchange

a developed credit system

fragmented agricultural holdings

capital/labor ratio

ratio of capital to output

the stock of capital

the investment ratio

the homogeneity of output

gross domestic product

leading sector

intersectoral technological linkages

Questions

1. Describe the symptoms of underdevelopment.

2. Explain why though the yield per acre of land is high, output per worker is low. When does this happen?

3. What is the relationship between a dual economy and a leading sector?

4. Does population growth hamper economic development or economic growth most?

5. What is the cost which developing countries have to pay in social terms for the assistance they receive from the richer countries?

CHAPTER IV

THE ECONOMICS OF GROWTH

>"Parsimony, and not industry, is
the immediate cause of the increase of
capital...It puts into motion an additional quantity of industry, which
gives an additional value to the annual
produce."

>Ad. Smith, Wealth of Nations,
Book II, Ch. 3

The purpose of this chapter is to study the
various conceptions and/or analyses of economic progress
as they were developed at various points of time, by different authors. In so doing, we will be looking at their
assessment of the relationship between the three main variables affecting economic growth, namely consumption, saving and income. Two points should be kept in mind in the
course of this study. The first is that economic progress is not an isolated process, but rather the result of
the interaction of many variables, some of them even outside the field of economics. It is the impact of these
phenomena on the reasoning and outlook of the economists
of their time, as much as the theories which they were
thus led to formulate, which are of interest to our study.
As Mitchell put it: "The thing which has most of all
stimulated the minds of successive generations of economists has been to endeavor to contribute to the understanding of the problems with which their generation as a
whole was concerned. ...These economic problems were
caused primarily by changes in the economic life of the
people, changes that were coming about through a

cumulative process." [1]

The second point to remember during this study
of the various schools of thought, is that the difference
between them is not so much a difference of objectives,
but rather of the means to realize such objectives.   As
a matter of fact, the objective of realizing a greater
national output, or income, is basically the same for all
the theories which will be reviewed.   It is in the means
to achieve this greater output, in the locus of emphasis
on the structural and the policy variables, as well as in
the vision and interpretation of all these factors, that
lies the difference between the theories to be studied.

Classical Growth Theories

Reference is often made to the Classical School
as if it were a homogeneous body of thought whereas in
actual fact there were wide differences of opinion within
it;   the only common denominator was the situation created
by the economic conditions under which its numerous authors lived and wrote.   Schumpeter[2] distinguishes three
entirely different types of 'vision' or outlook according
to the aspects which they stressed, namely: the pessimists, the optimists and the socialists.

In the first category, the pessimists, he
places Malthus, Ricardo and James Mill.   To these, it
was the pressure of population on means of subsistence,
decreasing returns from the land and hence its failure to
expand the food supply, which resulted in the decline of

_____

[1]Mitchell, Wesley C., Lecture Notes on Types of Economic
Theory, 1949.
[2]Schumpeter, J. A., History of Economic Analysis, 1954,
Part III, Ch. 5 and Part IV, Ch. 6.

net earnings from industry, low real wages, and increasing rent for the land. However, as these writers were formulating their pessimistic forecasts, important technological developments were taking place: the Industrial Revolution was heralding a new era of increased production, yet so preoccupied were they with what they saw around them of "cramped economies, struggling with ever decreasing success for their daily bread" that they failed to grasp the portent of the new developments. Eventually, real wages in England increased by 50 per cent between 1880 and 1900. Adam Smith was not as pessimistic as those mentioned above but he did foresee that economic progress would come to a stationary state soon. John Stuart Mill, the son of James Mill, though he harboured the same views about future prospects, was not as pessimistic as the others, only because he thought that people would follow the moral restraint preached by Malthus and that with the fall in the rate of population growth, normal consumption levels would obtain.

In the category of the optimists, Schumpeter places Henry Charles Carey, Friedrich List and Frédéric Bastiat. He traces the cause of their optimism to their vision of a capitalist society having the ability to create productive capacity and thus go on expanding. The holders of this view were not as famous as, or did not have the depth of Malthus and Ricardo, but their interpretation of events and their theories were proved to be more to the point.

In the socialist category, Schumpeter places Karl Marx only. Unlike the other economists of his time who looked upon economic progress as only one aspect of economic theory, Marx considered economic development

as the core of economic theory, and saw in its ever
changing aspects the causes of changes in the social
framework. Marx had a very clear conception of the
potential of capitalistic society, albeit a rather
biased one: he related development to technological
change fuelled by capital accumulation. The latter he
translated into the exploitation theory. He did em-
phasize though, the capacity-creating use made of capitalistic gains, whether they arose from the exploitation
of labor, or from re-invested profits. To Marx, the
value of every commodity was proportional to the quantity
of labor contained in it, provided that that labor was
in accordance with standards of efficiency in production.[3]

It should be mentioned that in the period immediately following the Industrial Revolution, or between
1873 and 1900, the effects of the expansion in physical
output resulting from new technical progress - when they
first made themselves felt - were reflected in falling
prices, labor unemployment and sometimes even business
losses. Consequently, the hardships generated in the
short-term by the prevailing economic conditions in manufacturing, obscured the view to the long-term advantages.

The economists of the marginalist school,
William Stanley Jevons, Leon Walras, Karl Menger and John
Bates Clark, related price determination to subjective
satisfaction and replaced the labor theory of value by
marginal-utility theory. In so doing they shifted the
emphasis from supply (of savings) to demand (for goods).
They defined competition, analyzed its workings in minute

---

[3]this was the labor theory of value developed by Ad.
Smith, Ricardo and other classics, but Marx as we shall
see later carried it to a further degree for reasons of
his own.

detail and from this base, they developed the theory of
deviation from competition, such as pure monopoly and
oligopoly.[4]   These men did not bring much change to the
theory of economic development per se, but a clearer perspective of such phenomena as population growth, capital
accumulation and the resulting increase in demand which
induces internal economies, such as technical improvements which reduce production costs.   The significance
of the marginal-utility theory was in its contribution
to the problem of resource allocation.

To these findings, Marshall added the effect
of non-induced and revolutionary inventions, unhampered
by the law of diminishing returns in production of food
and raw materials.   The classics had thought of such
evolution as a continuous and almost automatic process
which presented no problems.   He put the emphasis on
the entrepreneur,[5] as distinct from the capitalist and
his profit from interest.   The earnings of the entrepreneur were his reward for innovating, i.e. applying new
inventions to the methods of production and thus taking
the risk that any yet untried method presents.   These
returns were designated by various names: earnings of
management, (Alfred Marshall), wages of superintendence
(J. S. Mill), or rent of ability (Emil Mangoldt).[6]
Marshall's emphasis on the "two blades of the scissors"
(demand and supply) underlined the relationship between
consumption and production and at a time when other

----

[4]later, this was to lead Marshall to examine more closely
cases of decreasing cost curves.

[5]the owner-managed firm.

[6]Schumpeter, op. cit., pp. 645-47.

economists were busy arguing about different theories, Marshall's biggest contribution to development theory was his sense of perspective.

The notion that opportunities for investment would decline in the future, as compared with people's propensity to save, has been formulated by classical as well as modern economists, from Malthus and Ricardo, to Keynes, Hansen and Harrod, though it was expressed in somewhat different terms.[7] However, one should not forget that one of the outstanding features of modern economic growth, especially in the United States, is that technological progress and training have tended to offset the tendency of the marginal productivity of capital to fall because of the law of diminishing returns. Labor productivity has increased at least as fast as capital productivity, and the share of labor from the national income pie is still about 75 per cent.

Consumption, Saving and Income

Theories which consider consumption and/or saving as determining factors in output, date back to the first part of the 18th century. Richard Cantillon, the forerunner of much of what was to become economic theory, in his "Essai sur la nature du commerce en général" (c. 1730), stressed the importance of promptly spending the income accruing from agriculture in order to keep the economic process going. He considered that pure rent - generated by the productivity of scarce natural agents - was the only net income to society. This view was also held by François Quesnay, the founder

---

[7] the stationary state (classics); secular stagnation (modern). This is the underconsumption theory of which more will be said in the coming pages.

of the Physiocratic school.   In his "Maximes Genérales"
(1758) he emphasized the need to consume in order to has-
ten the flow of income into all phases of the annual circulation (production process).   He was against the
formation of pecuniary fortunes (capital accumulation)
and believed that saving would interrupt the flow of
income.

    With <u>Adam Smith</u>, the emphasis shifts from con-
sumption to saving,[8] but the objective of economic progress remains the same.   His treatment of the theory of
saving and investment in Book II of the "Wealth of
Nations" (1776) is considered the basis of a large part
of subsequent writings on the subject.   He is believed
to have written Book II after his visit to France during
which he was somewhat influenced by the concepts of the
Physiocrats - although he subsequently formulated them
in his own way.   For instance, in Chapter 3 (of Book
II), entitled "Of the Accumulation of Capital, or of
Productive and Unproductive Labour" (from which the
quotation at the beginning of this chapter is taken),
he makes the distinction between productive labor "which
adds to the value of the subject upon which it is be-
stowed" and, therefore, increases the stock of capital,
and unproductive labor which "does not fix or realize
itself in any particular subject or vendible commodity."
In the first category he includes mainly factory and
agricultural workers and in the second, menial servants,
the sovereign, public officers, comedians, musicians,
buffoons and all those whose services do not yield any

---

[8]an emphasis stressed by many of the economists which
immediately followed him.

profit.[9]   The capital which results from the efforts of
the productive workers must be saved in order to further
production.   This kind of saving was made up mainly of
stocks of durable goods, gold and silver, or a trade
surplus; there was no particular emphasis on capital
formation as such, or on the time lag needed in generating
it.

Jean Baptiste Say whose "Traité d'Economie
Politique" (1803) became famous because of its chapter
on the Law of Markets (loi des débouchés) stated that
supply creates its own demand.[10]   He meant that the demand for any product in general is a function of the income generated by the production of other goods - i.e.
the only way to obtain the goods we need, is to work, or
participate in producing the national output (supply).
This is just a different way of emphasizing the need for
capital accumulation.

Thomas Malthus in his "Principles of Political
Economy" (1820) - (not to be confused with his "Essay on
the Principles of Population", 1798, 2nd. ed. 1803)
strongly disagreed with Say and the principle of capital
accumulation 'per se'.   He maintained that the wealth
of an economy at any time is limited by its capacity to
consume.[11]   His disagreement with Say was based on his
principle of effective demand and he claimed that saving,
even if promptly invested, may lead to deadlock if carried

---

[9] the distinction really is between activity which results
in capital formation and that which satisfies consumption
needs only.   Compare, for instance, the case of a country
poor in resources which uses them to produce luxury goods.
[10] which according to Schumpeter (op. cit., p. 618-619) is
not an identity.
[11] in this he was probably influenced by Cantillon;   see
p. 5 above.

65

beyond a certain optimal point. The basis of the underconsumption theory is that aggregate demand may not be
sufficient to keep the economy progressing. As first
formulated, investment being the difference between
consumption and income, would provide for the normal increase in population and for replacement for worn-out
capital stock, hence a stationary economy. Contemporary
economists have added to this theory the notion of the
capacity-creating characteristic of investment, thereby
implying that there will be excess capacity in the following period unless consumption and investment are increased. If consumption is not increased, then business
firms will not invest in expanding production (the acceleration principle) and this will lead to a decline in
national income. There are several interpretations of
the underconsumption theory: Malthus attributed it to
oversaving (the paradox of thrift): saving reduces demand for consumer goods and at the same time increases
the supply of such goods when it is re-invested.[12]
Marxian theory attributed underconsumption to the fact
that the relative share of labor wages in total income
falls as income increases. Finally, the Keynesian interpretation which was also that of Alvin Hansen, was that
the decline in investment opportunities and the diminishing marginal efficiency of investment eventually lead to
stagnation.

A pupil of Malthus, William Nassau Senior, in
his "An Outline of the Science of Political Economy"

---

[12]this argument overlooks the possibility that the increase in the supply of consumers goods resulting from
more investment will lower their price, which is tan-
tamount to an increase in purchasing power.

(1836) disagreed with Malthus and established the same
distinction of productive and unproductive as Ad. Smith,
but he applied it to consumption.   Productive consumption is the "use of a product which occasions another
product."[13]   The concept was applied by him to households where commodities and services are not consumed
but provide services to members of the household, and
was later adopted by Wassily Leontieff who considers
households as an industry which consumes productively.
Senior's contribution was his theory of interest as a
compensation for saving ('abstinence' or deferment of
enjoyment).   This enabled him to speak of the productivity of capital and to carry out his investigation into
problems of interest and wages.   Saving (or capital
accumulation) is thus introduced as a factor of production which stands in the same relation to profit as
labor does to wages.

     Karl Marx (Das Kapital, 1867....1910) was the
last of the classic economists to cling to the labor
theory of value.   However, his theory of value does not
aim at explaining the prices at which commodities are
exchanged, nor does it explain the level of prices, or
the reasons of their fluctuations;   it aims only at explaining how labor is exploited in a capitalist economy.
According to Marx, the unemployment resulting from mechanization creates an industrial reserve army which de-
presses real wages to levels of misery and degradation
that might eventually lead to the final revolution.
As shown above, these predictions have been proved wrong
because of the progress in technology, but also because

---

[13]Senior, op. cit., p. 57.

of the emergence of powerful labor unions. To Marx, economic progress is propelled by the force of capital accumulation which proceeds at a rate faster than that of population growth. In the absence of technical improvement, this increase of capital per capita would decrease its productivity, and, with competition compelling producers to re-invest all their profits, would result in redundant capacity and an ever decreasing rate of profit. The desire for capital accumulation causes, then, a decrease in consumption, and leads to crises which are inherent in the contradictory nature of the capitalist system of production.

Marx's contribution lies in his description of the forces which underlie capitalistic development and in his suggestion of an alternative to it, i.e. planned economic development. In trying to give an analytical account of the evolution of economic institutions, he failed to allow for the process of ceaseless change of which human society is the product.

Modern Growth Theories

Chronologically, Joseph Schumpeter belongs in the classification of modern writers; conceptually, he stands by himself, both in terms of his contribution and of his interpretation of the economic process. With his work on The Theory of Economic Development, first published in German in 1911 and in English in 1934, he was the first to single out this field of economic theory for study and analysis.

Schumpeter emphasizes the role of the entrepreneur as an innovator who is willing to take the risk of trying out modern inventions for technical improvements

in production.   The profit he makes is his reward for
his initiative and results from his being the first to
reap the benefits of the new technology.   This profit
attracts new capital into production and thus raises
the rate of interest as well.   However, the profit
disappears as soon as competitors start imitating the
innovations.   Without other innovations or what we now
call technological progress, excessive capital accumulation and competition result in diminishing returns.
In this respect, we find Schumpeter expressing the same
view as Marx but for a different reason: the incidental
nature of the profit-inducing innovations and their interaction with the availability of credit and the role
of the entrepreneur, render the path of development in
capitalistic economies a jerky rather than a steady one.
He predicted that the very success of capitalism would
be the cause of its decline when the people would come
to prefer a welfare state system to a market economy.
Historical evidence has not corroborated his predictions.

It was stated at the beginning of this chapter
that the various theories which have been reviewed were
generally prompted by their authors' interpretation of
the economic conditions ruling in their times.   For instance, the kind of society which inspired Say's law was
one in which enterprises were small and producers in any
field were self-employed individuals, where proceeds from
sales were spent immediately on furthering production,
and thus saving was the same thing as investment.   By
comparison, in our modern society of big business corporations, ownership is completely divorced from management, factor markets are quite distinct from - though

influenced by - consumers markets, and saving and investment are two distinct processes having entirely different motivations.

The happy functioning of the society of the classics was based on two postulates which were supposed to operate under normal conditions, namely: a) the rate of interest which ensured full use of resources by adjusting investment to saving; and b) flexible wages which, by adjusting to conditions of supply and demand, ensured full employment.[14] The gradual evolution from the agricultural-industrial economic structure of the 18th century to the highly industrialized set-up of the advanced economies of today, was accompanied by a concomitant evolution in the vision and economic concepts which provide the tools of economic analysis. This transformation was corroborated by empirical evidence: the Great Depression of the 1930's proved that wage adjustment could not cure massive unemployment, nor would a low rate of interest stimulate investment if economic conditions - e.g. the level of demand - were not favorable.

The developed countries of the free world had reached the stage of mass production, but inherent in this progress lay the seeds of economic instability: mass production provided ever larger profits but required increasingly wider markets (demand) to absorb its output and keep employment at the optimal level. The emphasis, therefore, was no longer on the supply of savings (capital accumulation) but on (aggregate) demand for all goods and services. A new kit of tools was hence needed to gauge the new situation and provide recommendations and solutions.

---

[14]see Hansen, Alvin, A Guide to Keynes, 1953, p. 20.

The "new Economics"

Some writers among the classics had had the foresight to predict the eventual need to stimulate demand in order to keep the economic process going: Cantillon and Quesnay, among the early ones, later Malthus and Marx and more recently Wicksell. However, the decisive shift of emphasis on demand was brought about by John Maynard Keynes in his work "The General Theory of Employment Interest and Money" which came out in 1936 and revolutionized economic thinking.[15] Even those policy-makers who do not share Keynes's opinions have adopted his theoretical framework and adapted it with some modifications to their own economic systems. Keynes, who has been called "a many-sided genius"[16] was a policy-maker himself in his own country, England, and wrote his book at a time when the reduced output and massive unemployment of the Great Depression, had been plaguing the countries of the Western world. His recommendation for deliberate state action to take care of any recession or depression - even at the risk of sacrificing the time-honored balanced-budget concept - was meant to be a corrective to the laissez-faire attitude of 18th century capitalism which still prevailed. It was welcome to policy-makers hard-pressed between the necessity of giving relief to the great number of unemployed and that of starting their economies on the way to recovery, while vainly trying all along to balance their respective budgets.

---

[15]Keynes put together theories which had been already formulated, adding substance and precision to them.

[16]Samuelson, Paul A., Economics, 7th. ed., 1967, p. 195.

To go over all of Keynesian theory would be
like a repetition of the Principles course - so much have
his writings permeated present-day economics.   Instead,
let us look very briefly at the most salient points of
his contribution to the theory of economic growth namely,
the three new tools of analysis which distinguish Keynes
from his predecessors.   They are the consumption function, the investment-demand function and the liquidity
preference function.

The consumption function relates consumption to
income ($C = f(Y)$) and tells us that consumption increases
at a lower rate than income, or the marginal propensity
to consume ($\Delta C/\Delta Y$) is always smaller than unity.
This is because people's habits are such that some part
of income is saved, unless it is very low, and a larger
proportion of any addition to net income is also saved.
This gap between consumption and income representing the
community's saving, means that supply (income) does not
create a proportional demand - a refutation of Say's law.
Therefore, the ability of total potential output to be
marketed will depend on the willingness of business firms
to invest the amounts saved into the production of capital
goods - to increase future production of consumers goods.

However, the motivations of business firms to
invest are entirely different from those of the savers:
it stands to reason that they will not produce goods unless they have some expectation of being able to sell
them.   They are also concerned with the cost of investing
these savings, i.e. the rate of interest.   Hence the
investment-demand function[17] which relates the rate of

---

[17] $I = F(Y,i)$ where the function (F) stands for the marginal efficiency of capital, and (i) for the rate of
interest.

investment to the marginal efficiency of "capital in
general which that rate of investment will establish"[18] -
that rate itself being an aggregate of the marginal efficiency (schedule) of different types of capital goods.
The marginal efficiency of capital is, then, the ratio
between the expected yield from one additional capital
asset and its supply price.   The marginal efficiency
of any capital good will, therefore, decrease as investment in it increases.[19]

What if savers do not wish to lend their savings
but prefer to keep them in liquid form (hoard them)?
The reason may be that they are uncertain about the future, or that they are waiting for (speculating on) a
fall in the price of bonds - and a rise in the rate of
interest.   Here we find a third tool of analysis brought
about by Keynes, the liquidity preference function which
relates people's desire to hold cash (to hoard) to the
level of the rate of interest.[20]   People's demand for
cash may be for either one of three motives: transactions, precautionary and speculative.   It is the last
motive with which we are interested here: the first two
are not influenced by the rate of interest, but rather

---

[18]Keynes, J. M., The General Theory of Employment
Interest and Money, 1936, p. 136.

[19]investment is "autonomous" when it is independent of
the level of income, i.e. due to an external factor, such
as government spending, or new technology; it is
"induced" when it is due to consumers' demand.

[20]total liquidity preference function: $M = L(Y,r)$.
Speculative-demand liquidity preference function:
$M_2 = L_2(r)$; where (M) is the total money supply, (L)
the demand for money, (Y) national income and (r) the
rate of interest. $M = M_1 + M_2$ and $L = L_1 + L_2$.
Keynes, op. cit., p. 19.

by the level of income and do not, therefore directly
affect investment decisions.   The higher the rate of
interest, the less will people tend to hold on to their
savings in the form of cash and vice versa - the liquidity preference schedule is a declining function of the
rate of interest.   It can be seen here how the monetary
authorities can affect the liquidity preference function
by means of the tools of monetary policy.   Keynes's
contribution to the theory of saving is his assumption
that people save without having any particular intention
to invest and may not want to invest their savings;   in
which case such saving becomes a leakage out of the income stream in the sense that it does not contribute to
further the production process.

An analysis of the factors underlying consumption expenditures and investment outlays gives the aggregate demand function which is the cornerstone of
Keynesian theory and which "relates any given level of
employment to the 'proceeds' which that level of employment is expected to realize."[21]

Dynamic Growth Models

The understanding and recognition of the fundamental relationship between capital accumulation and
economic growth in a modern dynamic (and advanced) economy was first initiated by Sir Roy F. Harrod.[22]   Starting
from a Keynesian (static) framework, Harrod developed his
dynamic theory to explain how steady growth occurs over

_____

[21]Keynes, op. cit., p. 89.

[22]Harrod, R. F., "An Essay in Dynamic Theory", Economic
Journal XLIX March 1939, expanded and revised in Towards
a Dynamic Economics, 1963.

time and how it can deviate from its equilibrium path,
stating that investment depends upon the change in the
level of effective demand. In doing so he developed
the acceleration principle as a theory of investment,
thus making his (induced) investment more dynamic than
Keynes's autonomous investment.

Harrod's "natural" rate of growth

This is the more powerful tool of the two
models of growth rates that Harrod has developed: he
defines it as "the rate of advance which the increase of
population and technological improvements allow"[23] and
gives it in the following equation:

1) $G_n C_r = $ or $\neq s$

where G = the rate of growth, ($_n$ for natural), and $C_r =$
the capital-output ratio. It will be noticed that (s)
the rate of saving may or may not equal the desired
natural rate of growth. This model precludes involuntary unemployment and therefore assumes that an economy
which is growing at the natural rate would be a full employment economy. This is a condition which rarely obtains in an underdeveloped economy, albeit if the meaning
of full employment is correctly interpreted. The natural
rate ensures a level of production at which all producers
have made the right choice between work and leisure.

As regards the limitations on this rate of
growth, they are spelled out by Harrod as "the maximum
rate of growth allowed by the increase in population,
accumulation of capital, technological improvement and
the work/leisure preference schedule, supposing that

---

[23]Ibid., p. 87.

there is always full employment." [24]   In a high-saving
advanced economy, it is obvious that of the three lim-
itations mentioned it is the full employment of labor
ceiling which is the most real: if the growth of output
is limited by labor shortage, then the accelerator would
generate less investment and aggregate demand would fall.
A decline in total output would follow and at this point
the accelerator would tend to become negative. As regards the role of technology, Harrod does not specify
whether it is meant to save labor - and this again would
apply to advanced economies - or to improve production.
He seems to indicate a constant labor-output ratio as well
as a constant capital-output ratio and states that in the
long-run no growth can exceed the natural rate.

 To summarize, if an economy can maintain full
employment with the advance in technology, it can realize
optimal growth; but this cannot be achieved without capital accumulation and this is where the dynamic equilibrium condition is set out:

2) $$g^a = \Delta K/K = \Delta Y^a/Y^a = \Delta Y^p/Y^p = g^p$$

where K equals the stock of productive capacity, Y^a =
actual output and Y^p = potential output. Here the actual
rate of growth (g^a) equals the potential rate of growth
(g^p). Harrod takes capital accumulation for granted and
this is why he calls his natural growth rate the "welfare
optimum". This optimality implies that there is:
a) full employment, and b) rising labor productivity.

[24] Harrod, R. F., "An Essay in Dynamic Theory", (from
Economic Journal, March 1939), Hansen and Clarence,
Readings in Business Cycles and National Income, 1953,
p. 216.

As a tool of analysis, the terms of reference of the natural rate are not clearly defined: the role of technology, the connotation of population (whether it includes all population or only the active part of it, cf. choice between work and leisure). But Harrod is describing a kind of world which is plagued with economic instability and the more developed it gets, the more does the threat of instability become a possibility.

Harrod's "warranted" rate of growth

This rate is defined by Harrod as "that overall rate of advance which, if executed, will leave entrepreneurs in a state of mind in which they are prepared to carry on a similar advance. ... in the aggregate, progress in the current period should be equal to progress in the last preceding period." It is expressed by Harrod in the following equation:

3) $\qquad G_w C_r = s$

where G_w = the warranted rate of growth, C_r = the capital-output ratio and s = the rate of saving. This equation assumes that actual saving (S_t) during time-period (t) is a constant proportion (s) of (Y_t), the level of net national product resulting from the utilization of (K_t), the stock of real capital, at the warranted rate of growth (G_w), i.e. under full employment of capacity.

4) $\qquad S_t/Y_t = s \qquad$ (constant)

5) $\qquad (K_t - K_{t-1})/(Y_t - Y_{t-1}) = C_r \qquad$ (constant)

(C_r) is a constant proportion of the difference in output (Y_t) at period (t) and the previous year's output, or ($Y_t - Y_{t-1}$). (C_r) also represents the rate of net investment desired by the entrepreneur.

6) $\qquad I_t = C_r(Y_t - Y_{t-1})$

the model assumes the equality between actual saving and realized investment, or ex post magnitudes:

7) $\qquad I_t = S_t$

then

8) $\qquad (K_t - K_{t-1}) = I_{t-1} = C_r(Y_t - Y_{t-1}) = sY_{t-1}$

9) $\qquad G_w = (Y_t - Y_{t-1})/Y_{t-1} = s/C_r$

10) $\qquad G_w C_r = s$

Harrod's (G_w) which he calls the "entre-preneurial equilibrium" is the rate of growth which satisfies the profit motive and is in accordance with savers' desires. It allows for the possibility of "growing involuntary unemployment," because of productive capacity outrunning effective demand, although it guarantees full utilization of capital, and foresees that the "warranted" rate might exceed the "natural" rate, i.e. instability and/or stagnation. From the last part of its definition as given above, it can be seen that it takes into account the fact that producers plan output in advance and therefore have to guess what demand will be, so they increase their output by the same rate of increase of the preceding period. Finally, Harrod takes into account induced investment only and does not allow for autonomous investment. This latter point makes his G_w inadequate for developing countries, where massive public investment mainly in social overhead capital, is often necessary to start the growth process.[25] Another factor which makes G_w unsuitable for developing economies is that this leisurely rate of capital accumulation, even when capital is fully utilized, is not consistent with a high rate of population

_____

[25] although his "k" in $(GC = s - k)$ could be interpreted as including social overhead capital.

growth, especially when it is accompanied by rising labor
productivity.

Domar's Growth Model

Prof. Evsey Domar developed his theory of
growth in successive articles published in the American
Economic Review in 1947; they were later reprinted in
book form in 1957.[26]   Like Harrod, he had in mind an
economy with a high saving ratio and a high productivity
of capital, but, unlike Harrod, he does not say what investment would be, but rather what it should be.   He
defines his objectives as an attempt "to find the conditions needed for the maintenance of full employment
over a period of time, or more exactly, <u>the rate of growth</u>
<u>of national income</u> which the maintenance of full employ-
ment requires.[27]   The variables in Domar's model are
also functions of time but, unlike Harrod's variables
which are measured in finite time periods, Domar's variables are continuous over time.   In other words, Harrod
measures amount of flow during a time period and Domar
measures the rate of flow at any moment of time.   He
assumes that the ratio of savings (α) to net national
output, or effective demand (Y), is constant:

11) $S/Y = \alpha$

here Domar's (α) stands for the marginal propensity to
save and is the reciprocal of Keynes's (demand-expanding)
multiplier; as such, it is a 'demand-decreasing'
coefficient.   In this respect, it is different from
Harrod's (s) which stands for the average propensity to

---

[26]Domar, E., <u>Essays in the Theory of Economic Growth</u>,
1957.

[27]<u>Ibid</u>., p. 84.

save, is the reciprocal of a (resource-releasing) multiplier, and is an 'expenditure-reducing' coefficient.[28]
On the supply side, there is (σ) which Domar qualifies
as the "potential social average productivity of investment,"

12) $I = \sigma(dY/dt)$

explaining that " σ is concerned with the increase in
productive capacity of the whole society and not with
the productive capacity per dollar invested in the new
plants taken by themselves, that is with (s)" . . .
"the most important property of (σ) is its potential
character."[29]   Domar's investment is fixed, autonomous,
and does not include inventories, another difference
from Harrod's.

13) $S = I$

He assumes (σ) constant also and says that any difference between (α) and (σ) would mean inefficient, or
too rapid a rate of investment, compared with growth of
labor and advance in technology.   (Hence, he does not
assume the equality between actual saving and realized
investment.)

14) $\sigma Y = \alpha(dY/dt)$

15) $Y = (\alpha/\sigma)(dY/dt)$

16) $G = \alpha\sigma$

(G) is the growth rate of demand necessary to keep investment at the required level to achieve equilibrium
growth.

---

[28] see Kurihara, K. K., National Income and Economic
Growth, 1957.
[29] Domar, op. cit., pp. 89-90.

Domar stressed the inability of an economy to
sustain equilibrium growth unless the ratio of increase
in investment was equal at all times to the ratio of increase in output ($\Delta I/I = \Delta Y/Y$). This springs from his
emphasis on the dual aspect of investment: generating
effective demand and simultaneously increasing productive
capacity. He takes the constancy of a high (α) and
(σ) for granted and recommends that net investment be
adjusted to the values of both by means of fiscal policy
or other means. His main concern[30] is with the
capacity-increasing aspect of investment, so that if in
the following period investment were to grow at a lower
rate, added productive capacity would not be fully utilized. He also fears the competition of the new productive capacity for that equipment which is already in use
and may become obsolete.

Domar's required growth rate of investment
given by equation (16) is, like Harrod's G_w, a rate of
growth for advanced economies which have already built
up their capital stock of productive capacity and reached
the mass production stage. As such, it falls short of
what is required for a developing economy, although it is
of the autonomous type. Moreover, the constancy of (σ)
would not agree with the rising productivity and technological progress needed for development. Domar's
assumption of full employment is not consistent with the
capacity-creating aspect that he attributes to investment.

---

[30]inspired by Keynes's declining marginal efficiency
of capital doctrine.

Finally, Domar does not allow for the inter-dependence of (α) and (σ) while historical evidence tells us that there is a close positive relationship between capital accumulation and capital productivity.

REFERENCES

1. Blaug, M., _Economic Theory in Retrospect_. Homewood, Ill.: Richard D. Irwin, rev. ed., 1968.

2. Domar, Evsey D., _Essays in the Theory of Economic Growth_. New York: Oxford University Press, 1957.

3. Hansen and Clarence, _Readings in Business Cycles and National Income_. New York: W. W. Norton & Company, Inc., 1953.

5. Harrod, R. F., _Towards a Dynamic Economics_. New York: Macmillan and Co. Ltd., 1963.

6. Keynes, John Maynard, _The General Theory of Employment Interest and Money_. New York: Harcourt, Brace and Company, 1936.

7. Kurihara, Kenneth K., _The Keynesian Theory of Economic Development_. New York: Columbia University Press, 1959.

8. Roll, Eric, _A History of Economic Thought_, Third Edition. Englewood Cliffs, N. J.: Prentice-Hall, Inc., 1953.

9. Samuelson, Paul A., _Economics - An Introductory Analysis_, Seventh Edition. New York: McGraw-Hill, 1967, Part VI.

10. Schumpeter, J. A., _History of Economic Analysis_. New York: Oxford University Press, 1954.

11. Schumpeter, J. A., _The Theory of Economic Development_. Cambridge, Mass.: Harvard University Press, 1934 (English edition).

12. Smith, Adam, _An Inquiry Into The Nature And Causes Of The Wealth Of Nations_, Vol. I and II. Homewood, Ill.: Richard D. Irwin, Paperback Classics in Economics, 1963 - original edition 1776.

REVIEW QUESTIONS

Terms

a stationary economy

capacity-creating

the labor theory of value

the marginalist school

'earnings of management'

'wages of superintendence'

the marginal productivity of capital

pure rent

welfare optimum

the acceleration principle

the paradox of thrift

innovations

aggregate demand

the balanced-budget concept

investment-demand function

consumption function

liquidity preference function

the Physiocratic school

potential rate of growth

static versus dynamic theory

Questions

1. Describe the three types of outlook that Schumpeter speaks of. In what connection was his identification done?

2. What was Karl Marx's conception of capitalism?

3. Describe the conditions prevailing in factories and in the business world at the time of the industrial revolution.

4. Discuss the underconsumption theory and comment on its various interpretations.

5. Discuss the views and the contribution of Wm. Senior to the theory of economic development.

6. What was Schumpeter's main contribution to economic development theory?

7. In what way does modern, industrialized capitalism differ from that of the 17th and 18th centuries and how has this changed or affected the writings of the contemporary economists?

8. What was the main factor which motivated Harrod and Domar in developing their growth models?   In what do they differ from Keynes?

9. Make the distinction between Harrod's 'natural' and 'warranted' growth rates.

10. What is the important point that Domar's model tries to demonstrate?

CHAPTER V

CAPITAL FORMATION

Capital formation is the increase in a country's stock of productive capacity which will help it to expand its future output. It is made possible by saving (capital accumulation)[1] and the introduction of more roundabout methods of production. The relation between capital and economic development is demonstrated by the fact that per capita investment is high in the economically advanced countries and low in the developing ones. An economy undergoes significant changes as it develops: the physical composition of the stock of capital changes and so does the relationship between capital and labor. Theoretically, economic development depends upon capital accumulation; in practice, capital is created in the process of development and the latter may be sparked off, as seen earlier, by economic as well as non-economic factors.

The discussion in this chapter will cover the various aspects of capital formation, investment criteria and the priorities in project selection.

The Various Aspects of Capital Formation

A nation's rate of saving out of its current income is one of the main determinants of its rate of economic growth. Inasmuch as this saving results in capital formation, the nation is foregoing present consumption in order to increase its future consumption. The assumption then is that current saving is equal to

---

[1] in this text, the term capital accumulation stands for saving and that of capital formation, for the productive capacity which such saving makes possible.

current investment and the latter is required for growth.
Investment in social overhead capital will increase productivity; however, technological improvements can lead
to increased productivity without an increase in the
overall stock of capital but not without capital investment in research and in training.   By definition, saving
represents the part of disposable income that the people
do not spend on consumption (APS = 1 - APC).   The consumption function tells us that the main determinant of
consumption is income; there are other secondary determinants, such as liquid assets and bank credit, but just
now we will consider income.

Under equilibrium conditions, the gross national product must be such that private savings plus government tax collections equal autonomous spending - i.e.
private investment plus government expenditure.   Potential gross national product represents the level of output which could be obtained in a given period of time if
the economy were at full employment.   This maximum output depends on both the quantity of available resources
and the level of technology.   With technology taken as
given, the quantity of resources would, therefore, influence the level of an economy's potential g.n.p.
When an economy reaches the point of full employment, it
is faced with the choice of either allocating some of its
resources currently used in consumption to activities
which will increase its productive capacity and hence its
future output, or maintaining its level of consumption and
running the risk of a decline in its rate of growth.
This is the production-possibility concept which is the
basis of economic analysis.   The outlook is further
complicated by the absence of a clear line of demarcation

between present and future consumption, because of operational as well as temporal aspects. Consider, for instance, the difference in the production function and
time lag (gestation period) of the capital goods required
in the manufacture of such disparate consumer goods as
shoes and cars.

Demand and Supply

The demand for capital depends upon the incentive to invest; the profit motive is one such incentive
and probably the most powerful one; there is also the
urge to build up an enterprise for future benefit or
fame. In highly developed countries opportunities for
investment are taken up as they develop because capital -
in the sense of liquid assets - is abundant. In developing countries the opportunities to invest, or rather
the need for investment, exist, but there either is not
enough capital, or the size of the market is such that it
does not provide enough incentives for investment.

The supply of capital depends upon the ability
and the willingness to save: the ability or the propensity to save depends on income while the willingness or
the desire to save depends on various factors such as the
number of one's dependents, or the rate of interest - as
an inducement to part with one's liquid assets, or to
save on consumption. In developed countries, generally
the rate of saving is high because income is high, while
the contrary is the case in underdeveloped countries.
This is another way of saying that the propensity to save
is function of the level of income. There are instances
when the rate of saving can be increased in developing
countries and these will be examined in chapter VIII.

but, generally speaking, the shortage of domestic savings
is and has always been one of the most important imped-
iments to capital formation.

The demand and supply aspects apply to labor as
well as capital: large amounts of capital would not
benefit a country which does not have the trained labor
to operate it. The supply of labor is governed primarily
by the rate of population growth and by the opportunities
for education and training of the existing manpower.
The demand for labor depends generally upon the same factors which condition the demand for capital, namely the
incentive to invest and labor productivity. With modern
technology, another factor comes into the picture and that
is the alternative (opportunity) cost between the labor
factor and the capital factor.

The Measurement of Capital

If capital, taken in terms of capital goods, is
a means to further production of goods, then its measurement or its evaluation should be functional of the amount
of goods which it will produce. For instance, a machine
which will produce 100 units of a certain good is more
valuable than another which produces 90 units of the same
good. The value of a stock of capital then derives from
the future output of goods and services or the additional
delayed consumption which it makes possible. The calculation of what the future output and the value of such
output will be is necessarily an approximation and one
that may tend to be subjective because it is based on
conjecture. It is based on rates of productivity and
output which are determined. The calculation will also
have to take into account the rate, or rates, of interest,
for translating future values into present ones. Such

an estimate of capital, therefore, is not easy even if
enough data are available as to the number and age span
of specific assets and their productivity.

The question may be asked as to why estimate
the value of an asset from its future flow rather than
from its cost which may be a more solid base for calculation?   There are also a number of drawbacks to this
method.   First, in the case of assets with long lives,
such as roads, bridges and certain types of machinery,
the length of their prospective useful lives has to be
estimated.   Another drawback is the very nature of the
investment process: the commitment of capital and effort, for a specific purpose, in conditions of uncertainty about future demand.   These are factors which are
not included in the cash cost of an asset and any attempt
at putting a value on them tends to be subjective.   What
if the investment which seemed to be full of promise and
profitable turns out to be a loss?   Surely, it is better
to await the results which are dictated by market conditions before making any assessment of the value of the
asset.   The procedure of equating cost and value can
only give sure results under stationary conditions, i.e.
when population, income and tastes do not change.

The difficulties of valuation are faced whether
the calculation is concerned with a highly developed
country, or a developing one and they are aggravated
further by the problem of deciding which assets can be
considered as stock and which should be considered as
flows; in some cases the distinction is clear: a
machine is an asset and the goods it produces are flows.
But what about the cost of an education which would make
the student a more valuable factor in the production

process?   Surely, inasmuch as such an education will contribute to increase future output it is a capital stock,
but somehow the fact is not evident at first sight.
The line of demarcation is necessarily arbitrary and the
decision of what is a stock and what is a flow is dictated to a great extent by national norms and considera-
tions of statistical convenience.   The composition and
content of capital is not the same in all countries and
distinctions between capital and consumption expenditures
differ greatly between nations.

The Effect of Technology

In discussing the effect of technology on
capital formation a distinction must be made between the
realization of such a process in developed and in developing countries.   In the former, productive capacity has
already been built-up and the net increase in real capital is often the result of the improvement in the productivity of both capital and labor.   As a matter of
fact, some innovations do actually reduce capital requirement per unit of output.   This is obtained by means
of the technological progress embodied in more efficient
capital equipment and in better trained workers.   Then,
the increase in output needs little capital outlay, very
often provided by depreciation allowances and re-invested
earnings.

But how can the application of improved technology by itself increase output in a country where no
technological framework exists?   If the economy is
still in the process of building up its capital equipment, then any investment will require large capital outlays and, the more modern the equipment, the larger the

outlays.[2]   On the other hand, an abundant supply of
capital widening with no progress in technology, will
not result in improved output.   The same argument applies
to the effect of an increase in the labor force: in industrialized countries where capital deepening has been
going on for many years, any increase in the labor input
or in its productivity would tend to raise output.   In
developing countries where the capital/labor ratio is
low, it is doubtful whether an increase in the labor input would increase total output;   as a matter of fact,
it might set in the law of diminishing returns.[3]   On
the other hand, an improvement in labor productivity,
through education and training, may raise output in certain aspects of production which do not require large
capital outlays, but the contribution of such production
to capital formation would be small.   The foregoing
diverse aspects of the question only show the complexity
of the capital input and explain the differing points of
view.

        The developing countries have available to
them a large reservoir of technical progress from which
they can draw for the needs of their expansion.   Moreover, opportunities for investment are not lacking.
There are, though, certain qualifications to this statement: first, technical progress is assumed to be neutral
when it does not interfere with factor proportions or
their relative shares of income.   The prevailing view

---

[2]this point is often overlooked by authors on economic
development who are more familiar with the process of
capital formation in developed countries.

[3]this problem was described in Ch. III in connection with
the discussion of inadequate productive capacity as one of
the symptoms of underdevelopment.

about technical progress in advanced countries is that
it is of the labor-saving, capital-intensive type, a
fact which does readily fit in with prevailing conditions
in the developing countries.   Secondly, as such investment is more likely to be carried out by the public sector, it is feasibility and not profitability which is
the main determinant.   Other determinants may be connected with such intangible factors as the ability to
plan, coordinate and promote new enterprise.

Investment Criteria and Priorities in Project Selection

          Most developing countries have plans which set
up quantitative goals;   in the elaboration of these plans,
alternative objectives are studied for their efficiency
and their relative cost, until a final selection of targets is made.   These targets are usually defined in terms
of: a) a country's natural and human resources and their
degree of development;   b) its needs for both capital
goods and consumers goods, the former including social
overhead capital, and c) available capital imports, either
in the form of aid or loans.   In the final analysis, a
scale of priorities will have to be established in order
to make the best use of the capital funds available for
development, and also to avoid inflation.   The choice
will thus be made in terms of 'real' value, i.e. opportunity cost, and the problems of scarcities (capital and
resources) and redundancies (labor) have to be taken into
consideration.

Capital-intensive versus labor-intensive

          Capital-poor countries are usually intent on
giving preference to labor-intensive projects - or methods

of production - on the assumption that they have a low
capital/output ratio.   However, it was seen earlier that
the productivity of labor depends - except in a restricted
number of elementary industries - upon the quantity and
quality of productive capacity;   therefore, with the exception of relatively few projects which do not require
much capital,[4] there is a positive relationship between
the ratio of capital to labor and that of capital to
output.   Let (K) equal real capital, (Y) equal real output, and (L) equal the economically active labor, then

1) $K/Y = b$ (average capital/output ratio)

2) $K/L = \pi$ (average capital/labor ratio)

3) $Y/L = \theta$ (average labor productivity)

then

4) $K/Y = (K/L)/(Y/L) = b = \pi/\theta$

and if $\Delta\theta < \Delta\pi$ then $\Delta b > 0$.

In other words, if the increase of labor input in relation
to capital input decreases labor's productivity, then this
will tend to raise the capital/output ratio and nullify
the basis for the assumption of the suitability of labor-
intensive projects.

The choice facing policy-makers is not only
between capital-intensive and labor-intensive projects,
but between projects which are profit-making and the
creation of social overhead capital.   The latter type
of project is capital-intensive and, in less-developed
countries it is usually undertaken by the government.
With limited resources, the problem becomes one of resource allocation between the two sectors and this is

---

[4] such as the so-called "community development projects",
e.g. the building of cheap housing, hard-surface country
roads, etc.

discussed more fully in Chapter VIII. There are certain
characteristics which are peculiar to social overhead
capital projects, namely: a) because they constitute
the framework for development, they possess considerable
externalities; b) they provide services rather than
goods, hence they have to be produced locally and cannot
be imported; c) they are consumed collectively and
equally by all members of the community; d) their initial
investment is 'lumpy' and their marginal cost tends to be
constant even beyond the point of optimal social welfare,
i.e. where marginal cost = marginal revenue.[5] In the
final analysis, the selection of development projects
for government investment must be made on the basis of
economic judgment and political exigencies.

The Capital-Output Ratio

The orientation of development programs is
determined by the particular objectives which it is desired to achieve, e.g. an increase in per capita income,
the elimination of unemployment, balance of payments
equilibrium, or independence from foreign markets in regard to basic supplies. If the resources available are
not sufficient for the simultaneous realization of all
the projects needed, priorities must be established.
Planning then becomes an important part of the development program although, in order to be achieved, it has
to rely on some initial assumptions and basic data. The
assumptions are usually connected partly with a country's
economic conditions such as the availability of natural

---

[5] see Stephen Enke, Economics for Development, 1963,
pp. 321-22, and P. H. Herber, Modern Public Finance,
1967, p. 314.

and human resources, as well as capital for investment, and partly with its immediate and future needs. The basic data are those required to calculate and compare the productivity and feasibility of the projects planned. The tools most used in this connection are the investment ratio (δ) and the capital/output ratio (b); the first measures the percentage of national output which is allocated for investment, and the second measures the amount of capital required to increase output by one unit: it is the reciprocal of the productivity of capital (σ). The average capital/output ratio (COR) for the economy as a whole, is defined as the ratio of the total stock of capital (K) to the total flow of output (Y) in a given period of time. The marginal, or incremental, capital/output ratio (ICOR) relates net investment during a given period to increases in net output during the same period. Thus, if the capital/output ratio is shown as

5) $K/Y = b$

the incremental capital/output ratio will be

6) $\Delta K/\Delta Y = k$

(k) is a constant which "consists of current additions to capital (the value thereof to be expressed as a fraction of current income)";[6] it is supposed to represent investment of a long-term character. Originated by Sir Roy Harrod, the capital/output ratio was then designed for measuring short-run stability and growth problems in advanced economies, but is now currently used in planning development in the less advanced countries.

---

[6]Harrod, R. F., Towards a Dynamic Economics, Lecture 3, p. 79.

Harrod's argument is that the output which
would provide full employment of labor and capacity in
period (t) would not be sufficient in period (t + 1)
because of the additional capacity created by investment
in period (t).   The incremental capital/output ratio
can then be used to find out the level of net investment
(I) required in period (t + 1):

7) $$\frac{K_{t+1} - K_t}{Y_{t+1} - Y_t} = \frac{I_t}{Y_{t+1} - Y_t}$$

8) $$K_{t+1} - K_t = I_t$$

Then the rate of growth will be equal to the rate of
saving (s) divided by the incremental capital/output
ratio (k);

9) $$G = s/k$$

and, given a certain level of saving, the lower the incremental capital/output ratio, the higher the rate of
growth.   Assuming the Keynesian equality between saving
and investment, then capital formation can be accelerated
by either increasing the rate of saving, or by lowering
the incremental capital/output ratio - by technological
improvement, for instance.   Experimentally, the calculation of the capital/output ratio has proved to be more
reliable than that of the incremental capital/output
ratio.   In any case, both are meaningful only over a
long period of time and after allowance has been made
for the time lag between actual investment and final production.   Moreover, the ICOR for an enterprise or even a
whole industry does not measure its economic rationality
with regard to the rest of the economy.

Balanced versus Unbalanced Growth

The choice of the most adequate pattern of investment priorities is a controversial subject between development economists. There is the classical pattern which has the blessing of the United Nations and its specialized agencies, more particularly the World Bank, which would have development proceeding by stages:
1) increase agricultural production; 2) develop village industries or consumer goods industries; 3) social overhead capital projects undertaken by the government;
4) industrialization proper. This approach meets with objection on the ground that it is too slow and does not satisfy the need for drastic change; also, if "active participation in and support from the population is (considered) essential .... this support can neither be imposed from above nor imported from abroad." Therefore, "emphasis on agriculture and small-scale industries deprives development of dramatic character and makes it appear rather pedestrian."[7] Another criticism is that such a policy would not encourage additional investment and would save on capital formation rather than on capital.[8]

Theory of the Big Push

Another approach is that of the "big push" first developed by Higgins[9] but which is now more frequently identified with Rosenstein-Rodan.[10] This theory is based

---

[7] Alpert, op. cit., p. 173.
[8] compare this statement with argument on p. 92 re S.O.C.
[9] Higgins, B., Economic Development, 1959, pp. 643-44.
[10] Rosenstein-Rodan, P. N., Notes on the Theory of the "Big Push", reprinted in Morgan, Betz, Choudhry, op. cit., selection 15.

on the premise that a big effort (push) is required for
economic growth to overcome certain economic hurdles
which are more evident in underdeveloped countries.
These hurdles consist of indivisibilities which give rise
to external economies and of a certain degree of imperfection in markets.   The author makes a distinction between the indivisibilities in supply and in demand.   In
the former he includes the type of project which comes
under social overhead capital: the assumption here is
that such projects come first, necessitate large (lumpy)
capital outlays, have long gestation periods, and there
is a minimum number of such projects which must be created
at the same time.   These characteristics of S.O.C. projects are examples of indivisibilities in the production
function.

On the demand side, he includes the complementarity of demand, which means that several consumers goods
industries must produce together in order to provide a
market for each other, e.g. the wage-earners in each industry buying goods from the other industries.   However,
in an open economy imports and/or exports can achieve the
complementarity of demand, e.g. when a locally produced
good replaces an import, or when a new home industry finds
foreign outlets for its production.   Finally, the third
indivisibility mentioned is in the very low price elasticity in the supply of saving, e.g. low income will yield
little saving no matter how attractive the rates of interest, and the high income elasticity in the supply of saving, assuming that with the rise in income the marginal
propensity to save will also rise and thus provide the
funds needed for the high rate of investment.

The proponents of unbalanced growth point out that this was the pattern in the development of most of the presently advanced countries. Bottlenecks (shortages) which arose during the process of transformation induced new investments. This "genuine decision-making" [11] is, according to Hirschman, the most valuable prime resource of developing nations and, one way to view growth is as a chain of disequilibria. This view is also based on external economies and demand complementarity: "...the investment that is induced by complementarity effects may help to bring about a real transformation of an underdeveloped economy." [12]

Overview

From the foregoing discussion it would seem that the first priority in development is to devote a certain amount of capital funds for social overhead capital projects which provide considerable externalities, but no immediate fully recoverable earnings on capital invested. The next step would be to treat productivity as the most important criterion: investment should be allocated so that the ratio of current output to initial outlay be maximized. The allocation of investment will affect not only total output, but also the quality, supply and distribution of the labor force; finally, it will also affect the physical composition of capital. As regards the choice between either balanced or unbalanced growth, in the final analysis this will have to be

---

[11] Hirschman, op. cit., p. 68.

[12] Ibid., p. 65 - see also Ch. III.

dictated by each country's own peculiar conditions and the particular goals that it is seeking in promoting economic development.

REFERENCES

1. Alpert, P., *Economic Development*. New York: The Free Press of Glencoe, 1963, Chapter 11.

2. Enke, S., *Economics for Development*. Englewood Cliffs, N. J.: Prentice-Hall, 1963, Chapter 17.

3. Harrod, Sir Roy F., *Towards a Dynamic Economics*. New York: Macmillan & Co., Ltd., 1963, Lecture 3.

4. Higgins, B., *Economic Development: Problems, Principles and Policies*. New York: W. W. Norton & Co., 1959, Chapter 14.

5. Hirschman, A. O., *The Strategy of Economic Development*. New Haven: Yale University Press, 1958, Chapter 4.

6. Morgan, Betz, Choudhry, *Readings in Economic Development*. Selections 13, 14, 15 and 16.

7. Rosenstein-Rodan, P. N., *Economic Development for Latin America*, edited by H. S. Ellis, IEA Proceedings. London: Macmillan & Co., Ltd., 1951.

REVIEW QUESTIONS

Terms

the average propensity to save

the marginal propensity to save

the physical composition of the stock of capital

indivisibilities in capital outlays

externalities

gestation period

the production-possibility concept

incremental capital/output ratio

delayed consumption

opportunity cost

capital deepening

stocks and flows

labor productivity

capital widening

average capital/output ratio   capital productivity

capital-intensive   labor-saving

Questions

1. Discuss two ways of measuring capital.

2. Name the conditions which generally distinguish an asset from a flow.

3. Comment on the difference in the effect of new technology in developing and developed nations.

4. Discuss the various targets for priorities in planning development.

5. Make the distinction between the average and the incremental capital/output ratio.

6. Discuss the arguments for balanced versus unbalanced growth. Which of the two do you think is the best policy?

7. What are the basic premises on which the theory of the 'big push' is based?

CHAPTER VI

THE ROLE OF THE AGRICULTURAL SECTOR

A controversy seems to exist among economists as to the importance of land in furthering the process of economic development, no doubt because of the inelastic nature of its supply and its relative limitations in providing increased opportunities for employment and additional output. However, farming is generally the income-earning occupation of the major part of the labor force in underdeveloped countries and, whether agricultural output consists of subsistence foodstuffs or cash crops, it makes the largest single contribution to the national product. Moreover, in recent years technological progress has made it possible to sizably expand cultivation without necessarily increasing the acreage.

Objectives. The agricultural sector of the economy in a developing country fulfills a variety of objectives. On the supply side, it helps feed the growing urban population; it produces the raw materials for some of the manufacturing industries: e.g. cotton for textiles; it provides a surplus for exports; and, in many instances, it is the source of the capital funds invested in the new industrial ventures: this happens when rich landowners are looking for diversification in their investments. On the demand side, the agricultural sector constitutes a market for locally manufactured goods. This is usually the situation during the period of transition of the economy from its agrarian structure to an industrialized one, i.e. during the process of transformation. As the industrial sector develops, the

build-up of the capital stock of productive capacity will
gradually attract factors and resources out of agriculture into industry where their marginal product will tend
to be higher.

In evaluating the contribution of agriculture
to development, two aspects will be studied in this chapter: the first is the possibility of increasing output,
and the second is the rationality of a more widespread
distribution of such output, or of the main input producing the output, i.e. land. Before that, however, some
basic facts about agriculture should be noted.

The Facts About Agriculture

Population. In an underdeveloped country, the
usual pattern of distribution between urban and rural
areas is heavily weighted towards the latter: not only
is a large percentage of the labor force engaged in agricultural occupations, but a comparatively still larger
percentage of the population lives in rural areas, because of the many activities which are not strictly
agrarian but connected with agrarian populations. Foremost among these are the moneylenders, doctors and nurses,
social workers, school teachers, etc.[1] This heavy concentration of population in rural areas tends to generate
a special form of underemployment, the so-called 'disguised' unemployment which refers to small family farm
units where the same "output could be got with a smaller
labor force without any improvement in technical methods."[2] The marginal product of such redundant labor is

---

[1] see Bhagwati, J., The Economics of Underdeveloped
Countries, 1966, pp. 44-46.

[2] Nurkse, Ragnar, Problems of Capital Formation in Underdeveloped Countries, 1953.

obviously very low[3] and their opportunity cost should be
measured not only in terms of their meager contribution,
but also in terms of their attachment to this farm unit
which gives them a sense of security, if not much else.
It should be stressed here that this kind of unemployment is not the same as the Keynesian type which is due
to insufficient effective demand, but rather a type due
to insufficient capital accumulation.

    Land productivity. Land differs in its
capacity to produce: its productivity is dependent upon
geographic and climatic conditions, as well as physical
characteristics, such as the nature of the soil and types
of farming. Soils vary from the rich alluvial type
produced by the sedimentation of rivers in coastal plains,
particularly in deltas, desert soil suitable for the cultivation of citrus trees of all kinds, cereals and small
grains, and sub-desert soil, used primarily for pasture.
Yields are measured either in the simple direct form of
physical output per acre, also called the land/output
ratio, or in terms of the physical marginal product in
which case the inputs have to be taken into account.

Types of Farming

    Types of farming are classified according to
both their economic and their physical aspects, although
the two are to some extent interrelated. On the economic
side, it is the composition of agricultural output and
more specifically its ratio to the population which determine whether agriculture is at the subsistence level,
general or mixed farming, or plantation farming. On the

---

[3] see Ch. I, p. 9.

physical side, it is the availability of means of water
storage which makes the distinction between dry and
irrigated farming.

Under subsistence farming, the total output is
consumed locally and there is little or no surplus left
after the community's needs have been met; hence no
input-output contribution to other sectors. This is
the type of farm in which disguised unemployment would
be found. The output is usually of the kind which is
for immediate consumption, e.g. grains, dairy products,
etc. Under this kind of farming, family income is low
owing to either one or more of several factors: a low
land/man ratio, primitive or inefficient methods of cultivation, or a poor soil. Subsistence farming has been
prevalent at one time or another in the history of most
peasant communities.

General or mixed farming is the next stage
above subsistence farming and includes various forms of
more progressive land utilization. Not only is there a
surplus output after the needs of the community have been
met, but there is more diversification and part of the
produce may consist of what is called 'cash crops' such
as cotton, tobacco, etc. Here is where the transition
from a barter economy to a money economy takes place.[4]
Farms of this type are usually medium in size and the
presence of a surplus for sale gradually paves the way
for commercialized farming through the creation of markets, marketing bodies (e.g. credit cooperatives), and
means of transport and communication to reach markets.

_____

[4]Peter T. Bauer and Basil S. Yamey, The Economics of
Underdeveloped Countries, 1957, pp. 65-77.

The predominant characteristics of <u>plantation farming</u> are the following: 1) a very limited number of crops - often only one, e.g. rubber; 2) an intensive capital investment; 3) a commercial basis of production involving efficiency and economies of scale; 4) the bulk of the output is destined for export.   Their high degree of efficiency contrasts sharply with the neighboring subsistence farming and they appear as enclaves of plenty amidst poverty - hence the phenomenon of the dual economy.   Plantations are usually foreign-owned and competently managed concessions, originally obtained at low cost, e.g. most of the foreign-owned African plantations.[5]   As such, and because they repatriate most of their income instead of re-investing it in the country, strong criticism is often meted at them.   Moreover, inasmuch as they are institutional monopolies which perpetuate the status quo of concentrating on the production of one primary product, instead of diversifying production, they lead to a misallocation of resources and a delay in the development process,[6] notwithstanding their initial contribution to development.

Although size is one of the chief characteristics of plantation farming, not all large estates are plantations.[7]   In the Middle East (up to very recently) and in Southeast Asia, for instance, the pattern of a large estate under a single ownership, but leased in small units to tenant cultivators, is current but has no connection with plantation farming.   Neither is the form of

---

[5] see Alpert, Paul, <u>Economic Development</u>, 1963, pp. 11-13.

[6] because of the chronic decline in world prices of primary commodities.

[7] see Warriner, Doreen, <u>Land Reform and Economic Development</u>, 1955, p. 13.

traditional tribal land tenure widespread in nomad Africa.
The large estates, or latifundia, of Latin America which
are concentrated in the hands of a small feudal class,
are under extensive cultivation or used for cattle breeding and they produce for export.   However, not all of
them have the degree of efficiency of the plantations.

Dry farming is the type of agriculture which
relies on rainfall to water the crops.   It is found
mainly in countries lying in the temperate zone, or in
tropical areas with monsoon type of weather.   This reliance on the weather with its vagaries is often the cause
of the instability of output and can seriously affect the
level of the gross national product in agrarian economies.

Irrigated farming is that which gets its water
from a centrally controlled network of irrigation canals
and is thus ensured of a regular flow of water the whole
year round.   It is needed in areas of scanty or insufficient rainfall.   The advantages to any economy of the
latter type of farming are obvious, although its cost is
very high: it is considered that the capital-output ratio
in such projects is sometimes as high as 6 : 1.   The
advantages of an irrigation project would have to be
measured against the social overhead cost with a sufficient time lag to allow for the construction period.

A point about which experts do not seem to
agree is the degree of mechanization of agriculture which
is consistent with the optimal allocation of investible
funds and economic development.   On the one hand, mechanization of agriculture is by definition capital-intensive and labor saving; on the other, it tends to increase
output by means of more efficient methods of production.
It was seen earlier that in developing countries there is

a tendency for labor underemployment on the farms;
hence the two conflicting objectives of increasing land
productivity by means of mechanization and of reducing
unemployment, so long as no other sector in the economy
provides employment opportunities.

Agricultural Expansion

As the manpower needs of the new industrial
projects are gradually filled, there results some depletion among the labor force at the farms except in
cases where redundancy already existed. The extent of
the depletion is variable and depends largely on the
nature of the industrial projects: plants using capital-
intensive, labor-saving equipment do not require a large
labor force. However, as the volume of agricultural
production now has to be increased with what is a smaller
labor force, the need arises of an increase in the productivity of either the farmers or the land, or both.
Where possible, more land should be brought under cultivation.

Experience has shown that increasing the productivity of farm workers is only obtained with training
and requires both time and incentive. The latter is
provided by the prospect of higher gains from the sale of
the surplus production. Raising yields and expanding
the area planted to crops, both come under the subject of
agricultural expansion and constitute what is broadly
recognized as two different approaches to the problem,
namely vertical and horizontal expansion.

The choice between vertical or horizontal expansion depends on factors such as the nature of the soil
and its degree of fertility, the type of farming practiced

(dry or irrigated), the availability of virgin land, and, last but not least, the existence of rivers that offer the possibility of channeling their waters into dams. In the last resort, the capital productivity of each type of project and the amount of investible funds which can be allocated to agricultural expansion, will play a big part in the decision-making process.

Increasing Yields

Vertical expansion tends to increase the yield from a given area of land which gives comparatively low physical returns in relation to average gross output. This is achieved by improving certain aspects of agrarian exploitation; broadly-speaking, this involves the methods of cultivation and drainage, stocks and markets and the availability of agricultural credit.

The Methods of Cultivation. The problem of the proliferation of small holdings, in countries where the land/man ratio is low, together with what often proves to be a crop rotation inadapted to the nature of the soil in some areas, are two issues which affect the volume of production by diminishing productivity. Proliferation and fragmentation are the result of inheritance laws whereby each heir is given several plots of varying degrees of fertility in the same property. The cultivation of such holdings entails a waste of both labor and capital, as well as land. If the consolidation of holdings is not obtained through voluntary exchanges, it may be provided for by legislation. Alternatively, small estates can be grouped together in big farms and cultivated collectively - while preserving private ownership - under a single crop rotation system; such a system would avoid

the decline in yields resulting from fragmentation.
This is a case where collective farming would be dictated
by practical expediency rather than ideology, and should
not be confused with farm collectivization which completely eliminates ownership.   When land is scarce and
the soil good, more than one crop a year can be obtained
by means of fertilizers and an adequate supply of water.

Agricultural extension services manned by
experts provided by the government can bring to the farmer
new techniques which add to the efficiency of his production through increased and more knowledgeable use of fertilizers, selected high-yielding (hybrid) seeds, and the
control of cattle and poultry breeding.   The cost of
such services is high and often has to be borne by the
State;   however, its results are often rewarding, especially in areas where one of the main causes of low income
is the presence of unskilled workers.

Finally, the replacement of old open drains by
concrete-lined underground ducts also helps to increase
agricultural yields.   This applies particularly to land
watered by an irrigation network.   In addition, the
space vacated by the old surface drains makes available
an additional area for cultivation, and the water which
was previously lost through evaporation from the open
drains is saved.

Stocks and Markets.   The storing of perishable
agricultural produce is an expensive process well beyond
the means of individual farmers in developing countries,
unless they are big estate owners.   On the other hand,
the absence of properly organized markets in farming
areas, and the inelastic nature of perishable farm produce, often force the farmers to sell their crops at low

prices rather than lose them altogether. The construction of grain silos (elevators) and weather-conditioned
warehouses, owned and operated by agricultural cooperatives, helps towards a better preservation of the crops
and better marketing conditions.

The creation of markets for staple commodities
and the extension of credit in rural areas provide the
farmers with added security and increased incentive to
grow more food. The growth of markets needs primarily
the development of means of transport and communications;
it is stimulated by the growth of real income and, to a
lesser extent, by changes in people's tastes. In rural
areas, markets or "fairs" take place in the village
square, or some such location, at regular intervals on
appointed days. This very rudimentary form of marketing may be sufficient to dispose of small quantities of
perishable foodstuffs in the absence of proper means of
refrigeration and storage, but inadequate for staple commodities such as wheat, corn, soya beans, etc. For the
latter, a permanently located market (exchange) place
linked by means of communications with other markets,
would give the farmers a better chance of marketing their
crops at advantageous conditions.

Agricultural Credit. Farm incomes fluctuate
to a greater degree than non-farm incomes although agricultural production is more stable than industrial production, in spite of the vagaries of the weather. This
is due to the inelasticities of both supply and demand in
agriculture. With the uncertainty about their income,
one of the most pressing problems facing farmers is that
of the availability of both short and long-term credit,
the former to finance their production costs and the
latter for capital projects. Loans of varying maturities

are supplied by the commercial banks to farmers who have
a good credit rating.   The problem is in the availability
of credit, or lack of it, to small farmers who do not have
enough collateral or a good credit rating.   These borrowers of small means are chronically plagued with the ex-
horbitant rates of interest charged by non-institutional
money-lenders and most of them have lived through the
vicious circle of debts, loans to settle the debts and
more debts because of the usurious rates of interest -
sometimes reaching a level as high as 50% - charged them
by the money-lenders.   For these farmers the creation of
state-sponsored agricultural credit banks giving both
long-term and short-term loans at low rates of interest,
with their crops as collateral in case of the latter has
provided one answer to the problem in some countries.
Another solution is the formation of rural credit cooperatives which perform as small village banks.   The use of
such cooperatives is widely spread in Egypt and India.

Expanding the Area

The limit to agricultural production is set by
the quantity of water available for irrigation.   Dry
farming does not readily lend itself to expansion: it is
obvious that nothing can be done about the vagaries of
the weather where there is heavy dependence on rainfall.
As the aim of horizontal expansion is to bring more land,
i.e. a bigger area, under cultivation, additional water
resources have to be found.   These are obtained by one
or more of the following steps: 1) a more rational distribution of the existing water supply, 2) drilling
artesian wells, 3) a better use of drainage water, 4) the
construction of dams for water storage and/or diversion

weirs feeding a network of deep canals which retain the water during the dry season because they are deeper than the river bed. A rational and equitable distribution of the water supply is only possible if the water is obtained through a centrally controlled irrigation network.

The drilling of artesian wells taps underground water resources and has been known, in areas where such resources exist, to provide a sizable addition to the water supply. The additional water thus obtained is used sparingly by the installation of a sprinkler system. Drainage water, after some measures have been taken to cleanse it of its salt content, is certainly the cheapest, if not the best, method. However drainage water obtains in sizable quantity only in such areas which have an irrigation network.

The method which provides the most adequate means of irrigation is the building of storage dams, complemented by an irrigation network covering the additional area which is to be brought under cultivation. This is also the most costly way to agricultural expansion. A dam can be built only in a location where a river flows in a deep gorge. The river banks in this case provide the two side walls of the dam. After the dam is built a hydroelectric power plant can be installed to provide cheap electricity, thus making dual use of the irrigation project.

Systems of Land Tenure and Land Reform

An important institutional factor in the study of any agricultural structure is the system of land tenure. A pattern of land tenure often to be found in underdeveloped countries is that of the large estates belonging to an exclusively feudal class of wealthy

landowners who very often are absentee landlords leaving
the running of their estates to hired superintendents.
The land was probably acquired by their ancestors in return for some service rendered to the ruler of the country, or through conquest, or by buying it cheap and developing it over the years. Their offsprings, educated
abroad and used to good living, prefer to spend the income from their estate on the easier and pleasanter life
in the city, allowing their appointed superintendent to
run the estate in their absence. The big estates have,
no doubt, contributed in the past to the increase in
agricultural production because of the economies of
scale realized through large-scale farming, and also because of cheap wages. Nonetheless this pattern of
traditional land tenure no longer fits in with the requirements of modern economic development. Besides, it
creates a situation where weak incentive coupled with
farmer indebtedness lead to a low income elasticity of
supply.

      The farmers who usually cultivate such estates
are either one of two types: tenants, or wage-laborers.
The tenant farmers rent a plot of land from the landlord
and cultivate it with the help of members of their family
or hired laborers, often paying the exhorbitantly high
rent with part of the crop, hence the term sharecroppers.
Their lease is usually for one year, a fact which does
not encourage them to do anything about improving the
condition of the soil or preserving its fertility because
they have no security of tenure.

      Labor mobility being almost non-existent and
the opportunities of better employment rare due to the
absence of manufacturing industries, the agricultural

laborers have to accept what they find. It is significant that agricultural labor unions have not developed
anywhere with the same impetus that industrial ones
have. In a way this also reflects the differential in
the marginal productivities of capital invested in
agriculture and in manufacturing. Working conditions
of both tenants and laborers tend to be insecure as well
as unsatisfactory.[8]

As regards the actual benefit to the country's
economy from the agricultural production obtained from
the large estates, the surplus is sold on world markets
and the foreign exchange obtained therefrom is often
used to finance imports of luxury or non-essential goods,
when it is not merely spent abroad on travel and expensive living. The high returns obtained by this class
of feudal owners from their estates preclude the possibility of their investing in such ventures as new manufacturing industries: because of the risk involved and the
inevitable preliminary period of rising costs, the latter
hold no attraction for them.

Meanwhile, the farm population gradually grows
in size to the point where it exceeds its means of subsistence. At this point, the youths emigrate from the
rural areas and go to the big cities in search of employment, thus swelling the crowds of the unskilled and
unemployed and providing fertile ground for ferment and
discontent. It is against this background that the
prospect of land reform has become one of the tenets of
the revolution of rising expectations.

-----

[8] see United Nations, Land Reform and Community
Development. New York, 1962.

Land Reform

The main objective of land reform, generally, is to level the economic inequalities in rural areas, but it often has social and political objectives as well. Economic inequality is corrected in either one of three ways: 1) by providing wider opportunities for land ownership through the expropriation of large estates and their redistribution to landless peasants; 2) by improving conditions of tenancy for tenants and share-croppers; and 3) by setting a minimum wage for rural laborers.

Because of the pattern of land tenure des-cribed above, landless peasants usually form the backbone of the rural population in an underdeveloped economy. It has been found that when they become beneficiaries from land reform they achieve a higher degree of social stability with the assurance of a steady and rising in-come. Finally, by breaking up the big estates, land reform tends to diminish the political power of the wealthy landowners: with their holdings reduced to a fraction of what they were, their influence over the peasants who formerly worked for them or were their ten-ants gradually wanes. We therefore really have three aspects to any land reform program: economic, social and political.

Implementation: Land redistribution

The first and the most important step taken under any land reform program is that of expropriation. The big landowners are usually allowed to keep a certain area, say 200, or 100, or even 50 acres of land according to its degree of fertility, and the rest is taken over by

the government who promises to compensate the owners by
some long-term means. The land is then parcelled out
in lots, ranging in area from 2 to 20 acres, according
to its degree of fertility and to the number of beneficiaries to be included in the distribution. Priority
in distribution is given to the landless and the poorest.

The price of the land thus distributed is set
at a modest rate based on either land tax, or land yield,
rather than market price, which is usually high prior to
the reform because of the pressure of demand by the
wealthy landowners in their quest for land. The same
modest rate is also applied in calculating the compensation paid to the dispossessed landowners.

Giving a plot of land to a farmer who has never
owned any before has great psychological and social as
well as economic connotations for him. However, as
empirical studies have proved, this is only the beginning
of the story. The new beneficiary has usually no financial means whatsoever; he has no implements and still
less practical experience as to how to manage a farm,
especially if he was previously a laborer and not a tenant. He has to buy the seeds and the fertilizers, pay
for the water, and generally organize the exploitation
of the land according to the most efficient way. His
biggest problem is lack of funds. There are also instances where the breaking up of the big estates - no
matter how productive the estate may have been as a
whole - may result into small lots which are of varying
degrees of fertility. Such lots may prove to be un-
economic in their exploitation. The resulting financial
problem to the new owner is further aggravated by the
installments that he is pledged to pay for his newly

acquired estate.   At this point, the land reform authority finds itself faced with the choice of either helping
the farmer out of his predicament or witnessing the failure of the reform.

Land Reform Cooperatives

          The agricultural cooperative has proved to be
the best way by means of which the land reform authority
can extend both funds and technical advice to the new
beneficiaries.   The cooperative usually includes all
the farmers who have been given land, as members.   One
cooperative is formed in every village and an agricultural
expert is delegated as consultant to it.   He attends the
meetings and gives advice to the farmers, but he is not
a member and has no voting rights.   His only point of
leverage is in his recommendation for credit for the
cooperative.

          Credit is extended as a rule by an agricultural
credit bank.   In many instances such a bank is state-
owned or sponsored because of the low rates of interest
it is committed to charge.   The possibility of obtaining cheap credit to finance agricultural production is
one of the basic requirements for the success of any land
reform program.   The credit is usually granted to the
cooperative which is thus enabled to supply the farmer
with his requirements in the way of seeds, fertilizers,
etc.   Farming implements are bought and owned by the
cooperative who loans them to the farmers.   When crops
are harvested they are sold by the manager of the cooperative who then deducts from the proceeds the amount of
the farmer's loan plus the yearly installments, making
sure that enough is left for the subsistence of the
farmer.

Conditions of Tenancy

Though land redistribution is the most spectacular aspect of land reform, it is by no means the one
which benefits the largest number of farmers. The
reason is simply that there is never enough land to go
round and, no matter how small the lots which are distributed, there are usually more people left out than
there are happy beneficiaries. One of the more important objectives of land reform is to provide security
of tenure - and a reasonable level of rent - to tenants,
i.e. to those farmers who lease land and cultivate it
for their living. The rent is calculated on the same
basis as the price of the land. It may be paid in
actual cash or in kind when the farmer gives a share of
the crop to the landowner. In any case, the rent is
much lower than that paid under the previous system:
middlemen have no place in a land reform program.
Moreover, the previous contract was usually only for
one year and the tenant who had no assurance of tenure
was inclined to get the most out of the land without
any regard for its upkeep or for the danger of erosion
from too excessive cultivation. The longer tenure
stipulated by the land reform legislation achieves,
therefore, a dual purpose: it gives security to the
tenant and, by so doing, it provides him with an incentive to take better care of the land. As the tenants
or sharecroppers usually constitute the bulk of the
rural population, this second basic objective of land
reform benefits a greater number of families and a
larger area of land even though it does not make big
headlines.

Wage Laborers

The third objective of any land reform legislation is to assure agricultural laborers of a wage
which provides them with a livelihood somewhere above
subsistence level. Although most countries have laws
stipulating a minimum wage scale for urban workers, it
has proved difficult to enforce the same regulation for
agricultural workers. The latter generally have weak
or no trade union affiliations;[9] the returns from
agricultural production are far from having the same
margin of profit as those from large-scale manufacturing.
Child labor is prevalent in rural areas and cannot be
controlled to the same extent as in big factories. The
result is that adult laborers face competition from
younger ones. The new beneficiaries do not need any
hired help: they farm their new lots themselves with
the help of their families. The shrinking of the big
estates therefore tends to reduce job opportunities for
laborers.

Land reform legislation usually includes stipulations fixing minimum wages for both adults and children; the stipulations are included because the declared
objective of the reform is that of improving economic
conditions for the rural population. However, what
usually happens is that the forces of supply and demand
in such cases work against the agricultural laborers
and, with reduced opportunities and the need to earn their
living, the workers not only accept but offer to take jobs
at wages lower than the minimum. As a matter of fact, it

---

[9] this applies also to workers in advanced countries,
e.g. the United States.

is not unusual to see adults figuring on the wage list as boys and accepting the lower wages stipulated for boys. In countries where economic development plans include projects for agricultural expansion, new employment opportunities are provided; but where land reform is implemented without expanding the land area, experience has shown that the laborers do not benefit as much as the other farmers from the reform.

Assessment

It has been shown that land reform has a political as well as a social and an economic impact. The first is particularly felt in the early stages of expropriation and redistribution; it works in two ways: it reduces the power of the big landowners over the farmers who used to depend on them for their living; it also tends to create a new class of small landowners constituted by the new beneficiaries. As regards the social impact, it is evidenced in the sharecroppers' security of tenure and the social status acquired by the new landowners.

Does the objective of leveling income from agriculture and thus achieving greater social equality, conflict with the need for increasing efficiency in agriculture? It is often said that the parcelling out of the big estates leads to a decline in production. Not so, says an expert on the subject who thinks that "if we use the methods of economic analysis, and are careful to define our assumptions, we can perhaps show that there is a positive relation between reform and development, in the conditions of 'underdeveloped countries'."[10] In any case the above argument is subject

---

[10] Warriner, op. cit., p. 10.

to strong qualifications regarding the type of the land
being redistributed and its former level of production.

Hence the economic impact of land reform is
somewhat more difficult to predict than the political
and social ones.   It depends not only on the efficient
management of the reform, and on the supply of ample
credit in the early stages to the new landowners, but
it depends also to a great extent on the quality of the
land which is being distributed and, last but not least,
on the availability of water.   A soil, no matter how
fertile, which depends on rainfall for cultivation,
becomes a pretty risky venture when parcelled out and
distributed, as numerous examples have proved.   An
adequate water supply, preferably through some means of
irrigation, is therefore necessary to ensure the economic success and, in the long run, the political and
social fulfillment of any land reform program.

Overview

This chapter has dealt with the role of
agriculture in developing countries only.   Industrialized countries have an entirely different problem in
connection with agriculture: a problem which is not
related to its degree of development but is due rather
to such factors as agricultural surpluses, the large
number of marginal farms, and more particularly the
disparities existing between the agricultural and the
industrial sectors in terms of comparative productivity.
Unless it is decided to allow the working of the market
mechanism to prevail and face the resulting temporary
hardships, the solution of such problems is more of the
competence of the sociologist and the politician.

122

In developing countries, the problem which begs an answer is the distinction to be made between the economic interpretation of what is a feudal estate, or a feudal system, on the one hand, and the political and social connotations of such a system on the other. The latter apply to cases of intensified social stratification in rural areas which precludes constructive community activity. However, where economic production is concerned, a large estate organized as an efficient commercial enterprise and enjoying a high degree of productivity, is not feudal.

Land reform, if successfully implemented, can have an income effect in the long run through the increased returns to the beneficiaries. But the scope of land reform is limited by the basic problem of population pressure: there is never enough land to parcel out in economic holdings to even half the number of landless peasants. There follows, therefore, the need of either intensifying production on the existing area (vertical expansion), or of increasing the land under cultivation (horizontal expansion). As shown earlier in this chapter, both methods require varying degrees of planning and financing.

REFERENCES

1. Alpert, Paul, _Economic Development_. New York: The Free Press of Glencoe, 1963. Chapters 7 and 8.

2. Bauer and Yamey, _The Economics of Under-Developed Countries_. The University of Chicago Press, 1957. Chapters 4 and 14.

3. Bhagwati, J., _The Economics of Under-Developed Countries_. World University Press, McGraw-Hill Book Co., 1966.

4. Garzouzi, Eva, Old Ills and New Remedies in Egypt. Cairo: Dar Al Maaref Press, 1958. Chapters 3, 4 and 5.

5. Kindleberger, C. P., Economic Development. New York: Economics Handbook Series, McGraw-Hill Book Co., 2nd. edition, 1965. Chapters 4 and 12.

6. Nurkse, Ragnar, Problems of Capital Formation in Underdeveloped Countries. Oxford: Blackwell, 1953.

7. United Nations, Progress on Land Reform, Third Report, 1963, Sales No. 63. IV. 2.

8. United Nations, Community Development and National Development, 1964, Sales No. 64. IV. 2.

9. Warriner, Doreen, Land Reform and Economic Development. Cairo: National Bank of Egypt Lecture Series, 1955.

REVIEW QUESTIONS

Terms

labor's opportunity cost	cash crops
land/output ratio	land/man ratio
subsistence farming	general farming
plantation farming	dry farming
irrigation farming	crop rotation
collective farming	diversion weirs
land reform	land redistribution
absentee landlord	security of tenure
tenant farmer	sharecropper
agricultural credit	agricultural (rural) cooperative

Questions

1. How does the presence of commercial plantations, whether they are foreign-owned or locally owned, affect economic development?

2. Discuss the various types of farming.

3. Discuss the mixed effects of the mechanization of agriculture.

4. What is the difference between increasing the volume of production and increasing productivity?

5. What is the distinction between vertical and horizontal agricultural expansion?

6. How important is the supply of agricultural credit for developing countries?

7. What is meant by the elasticity of agricultural supply and demand?

8. What are the objectives of a land reform program and which one is the most important for development?

9. Describe the role of cooperatives in a land reform program.

10. Do agricultural wage laborers benefit from land reform?

11. What are the conditions necessary for the success of a land reform program?

12. Why is land reform a phenomenon of underdeveloped countries only?

125

CHAPTER VII

INDUSTRIALIZATION

It was seen in earlier chapters that the process of economic development involves a structural change in a country's economy and that this structural change means the transition from an agrarian economy to an industrialized one. Industrialization, then, becomes almost synonymous with economic development. While the prerequisites and the stages of the process of industrialization are the same for all developing nations, actual realizations and the time lag needed, may differ between one country and another due to any of several reasons. Endowment in natural resources, sources of cheap energy, e.g. rivers, waterfalls, a labor force more receptive to training, the availability of technical assistance, and, last but not least, the presence of certain sectors which are already developed and provide a starting point, (also called 'leading sectors'),[1] all these factors may account for the difference in degree of success between one industrialization plan and another.

In this chapter we will study the economic and some of the social problems connected with industrialization. These will include first the assessment of capital and manpower requirements, and, as regards the latter, the educational facilities and vocational training needed; then, under project rationalization, the demand and supply aspects of industrialization including resource allocation, and finally, the growth of markets and their interaction with the industrialization effort.

---

[1] see Ch. III pp. 50-51.

Assessment of Requirements

Assuming that with the increase in effective
demand, capital accumulation and foreign aid make funds
available for investment, then the direction of such investment might take two different paths: the first is
to let it be guided by the increment in demand in the
various industries and this would achieve the dual
purpose of meeting the needs of the population and of
assuring returns on the capital invested.[2] The second
path has as its objective the supply of the framework
for economic projects, such as power plants, communications, etc...i.e. social overhead capital projects.
When the choice has been made the application of the
tools explained earlier and more especially the average
capital-output ratio will help in assessing capital requirements. Apart from S.O.C., one can say generally
that consumer goods industries (textiles, food processing) will develop first, while capital goods industries
will appear at later stages.

However, in planning these projects two factors have to be taken into consideration; the first is
the time element: projects which have a short life span
may appear to have a low capital-output ratio in the
short-run, but that would most likely not be so in the
long-run. The second factor is the ability of the
planned industry to provide other industries with raw
materials inputs and to provide workers with more productive power. In other words, the optimum objective
of industrialization should primarily be to increase
output per capita in the future rather than increase
national income in the present.

---

[2]this statement may be found to conflict with the principle of comparative advantage developed in Ch. IX.

Capital requirements then depend on the kind
of industries which are developed and on the type of
equipment used.   It takes several years to identify
and prepare a number of projects sufficiently large to
offer a choice in selection.   Pre-investment and investment studies are required to carry the planning
process from the aggregative stage to the individual
project level.   Although modern technology has made
possible the adaptation of certain handicrafts in which
relatively large gains in productivity can be realized
without heavy installations, the bulk of modern industry
tends to become more and more capital-intensive.   However, it is in large-scale manufacturing that the advantages of technical progress are available and to
keep investment per worker at a low level might lose
the advantages of the increase in productivity.   When
total capital is limited, the gain in aggregate income
due to higher employment per unit of capital may offset
the loss in efficiency, but there comes a point where
the use of inferior equipment would mean the same thing
as disguised unemployment.

Labor.   A factor which constitutes the second
prerequisite for industrialization is labor.   Here a
distinction must be made between the quantity and the
quality of labor.   The quantity of labor in developing countries is always sufficient, if not overly so.
However, in most countries, labor is measured by numbers, with merely a classification between men and
women.   The quality relates to the ability of the nation's manpower to assimilate the body of knowledge accumulated from tested findings and the discoveries of
empirical science - i.e. to benefit from vocational

training programs. Basic education and special training are needed.   Coefficients of educational requirements for specific jobs exist in the U.S. and elsewhere
and they serve as a basis for calculating manpower requirements.   The U.S. Department of Labor has prepared
lists of the "specific vocational preparation" (SVP)
meaning training acquired through experience on the job,
a "general educational development" (GED) meaning years
of formal education, for a variety of jobs in the U.S.[3]
While these lists may not quite apply to presently developing countries, because they cater to a highly industrialized economy, they are, nevertheless, models
which they can adapt to their own conditions.

Many of the elements which influence the trend
of development bear on the pace of industrialization.
Work in factories may use physical and nervous energy
to a greater degree than work on the farm but it also
requires a higher level of discipline and its effectiveness is influenced by the incentive of the workers.
Factors to be considered in the quality of the labor
force are primarily technical skill, followed by the will
to economize, workers' interest in output and the spirit
of teamwork.

Production.   Apart from capital and labor,
the process of production involves also management or
the entrepreneur, and technology.   The classical notion
of the entrepreneur is that of a businessman who has the
ability, experience and know-how to undertake any project.
He is also willing to shoulder the risk involved in trying out methods which have not been tried out before, by

-----

[3] Eckaus, R. S., "Economic Criteria for Education and
Training" Review of Economics and Statistics, vol. 45,
No. 2, (May 1964), pp. 181-190.

introducing innovations, for instance, in the methods of
production.   The entrepreneur does not provide the inventions himself, but he puts in practice the findings
of scientists and researchers and, by so doing, contributes to technological progress and economic development.   The profit he makes is his incentive.   In modern
times, the entrepreneur has been replaced by the group of
experts who are called upon to manage an enterprise:
they take no risks and make no profit, but they usually
earn high salaries which are commensurate with their usefulness to the enterprise.   In present day discussions
of production under free enterprise, the term entrepreneur still tends to have the connotation of the businessman who is willing to risk his capital in an untried
project, even though he may have to rely on others who
possess the technical skill necessary to carry out the
project.   However, private entrepreneurship still carries the assumption of initiative, profit and social
mobility.   The quantity and quality aspects of organization help explain differences in output among the various countries and improvements explain the speed of
growth.   Having discussed capital and labor separately,
let us now have a look at the result of their combination
together in the production process.   This is what is
called the production function[4] which also gives us the
scale of the enterprise and is an important factor in
planning development.   A simplified formula for it would
be:

$$Y = F(K,L,R)$$

which means that the level of output (Y) is function of
the capital (K), labor (L) and land or resources (R)

---

[4]the relationship between various combinations of inputs
to produce a certain output.

inputs.   To this simple formula could be added another
variable, T, for technology to show the improvement in
output due to technology and the progress from one year
to another could be shown by separate coefficients in-
dicating the productivities of capital and labor.   If
factor proportions are constant, the production function
is said to be homogeneous of the first degree.

　　　　Technology.   Technological progress has contributed in recent years an increasingly larger part to
economic growth, while for developing countries it is
a matter of adapting already existing technology to their
own economic conditions wherever that is possible.   In
calculating the rate of growth, after increases in capital
and labor have been taken into account, technology is the
residual factor.   In the United States, for instance, it
is considered that technological improvement has not only
contributed to the growth process, but it has delayed the
effect of the law of diminishing returns[5] where capital
is concerned, because the latter has been growing faster
than labor.   The new technology is manifested in two
ways, namely, new methods of production and new equipment,
or to put it differently, technical progress can be embodied in the performance of management and labor through
the adoption of new methods, or it can be embodied in the
new more efficient, labor and time-saving equipment.
Technical change is considered neutral when the factors
of production are still used in the same proportion after
its introduction, and non-neutral when the proportion of
one factor to the other changes after the introduction of
the new technique, e.g. when an innovation is either
capital-saving, or labor-saving.   The effects of

---

[5] or the law of variable proportions where industrial
production is involved.

technology on development can be felt generally in either one of two ways, according to whether the new inventions apply to consumers goods or to capital goods. In the former, the assumption is that the invention has reduced the cost of the good to the consumer, or improved its quality, and that makes it more desirable; in other words, it stimulates the demand for the good. In capital goods, the new techniques reduce the cost of production and tend therefore to increase the level of output without a corresponding increase in inputs.

Large projects tend to develop slowly while in the meantime other projects may be delayed. If investment is channelled to huge projects only, the possibility arises of wrongly estimating outputs. Another risk lies in financial resources falling short before the project is completed. The pace of industrialization is also significant. One objective should be to establish a pace which would coincide with the expected increase in income. When the choice is between technologies requiring different proportions of the productive factors, a rational choice would be the combination using quantities of the productive factors according to their availability, because the overall objective is to obtain maximum output from all the resources available to an economy, combined together.

Project Rationalization

Rationalization here is concerned with reconciling long-term economic objectives with present needs and ruling conditions and the overall purpose of industrialization with its practical aspects. Experience has proved that the most important practical aspect in the planning of new industries is the limited scope of the market.

The Demand Aspect

The limited scope of the local market, or the lack of effective demand, is one of the first obstacles to be taken into consideration in an industrialization program. Domestic investment in large-scale industries required to reach the stage of mass production and sell at popular prices, is usually deterred by the small demand for consumer goods. There is also the assumption, in countries which have been open to foreign economic penetration, that foreign capital would have undertaken these projects if the expectations from sales had been adequate. In other words, there is no point in producing goods if prospective customers do not have sufficient income to buy them. What is, then, the solution to the problem?

This obstacle can be overcome either by finding outlets for the output of the new industries in spite of the size of the market, or by expanding the latter through an increase in consumption. Outlets can be found either internally, or externally. First, the country which is industrializing should attempt to produce goods which would replace those which it is importing, while keeping exports at the same level. In the early stages of production, the home-produced goods will probably be more expensive than the imported ones and not as good in quality, so they will need protection in the form of import restrictions: either tariffs or import quotas. This is what is referred to usually as the protection of infant industries and about which more will be said under Foreign Trade. Such restrictions should be of a temporary nature. Another alternative is to create new industries which would produce for export and

compete with foreign goods. This is a case where protection will have to be provided to the new industries
in the form of subsidies to exporters.

These two solutions, though sound theoretically,
would probably prove to be very limited in scope practically, the first because the propensity to consume any
items other than food is feeble when income is low and
would not be enough to make the local production economically viable. As for exports, unless the newly manufactured goods have some inherent advantage, such as a
higher quality raw material, it is doubtful whether they
will be able to compete successfully in workmanship with
foreign goods which have the advantage of long experience.

The way to expand effective demand is to increase consumption and this inevitably results from the
large investments made necessary by development - mainly
by the public sector. Investment creates employment and
employment provides income; a very large proportion of
additional income in the lower bracket range is usually
spent on consumption, so the marginal propensity to consume manufactured goods would be higher than the average
propensity for such goods. The secondary and tertiary
effects of the increase in income could serve as guide-
lines in the selection of the new industries. The public
investment which would lead to an increase in consumption
might be in social overhead capital: roads and canals,
bridges and power stations, housing and schools, without
which no industrial progress can take place. In this
connection, mention should be made of a measure which
might tend to increase the income of the poorer class,
that is the reform of the fiscal system which is covered
in another part of the book. In most underdeveloped
countries taxation is regressive, i.e. a sizable

proportion of public revenue comes from indirect taxes
levied on consumption; a reform of the taxation system
which would put more of the burden on the higher income
brackets by means of direct taxes, would free more of
the lower bracket income for consumption. This redistribution of income should be accompanied by a policy
to encourage or induce saving in order not to reduce
capital formation.

The creation of industries for the home market depends, therefore, on the improvement of the productivity of the other economic activities. With the
growth of the income derived from road construction and
other public works, agriculture and mining, the local
market for manufactured commodities grows also. One
path to progress then is by increasing the productivity
of the farmers: in poor countries, a large percentage
of the population is required on the farms just to produce enough food; this percentage declines as efficiency
in food production increases. As a matter of fact, the
percentage of the labor force needed on the farms to
feed the country is an elementary index of a country's
degree of productivity. In the more advanced countries
it is low: in the U.S. it is less than 5 per cent, in
England which cannot produce all the food it needs 3.1
per cent, in Australia 8.5 per cent, while in the underdeveloped countries, this percentage is anywhere between
50 and 75 per cent.

The Case of Import Substitution Industries

Industries producing goods which replace imports come into existence as a result of either one of
several conditions; such conditions could be induced
by the developing country or they could happen through

no direct attempt on its part.   The first category includes government development programs which by means of
a combination of credit and fiscal policies, e.g. low-
cost credit from state-sponsored development banks, tax
credit on investment, exemption from customs dues on imported capital equipment, etc...promote such import substitution industries;   also, the establishment of government corporations for the purpose of carrying out
specific projects.   The second category includes situations resulting from world wars which close the sources
of imports and force the country to replace them by
domestic production;   balance of payments difficulties
which induce cut-down on non-essential imports;   finally,
growth of income which leads to the expansion of the market and which usually is a corollary of economic development.

The general pattern is that import substitution
industries start by producing finished consumers goods -
preferably those which offer some advantage from the
point of view of available raw materials, or a high
social rate of return as compared with a private rate of
return on investment.   Next, as the contribution of the
industrial sector to total output rises, comes domestic
production of intermediate and basic industrial materials
for these industries;   this is the backward linkage effect.[6]   However, the creation of these industries with
imported techniques, equipment and experts, for the purpose of expediency rather than through normal evolution,
becomes an imitation process which can be very smoothly

---

[6] see Meier, Leading Issues in Economic Development, 2nd.
edition, 1970, pp. 403-4.

carried out but which precludes innovation and learning
by experience.   It also precludes the adaptation of the
new technology to conditions prevailing in the developing country, e.g. labor-intensive versus capital-intensive.[7]

The above point has particular significance
in the case of the first situation mentioned above, i.e.
deliberate government development programs, because of
its impact on the whole industrialization effort: if
the goods produced by the new industries do not find
acceptance in the market, they quickly become an expensive burden on the whole program.   Their non-acceptance
may result from inferior quality or workmanship, lack of
choice to consumers or too high costs of production.
In any case, these new industries have to be protected
by tariff walls.   All the foregoing facts make the choice
of import-substitution industries a somewhat controversial subject with both policy-makers and their economic
experts.

Conclusion: The Case for Industrialization

To conclude, the fact that the developed countries of today have achieved their development through
industrialization should not by itself be a compelling
reason for the developing ones to industrialize.   There
are, however, three other major reasons which are sum-
marized below:
1)   the marginal value product of labor is generally
higher in industry than in agriculture, with a resulting

---

[7] see Hirschman, A. O., "The Political Economy of Import-
Substituting Industries in Latin America" in Nisbet,
C. T., op. cit., chapter 10.

increase in national output.

2)   industrialization has external economies: in
training, in stimulating incentive and interaction, in
the demonstration effect in consumption and in production,
which agriculture does not have.

3)   improvements in and mechanization of agriculture
rely on industrial products which should be produced
locally rather than imported.

        Moreover, there is the psychological factor;
the new nations think, for instance, that industrialization goes together with the achievement of nationhood;
consider the prestige symbol represented by the possession
of a brand new steel mill! even if the prerequisite raw
materials are not available within the country.
Finally, the spirit of nationalism which dictates self-
sufficiency and non-reliance on outsiders for essential
commodities, plays a big role in planning decisions.

REFERENCES

1.   Eckaus, R. S., "Economic Criteria for Education and
      Training," Review of Economics and Statistics, vol.
      45, No. 2 (May 1964).

2.   Eckaus, R. S., "Technological Change in the Less
      Developed Areas," in Robert E. Asher (ed.) Develop-
      ment of the Emerging Countries. Washington, D.C.:
      The Brookings Institution, 1962, pp. 126-128.

3.   Grunwald, K. and Ronall, J. O., Industrialization in
      the Middle East. New York: Council for Middle
      Eastern Affairs, 1960.

4.   Lewis, Wm. A., Aspects of Industrialization. Cairo:
      National Bank of Egypt Commemoration Lectures, 1953.

5.   Nurkse, Ragnar, Problems of Capital Formation in
      Under-developed Countries. Oxford: Basil Black-
      well, 1953.

6. Tinbergen, Jan, The Design of Development.
   Baltimore: The Johns Hopkins Press, The Economic
   Development Institute (International Bank for
   Reconstruction and Development), 1958.

7. United Nations, E.C.A.F.E., "Criteria for Allocating
   Investment Resources Among Various Fields of Development in Underdeveloped Countries," Economic
   Bulletin for Asia and the Far East, June 1961, pp.
   30-33.

REVIEW QUESTIONS

Terms

structural change

coefficients of educational
requirements

specific vocational
preparation (SVP)

the entrepreneur

labor coefficient

law of diminishing returns

neutral and non-neutral
technical change

infant industries

a vocational training
program

manpower requirements

general educational
development (GED)

innovations

capital coefficient

embodied technical
progress

project rationalization

the production function

Questions

1. Comment on the importance of keeping investment per
   worker high during the development process.

2. What is the relationship between the entrepreneur
   and technical progress?

3. How are the effects of new technology on economic
   development felt?

4. When and why is technical change non-neutral?

5. What should the pace of industrialization be?

6. Discuss the effect of the size of the market on
   industrialization.

7. Explain the difference between the average and
   the marginal propensities to save in a developing
   country.

8. Why is it said that taxation is regressive in under-
    developed countries?

9. Does the difference in the proportion of the labor
    force working on the farms between countries prove
    anything?

10. Are there valid reasons why a developing country
    should start an industrialization program?

CHAPTER VIII

MONETARY AND FISCAL POLICIES FOR DEVELOPING COUNTRIES

The rules of either monetary or fiscal policy as they appear generally in Economics textbooks were devised for conditions ruling in developed and highly industrialized countries. They have to be modified when they are applied to developing countries. The objectives to be attained may be the same for both groups of countries, though their order of importance may differ. Of the three goals of price stability, a rise in per capita income and equilibrium in the balance of payments, advanced nations may want to give priority to the first and the third, while the others would put all their emphasis on the second. However, the main difference really lies in the means to achieve these goals. Let us first consider financial conditions in developing countries.

The Financial Background

The situation of developing economies is different from that in the developed ones in that they are still going through the process of transformation, i.e. building up their social overhead capital as well as their productive capacity. The level of their national output is low, and so is that of their capital accumulation. But if they were to save enough - in terms of foregoing present consumption out of current income - they cannot invest in productive equipment because such saving would not have the degree of homogeneity required for capital formation. Translated in terms of sectoral input-output analysis, these economies do not have the capital equipment and skilled labor which, if transferred from the production of consumption goods would be adequate for the

production of capital goods. This is a case where factor
substitution is precluded by the heterogeneous character
of modern output. It is, therefore, a vicious circle of
slow capital accumulation, weak technology, and a resulting low productivity of investment which is the cause of
a low rate of economic growth. Consequently, what these
countries need badly is a high rate of capital accumulation as well as technology, in order to increase their
productive capacity.

Basically, capital formation is possible only
when a society produces a surplus (saving) out of current
production to form capital. A usual symptom of economic
development is the rise in the rate of saving in the early
stages of development. The source of voluntary saving
is complicated by social attitudes towards economic
mobility, by uneven income distribution and by the level
of income. The effort made by the developing countries
of today to overcome the internal obstacles to their development is closely watched by the outside world and
more particularly by international lenders: this is
partly due to the idea that self-help must come first
and partly to the recognition that a country's ability to
service and repay external debt depends largely on:
a) its success in achieving a sustained increase in its
national output, and b) its ability to save an increasing
portion of its income.

In the monetary field, a developing country has
usually got over the barter stage but has not yet reached
that of a well developed credit system. Its money market is weak and hardly existent except for government
securities. Barring the vagaries of the weather which
affect their crops and over which they have no control,
the less developed countries do not experience business

cycles as such but they are affected by the cyclical
fluctuations which occur in the developed countries who
buy their primary products.   These are situations which
it is not in their power to remedy.   Fluctuations in
foreign trade affect their reserves of foreign exchange
and their money supply, thus weakening the control of
the central bank over the latter.   Changes in the
volume of credit that the central bank can extend to
the government also affect the money supply.   This is
because banking habits are not widespread except among
institutional customers and currency in circulation constitutes about 50 per cent of the total money supply.[1]
Consequently, the commercial banks' capacity for credit
creation is limited and the expansion ratio tends to be
very low.[2]   Moreover, unless they are foreign-owned,
the existing independent commercial banks carry out
small-scale operations and their weakness lies in a
possible undue concentration of business risks.

　　　Another trait of monetary conditions in developing countries is the non-homogeneous structure of
interest rates which show wide disparities between the
organized and the non-organized markets.   In fact, usury
rates are sometimes charged by moneylenders in the latter
market, notwithstanding strict legislation forbidding
usury.   Commercial banks favor short-term loans to institutional borrowers and the supply of medium and long-
term credit is so restricted that such credit has to be
extended by government-owned or sponsored development
banks of various types: agricultural, industrial and
commercial.

------

[1]when it is about 20 per cent in the United States.

[2]see Bloomfield, A. I., "Monetary Policy in Underdeveloped Countries," in Morgan, op. cit., selection 32.

In the fiscal field, the less developed countries usually suffer from an archaic system of taxation,
a strong elite of entrenched vested interests who are
adept at evading taxes, and a per capita income for the
majority of the population which is so low that it
leaves little margin for either forced or voluntary saving.   On the other hand, an adequate amount of funds is
needed to provide a non-inflationary means of financing
development expenditures.   At the same time, the taxes
which are collected must be selected with a view to their
effect on the people's ability and willingness to work,
to save and to invest.   Moreover, conditions of carrying out business must be made attractive to foreign
investors.   As regards consumption, contrary to what
is the desired objective in rich countries of stimulating
it, the purpose in poorer countries is to restrain it,
first because the demand is usually in excess of the
supply and then because saving should be encouraged.

Voluntary Saving and Compulsory Lending Out
of Real Income

The application of the investment multiplier
theory without modification to the problems of employment
and capital formation in underdeveloped economies, can be
misleading because in such countries it is difficult to
increase total output in the short run.   This is because
of the lack of proportion between productive factors,
mainly labor, compared to capital and the lack of homogeneity in the composition of the latter.   The increase
in income generated by investment will not increase consumption in the short-run; it will, rather, only tend
to raise prices.   Moreover, the disproportion among the
productive factors, e.g. labor and land, will preclude a

rise in output from the agricultural sector which is the most important; hence total output will be almost completely income inelastic in the short-run.

Voluntary saving may take one of several forms: additional factories, extra or more modern equipment to existing ones, inventories of both consumers and capital goods, export surpluses, saving by businesses reflected in the increase in their net worth. Surpluses of premiums received by insurance companies over benefits paid can constitute an important source of saving. Investment in a developing society is undertaken by farmers, by domestic and foreign entrepreneurs and by the government. Where housing is owned by the occupants, this is another channel of investment. Inventories in such an economy are rare except where the term applies to goods in the process of production. Saving and investment can be effected in either one of two ways: the first is to save on consumption and increase the production or import of capital goods, substituting the latter for part of the former. The second way is to leave consumption unchanged and to devote any increase in output to capital formation. In either case total income will exceed total consumption, the difference between the two representing newly created means of production. Over time, this will lead to structural change and economic development.

In actual practice, voluntary saving does not necessarily find its way into investment for development if not nudged to do so. For instance, the savings of the rich elite are attracted into loans to consumers and farmers at high rates of interest, rather than the more risky development projects. Savings may also be used to hoard goods in the hope that prices will rise. In fact, if hoarding is considered synonymous with withholding

savings from developmental investment, then it can take
any of several forms and be carried out by the poor as
well as the rich.   Buying land as a hedge against inflation and leaving it idle, buying jewelry such as the
many bracelets working women wear in poor countries, or
even the gold fillings they have fitted to their teeth
even when they do not need them,[3] or holding cash or
unused bank balances, are some of the many instances of
hoarding.

It is considered by some[4] that the monetary
authorities could extend credit for development against
the money withdrawn from circulation into hoards, without generating inflationary tendencies, that is if they
can be sure that the cash will remain into hoarding, which
of course is unlikely.   The only way, then, that voluntary savings can be nudged into financing development, is
to attract them to credit institutions which would channel
them into loans for production rather than for consumption.   However, the process of saving has to take place
first because the existence or the creation of credit institutions is no substitute for the necessary act of real
saving which is anti-inflationary, while credit is inflationary.

A compulsory lending scheme is defined as one
in which "people coming under some wide classification
(e.g. liability to pay income tax) are obliged to deposit
with the government a given sum of money for a period of
time, on the understanding that it will be returned to

---

[3] a practice this writer has witnessed in a Middle Eastern
country.

[4] see Higgins, B., Economic Development.   New York:
W. W. Norton and Company, Inc., 1968, Ch. 23.

them relatively soon."[5]   Examples of such schemes are
the reserve ratio requirements for banks, regulations
requiring insurance companies to invest part of their
assets into government bonds, compulsory deposits on
imports, etc.   The stipulation that the funds will be
returned soon leaves out such items as contributions to
social security schemes and pension funds, although if
the definition were to be applied with this broader connotation the resulting kitty would be a much bigger one.
The developing nations of the 20th century have adopted
for the most part the complete kit of welfare measures
including employment insurance, medical care, dis-
ability and old age pensions.   The contributions to
these schemes are paid by employers and employees from
whose paycheck they are deducted, and they are channelled
to one or two big institutions which are either state-
owned or state-supervised.   Thus large sums are accumulated and in the absence of a well developed money
market, these institutional investors contribute to the
production process by means of the long-term loans they
extend to big industries.

        Against the background of the foregoing con-
ditions, one must remember that the stepped-up rate of
investment is likely to generate inflationary tendencies
which would hurt the economy by reducing saving on the
one hand, and raising the prices of productive factors on
the other.   What, then, is the best policy, either in
the monetary or the fiscal field, under such conditions?
The answer is that there is no well defined, articulate

---

[5] Prest, A. R., "Compulsory Lending Schemes," Staff Papers,
International Monetary Fund, Vol. XVI No. 1, March 1969,
pp. 27-50.

policy, but a number of steps which will work under certain conditions. To explain these, the respective roles of the Central Bank and the Treasury should be discussed separately.

The Role of the Central Bank

An initial step to promote the development or the adequate functioning of the banking system is the creation of a central bank. Some developing countries have inherited from the time of colonial rule some highly developed, foreign-owned and managed, commercial banks. The presence of these establishments, though it can help the formation of domestic banks by means of the demonstration effect and by training local personnel, emphasizes rather than otherwise, the need for the creation of a central bank: the foreign banks are usually branches or subsidiaries whose policy is geared to that of their head office abroad and not to the particular needs of the country in which they are operating. To the newly established central bank falls the task of managing the country's finances during the stage of development. It has to thriftily allocate, or even ration, the use of its limited supply of foreign exchange; it has to set the level of interest rates best suited for development and, create incentives for saving - two seemingly contradictory objectives - generally control the heavy credit expansion and the inflationary tendencies which seem to be the inevitable corollary of development. Another area where the new central bank will have to exercise its prerogatives is to put a brake on borrowing by the public sector; it will also have to restrain the latter's propensity to make an excessive use of the "printing press."

The conventional tools of monetary policy as they are used in the richer countries are not very effective in the poorer ones. The scope for open market operations is constrained by the small size of the money market and the still smaller reserves of the commercial banks. The use of the discount rate is not very effective because the commercial banks do not borrow readily from the central bank - if they are branches of foreign banks, they borrow from their head offices. For the same reasons, a change in the reserve requirement would not have a great impact. However, there are certain responsibilities that the central bank can effectively assume. The first of these is its participation in balance of payments management by its control over the rate of exchange and over capital movements. Another responsibility is the control of domestic bank credit, both public and private, taking into consideration the policy of the Treasury and the loans extended by other credit institutions. In controlling the volume of credit, the central bank in a developing country also regulates its allocation to the uses which would best promote economic growth.[6] Finally, the central bank has the responsibility of overseeing the level and structure of interest rates and of indirectly stopping the flight of capital caused by inflation; this is accomplished by its monetary policy and also by its decision about the proper mix of foreign or domestic, public or private, long-term or short-term assets in its portfolio. For instance, purchase of domestic

---

[6] see Southard, F. A., "The Central Bank in the Policy Making Process," *Finance and Development*, The Fund & Bank Review, No. 2, 1968.

assets (credit creation) would be limited to the increase
in currency in circulation desired by the people, unless
it wants to reduce its foreign exchange reserves.

All this will prove to be a difficult test
for the newly created central bank, but only by so
doing can it prove its effectiveness. When these factors have been duly taken into consideration, credit
creation by the banking sector, either for public use in
creating social overhead capital, or for private use in
productive investment and consumer loans, will stimulate
economic activity and encourage entrepreneurial risk
taking. As regards consumer credit, the trade-off is
between stimulating production by encouraging consumption and reducing credit in order to avoid inflation
when the supply of goods is not coming forth fast enough
to meet demand. In general, the role of the banking
sector, in the absence of a well organized capital market
is to mobilize the fragment of aggregate income that
people do not spend on consumption and to allocate it
among the alternative proposals for adding to productive
capacity.

The Role of the Treasury

As a country develops and its per capita income
rises, the responsibilities of the public sector grow in
proportion to total economic activity. Moreover, the
process of economic development is far too important to
be left to depend entirely upon the decisions of profit-
motivated businesses; it should be the responsibility
mainly of the state. This does not mean that private
enterprise should be eliminated, but that the necessary
infrastructure for development would be provided. In
other words, the government should help provide the

maximum of productive capacity which is consistent with
the level of effective demand, rather than to stabilize
such demand as it does in developed economies. The expansion of industrial production which is thus initiated
by the government when it does not hold enough attraction
for private business is a prerequisite for, rather than a
consequence of economic development. It is also not
necessarily a symptom of increasing personal welfare:
given a certain production-possibility curve, the government can, by increasing taxes, force consumption down to
a lower social indifference curve. This is an extreme
application of Galbraith's "social balance" concept.[7]
To repeat, expansion of the public sector need not occur
at the expense of the private sector, since the two sectors are complementary rather than competitive.

In the opinion of many experts, the funds for
development can be obtained only when government reduces
personal consumption by means of taxation. Tax revenue
for financing is preferred to voluntary saving because
it creates no claims on future increases in output, while
private savers would have such claims in the form of
bonds or other financial investment media. It is considered that the servicing of this internal debt would
hamper public revenue and spending policy in the future.
Hence, during the past two decades, the developing countries have been encouraged to raise the level of taxation
in their countries; the International Monetary Fund and
the World Bank, among others, attach a great importance
to this policy. In fact, the ratio of tax revenue to

---

[7]Galbraith, K., The Affluent Society. Boston, 1958,
pp. 255-262.

gross national product is considered one of the most
important criteria for assessing a country's economic
importance.[8]

Consequently, in a number of countries public
revenue has increased and now accounts for between 12
per cent and 27 per cent of gross national product.
However, it would appear that the increase in public
revenue has not found its way into development, but it
was rather absorbed into current expenditure.[9] While
there is no doubt that public spending must rise, particularly during the early stages of economic development, there is also the necessity of giving unquestioned
priority to capital rather than current expenditure.
It may be politically difficult for the government to
resist pressure for increased spending, say on salaries,
or national defense, when the funds are already available. This difficulty can be overcome by more rationality in the budgetary process, accompanied by better
accounting techniques, so that the increase in revenue
be channelled to the desired objectives. Another way
would be to earmark revenue from certain taxes to
specific projects, but this method is limited in its
scope. A better way still is to assign certain revenues
to a development fund.

What about the choice of the right tax? It
was said earlier that taxes should be so selected that
they would provide the means to finance development but
not discourage either saving or investment. An

[8]Please, Stanley, "Saving Through Taxation - Reality or
Mirage?" Finance and Development, The Fund and Bank
Review, Vol. IV, No. 1, March 1957, p. 25.
[9]Ibid., p. 26.

experiment carried out by an expert of the International
Monetary Fund who used economic analysis to determine the
potential value of a given tax, shows that the problem
can be dealt with by the selection of a tax base which
has a high income elasticity, i.e. which would rise more
than proportionately with the rise in national income,
as development proceeds.[10]   For this purpose, one or
more hypothetical tax bases, e.g. disposable income,
property, sales, - such tax bases exist whether they are
taxed or not - would be selected and their trend in relation to that of national income, over a past period of
time, would be studied as to changes in size, incidence,
revenue criterion and the degree to which they are affected by the structural change resulting from economic
development.

  The above-mentioned experiment was carried
over the general sales tax in a Latin American country,
which excluded only food and services.   The findings
from a study covering forty years showed that 1) the size
of the base grew faster than national income, because of
changes in the composition of expenditures;   i.e. people
were spending relatively less on food and more on goods;
2) its incidence was proportional to total spending, but
regressive in relation to income because of savings;
this was because of the exemption of services from the
tax;   3) the revenue criterion which had included customs
duty, declined in relation to national income, because of
a change in the composition of imports and more exemptions for raw materials needed in production;   finally,

_____

[10] see Levin, Jonathan, "Will Sales Taxes Work in Developing Countries?"   Finance and Development, No. 1, 1968,
pp. 19-23.

4) there was no change in the tax base at the manufacturing level, although there was some improvement at the
retail level.   This is an interesting experiment and
would be very useful if accurate data of past economic
performance in a developing country could be obtained.

Apart from providing social capital, the
government can create the atmosphere which is propitious
to private investment: by facilitating the development
of a capital market and issuing the regulations necessary to protect investors; by making saving attractive
to small investors, e.g. through the post office or
other such institutions.   The most important service
which can be rendered by the government in this area is
the sponsoring of development banks.[11]   This is an area
in which it can get ample advice and expert service from
the World Bank which now has a branch specialized in this
field.   This type of institution which has become a
common feature in many developing countries, extends low-
interest loans to small investors in the fields of agriculture, industry and commerce.   The working capital
for development banks is supplied by the government out
of tax receipts; thus a redistribution of income is
effected.

REFERENCES

1.   Galbraith, K., The Affluent Society.   Boston:
      Houghton-Mifflin Co., 1958.

2.   Higgins, Benjamin, Economic Development:
      Principles, Problems and Policies, Revised Edition.
      New York: W. W. Norton and Company, 1968.

---

[11] see Ch. VI for the role of agricultural banks.

3. Levin, J., "Will Sales Taxes Work in Developing Countries?", Finance and Development, No. 1, 1968.

4. Lieftinck, Pieter, "Monetary Policy and Economic Development," Finance and Development, The Fund and Bank Review, Vol. 1, No. 3, December 1964.

5. Meier, Gerald M., Leading Issues in Economic Development: Studies in International Poverty, Second Edition. Oxford University Press, 1970.

6. Morgan, Betz, Choudhry, Readings in Economic Development, selections 32 and 33.

7. Please, Stanley, "Saving Through Taxation - Reality or Mirage?" Finance and Development, The Fund and Bank Review, Vol. IV, No. 1, March 1957.

8. Southard, Frank A., "The Central Bank in the Policy Making Process," Finance and Development, No. 2, 1968.

9. Prest, A. R., "Compulsory Lending Schemes," Staff Papers, International Monetary Fund, Vol. XVI, No. 1, March 1969.

REVIEW QUESTIONS

Terms

monetary policy

open market operations

changes in reserve requirements

changes in the discount rate

commercial banks' reserves

development banks

money supply

the structure of interest rates

currency in circulation

fiscal policy

sales taxes

excise taxes

the income elasticity (of a tax)

vested interests

flight of capital

the "social-balance" concept

social indifference curve

the tax base

the revenue criterion

Questions

1. Compare conditions in the monetary and fiscal
   fields between developing and developed countries.

2. Why is a developing country's ability to save and
   invest closely watched by its prospective lenders?

3. Does a central bank in a developing country have
   more or less responsibility than in a developed
   one?   How do the two compare?

4. What is the function of the government in a
   developing country?   Can it in any way affect
   the development process?

5. Comment upon the choice faced by the government
   of a developing country between immediate social
   welfare and capital formation.

6. Comment on the fact that the ratio of tax revenue
   to G.N.P. is important for assessing economic
   importance.

CHAPTER IX

INTERNATIONAL TRADE AND DEVELOPMENT

The contribution of international trade and payments to economic development is a fact which no longer has to be proved and is well recognized. It is rather the study of how such trade can best be made to serve the purpose of development which is the object of this chapter. It was seen in Chapter II that after industrial expansion started in England and spread out to the other countries of the western world, England, with its expanding industries but limited natural resources, had to grow outwards; there emerged then the classic pattern of exchanging manufactured goods from industrial centers for primary commodities from what it has become customary to call "peripheral" (underdeveloped) countries. Imports of such items into the United Kingdom gradually increased and so did the share of foreign trade in national output. The overall import coefficient rose from approximately 18 per cent in 1850 to the rather high level of almost 36 per cent in 1880-84, as a result of free trade. As a matter of fact, during the last quarter of the nineteenth century, the United Kingdom was the world's leading trade center, accounting for about 36 per cent of world exports of manufactured goods and 27 per cent of the imports of primary commodities.[1]

---

[1] see United Nations, "Towards a New Trade Policy for Development," Report by the Secretary General to the U.N. Conference on Trade and Development, February 1964.

During that period, the general philosophy which underlay trade policy was based on a conception that the expansion of trade worked to the mutual advantage of all countries concerned if all obstacles which impeded free trade were removed. This philosophy was based on an abstract and rather delusory notion of economic homogeneity which concealed the great structural differences between industrial nations and their sources of raw materials and food supplies. Development in the periphery during the 19th century and the early decades of the 20th was a repercussion of the spontaneous development of the western world, but it lacked its spirit of initiative and its economic and social implications. Moreover, it was prompted by a unique combination of external factors which have since ceased to exist. While it lasted, the remarkable expansion of world trade and multilateral exchange acted as a strong catalyst for the less developed countries' production of primary commodities.

The Great Depression brought about the end of this order which already had been undermined by the impact of World War I. Since then, various factors have been at work to change the pattern of exchange: technological progress which has greatly modified the methods and the proportions of inputs in production, the invention of synthetic fibers, exclusive trade groupings, to mention only a few, have reduced or modified the demand from the industrialized countries for the products of the others. On the other hand, structural change in the developing countries necessitating large imports of equipment goods, has increased their demand for the products of the industrialized ones. The result has been a deterioration in the terms of trade of the peripheral nations and the gap will keep growing if the pace of development is to be speeded up.

The causes underlying this situation are difficult to pinpoint, but some facts will become evident during our study. First, the point has already been made that the developing countries have to achieve their development in a much shorter span of time than did any of the industrialized ones: as obvious determinants for such a policy, one could readily mention the pressure exerted at home by the awakened masses claiming a better way of life, and then the enormous potential of modern technology available to them. Secondly, for complex reasons which will be looked into later in this chapter, most of the peripheral countries have not made an adequate effort to diversify their output - and exports - by building up their productive capacity, although there are notable exceptions to this statement.

Our study, then, should start by the recognition that it is dealing with countries which have different levels of development and that their economies are growing at different rates. This recognition should then lead to some modification in the interpretation of the established theory of international trade in order to allow for the dynamic conditions of modern times, and to make possible the assessment of the long-run impact of international exchanges on the evolution of economic development. Of particular interest will be the growth in the level of both aggregate supply and aggregate demand, the effects of technological progress and the direction of, international capital movements. Changes in any of these parameters affect international trade as well as

the development process. These problems concern all
countries, whether they are on the path of economic
development, or of economic growth, but they are of
more immediate importance to the former because foreign
trade makes a bigger contribution to their gross national
output.

This study of how foreign trade can best contribute to economic development will concentrate on those
of its aspects which affect and/or are affected by it,
such as the theory of comparative advantage, the significance of the terms of trade, foreign exchange for
development, the problems arising from the decline in
the prices of primary commodities on world markets and
the suggested solutions to them. To conclude, a brief
look will be taken into the objectives and actual realizations of the United Nations Conference on Trade and
Development.

Comparative Costs

The traditional basis for the theory of international trade is Ricardo's Theory of Comparative Costs,
spelled out in Chapter VII of the 1817 edition of his
"Principles." This theory has a positive economic
aspect, as well as a normative (welfare) one; it is the
latter which is of more concern to developing nations.
According to this theory, each country will specialize
in making goods which it can produce relatively cheaply
and import those in the production of which other countries have a comparative advantage. The theory assumed
conditions of free trade and complete internal mobility
and external immobility of the factors of production.
Finally, it was based on the labor theory of value which
assumes that labor is the only factor of production.

International division of labor and international trade, which enable every country to specialize and to export those things that it can produce cheaper in exchange for what others can provide at a lower cost, are factors which are basic to economic growth.[2]   However, care should be taken as to how costs are calculated: direct costs are those incurred in producing the goods and the tendency, generally, is to take these costs only into consideration; indirect or "real" costs, such as the social disutility of producing for export, the scarcity of raw materials, the development of the export sector at the expense of budding industries catering for local consumption, are of much more permanent effect and should be taken into consideration.

The advantages of the principle of comparative cost for developing countries lie mainly in the comparative differences in the cost of production of industrial products, foodstuffs and raw materials, between them and the industrialized countries, which are likely to be of some magnitude.   In certain cases, of course, countries of one group cannot produce at all what those of the other group have to sell.   The main disadvantages of the application of the principle of comparative cost reside in three points which are important and should be kept in mind through our study of international exchange. The first two points spring from the fact that the classical theory is static: although more of a developing country's resources may be invested in the industries producing for exports than in those producing for local

---

[2] this holds true for developed as well as developing countries, no matter what their rate of growth is.

consumption, external economies are more likely to be
achieved when development is directed towards import-
substitution than export-expansion. In this connection,
it is often difficult to tell where the comparative advantage lies because if industries producing for local
consumption have not yet had the chance to expand and
reach the stage of mass production and least cost, then
a comparison of costs between these industries and foreign
ones would be misleading.

Comparisons would also be out of place because
of the assumptions which underlie the static theory and
which are: 1) identical production functions[3] in the two
trading countries, 2) conditions of full employment and
3) free market conditions. The first of these assumptions seems to be the one least likely to obtain between
developed and developing countries, for the very reasons
which are presently basic to international exchange between them. In developing nations labor wages are low
and capital scarce; they therefore tend to concentrate
on a labor-intensive rather than a capital-intensive type
of production, and that is the contrary of what is the
case in the industrialized nations. As regards the
second assumption, it should be remembered that the fact
that a country is not yet industrialized precludes, by
definition, the realization of real full employment conditions, because when a country has not yet built up its
productive capacity, it is not capable of fully employing
all its resources, especially if you remember that here
full employment involves resources as well as labor.

_____

[3] the production function is the technical relationship
between a given output and various combinations of
inputs.

The third assumption may or may not obtain in either
type of country, but it is less likely to be found in
the developing countries.

From the first argument against the principle
of comparative cost, there follows that of the protection
of infant-industries: not only must those factories producing for local consumption be allowed to expand by obtaining all the resources and productive agents which
they need, but they must be protected in the early stages
of their development from competing foreign imports.

Another important argument against the theory
of comparative cost is the instability of world prices
of primary commodities. The main items of export of
developing countries are either agricultural or mineral,
in either case they are primary products, as compared
with the manufactured articles traded by the industrialized nations. Historical evidence is that the prices
of primary products have been falling steadily with few
upward fluctuations, since the beginning of this century.
Furthermore, the developing countries' concentration on
the primary products which the law of comparative costs
would suppose them to do, would nail their reliance for
the greater part of their export earnings on factors over
which they have no control, such as price fluctuations on
world markets - to say nothing of the lack of diversification in their exports. Moreover, if one remembers the
relatively more important contribution of proceeds from
export to the gross national product of these countries
than to that of the developed ones, the problem acquires
added importance.

Finally, there is the argument concerned with
the inequalities in means of transport, more particularly
shipping: developing countries generally have to pay for

freight in foreign currencies to the developed countries
on both their exports and imports while the latter receive substantial earnings in foreign exchange from
shipping.

Beside determining the articles which countries
should export and import, the comparative cost rule also
decides to some extent the products in which they actually
trade, so that notwithstanding any obstacles that impede
free trade such as the various restrictions on imports,
the main changes in world trade are still interpreted as
related to changes in comparative cost.

In this century, Ohlin[4] has introduced the
notion of factor-scarcity as a result of interregional
differences in productive factor endowments. According
to this theory the comparative advantage is simply a reflection of the relative scarcity (or abundance) of the
factors of production: a country exports those goods
which require a comparatively large proportion of the factors of production and/or resources which the country
possesses in ample supply, and the contrary applies to
the goods which it imports. This theory seems to be vin-
dicated in the case of developing countries which specialize in primary products and of which examples abound: e.g.
Kuwait's oil exports, Brazil's coffee exports, Egypt's
cotton exports, Chile's phosphates and copper and, to go
back to Ricardo's example, Portugal's wine exports.

The Terms of Trade

The terms of trade are defined as the ratio of
exchange between commodities exported and imported; in

_____

[4]Ohlin, Bertil G., International and Interregional Trade,
Cambridge: Harvard University Press, 1933.

practical terms, it is the extent to which the proceeds from a country's exports will pay for its imports. There are different concepts of the terms of trade, according to what particular aspect is singled out for analysis.   The aspect which is most currently used is that which relates the ratio of exchange between commodities and this is expressed by the gross barter, the net barter and the income terms of trade.   The second group of parameters is concerned with the exchange between productive resources and includes the single-factoral and double-factoral terms of trade.   The third group studies the influence of trade transactions in terms of marginal utility analysis, i.e. the real cost and utility terms of trade.[5]

The commodity or net barter terms of trade (N) are calculated by dividing the index of export prices (P_x) by the index of import prices (P_m) or $N = P_x/P_m$. A rise in (N) would indicate that a larger volume of imports could be received, on the basis of price relations, in exchange for a given volume of exports.   This index is relevant when only merchandise is exchanged.   The commodity gross barter terms of trade (G), give the ratio of physical imports (Q_m) to physical exports (Q_x) or $G = Q_m/Q_x$.   A rise in (G) is favorable because it means that a greater volume of imports would be received for a given volume of exports.   (G) would equal (N) only if the value of imports and the value of exports were to be equal.   Based on the two foregoing indexes, the income terms of trade (I) correct movements in the net barter

_____
[5]Meier, Gerald M., The International Economics of Development, New York: Harper & Row, 1968, Ch. 3.

terms of trade (N) for changes in the volume of exports Q_x or $I = N \cdot Q_x$ because it is important for a poor nation to keep track of changes in the volume of its exports. A rise in (I) would mean that the country can obtain a larger volume of imports from the sale of its exports, i.e. an increase in its propensity to import based on a surplus on the payments side of the balance of payments. Consequently, if export prices fall but export volume increases by a higher proportion, this will mean an improvement in the income terms of trade in spite of a deterioration in the net barter terms of trade.

The <u>single-factoral</u> terms of trade (S) multiply the net barter terms of trade (N) by an export productivity index (Z_x) or $S = N \cdot Z_x$ to find out the quantity of imports which can be obtained per unit of factor-input which enters in the production of exports. A rise in (S) would be favorable because it would mean more imports. The <u>double-factoral</u> terms of trade (D) use an import productivity index (Z_m) as well as the export productivity index (Z_x) and are expressed as $D = N \cdot (Z_x/Z_m)$. A rise in (D) would mean that the unit of domestic factors embodied in exports exchanges for more units of foreign factors embodied in imports. If (D) diverges from (S) this indicates a change in the factor cost of imports and a change in productivity of the foreign country, but has no welfare significance for the importing country. What matters to the importing country is the volume of goods it receives per unit of its exported factor input. If a deterioration in the commodity terms of trade is accompanied by a deterioration in the factoral and income terms of trade, this would constitute an obstacle to

development. However, if the single factoral terms of
trade improve in spite of the imbalance in the commodity
terms of trade, then the latter is due to increased productivity in the export sector. In other words, a country's gains from trade will continue if the rise of productivity in its export sector is more than proportional
to the deterioration in its commodity terms of trade.

The majority of the developing countries have
been suffering from an adverse long-term trend in their
terms of trade. The decline in the prices of primary
products, which was particularly strong for the exports
of these countries, set in after the temporary Korean
boom. Meanwhile, the prices of manufactured goods were
moving upwards so that during the 1950's the ratio of
prices for primary products to those of manufactured
goods declined by more than 20 per cent and has remained
stationary since. The following table gives data on the
trend of the developing countries' exports compared with
those of the rest of the world.

Table IX/1

DEVELOPING COUNTRIES SHARE OF WORLD EXPORTS: 1960-66

	1960	1961	1962	1963	1964	1965	1966
Value (billion $'s)	27.5	27.7	29.1	31.7	34.7	35.7	38.4
% of world exports	21.1	20.6	20.4	20.5	20.0	19.2	18.9
% change yearly		-0.5	-0.2	0.1	-0.5	-0.8	-0.3
% increase in world exports		4.5	5.7	8.8	11.6	7.3	9.3

Source: I.M.F. International Financial Statistics,
March 1968, 'World Trade'. Figures adjusted
to include Soviet bloc, Mainland China and Cuba.
Exports are f.o.b.

Funds for Development from Foreign Trade

Proceeds from exports of primary commodities
are a chief source of foreign exchange for development:
they provide about four times as much as international
public loans and grants, and private investments combined. The sharp decline in prices of primary commodities of the 1950's was followed by a decrease in the
developing countries' share of world exports since 1960,
except for the year 1963, as can be seen from table IX/1.

Export expansion does not seem to have affected
development in all countries to the same degree and the
interpretations of the effects of foreign trade on economic development have been almost as varied as the authors
who treated this subject. For instance, Raul Prebisch
stresses the disparity created by the developing countries' increasingly higher ratio of manufactured imports
to their exports of primary commodities; he deplores the
fact that little technological progress can be gained by
the less developed countries as long as they limit their
exports to primary commodities, and thus concludes that
foreign trade has inhibited the expansion of the industrial sector in the developing world. Prebisch also
thinks that the subsidies given farmers in most industrialized countries encourage them to increase production - even though at inflated prices - and this restrains
imports of agricultural products from the developing
nations.[6] Gunnar Myrdal thinks that free trade does not
tend to achieve income equality between factors of production in the developed nations and those in the

---

[6]Prebisch, Raul, Towards a New Trade Policy for Development, Report by the Secretary General of UNCTAD, United
Nations, 1964, pp. 11-16.

underdeveloped, but rather that the process of economic
development would work to accelerate inequalities. As
a matter of fact, trade, if unregulated, can cause setbacks in development: imports of non-essentials using
up scarce foreign exchange, flights of capital, are some
proofs of the need to regulate trade.[7]

Taking a middle of the road view, Ragnar Nurkse
recognizes the lop-sided effects of economic growth when
it is induced by international trade, that is when export
industries are developed by means of foreign investments
to the detriment of the industries producing for home
consumption; however, he concludes that even unsteady
growth is better than none.[8] Gottfried Haberler takes
the view that undue emphasis has been placed on the negative aspects of foreign trade on economic development
and that its benefits have been overlooked. Of the two
types of changes which he says characterize economic development, namely the autonomous changes which are independent of international trade and the changes in productive capacity brought about by trade and favorable change
in trade policy, he particularly stresses the indirect or
dynamic benefits of the latter, such as gains in technological know-how, movements of capital goods and the
fight against monopoly.[9] Finally, Gerald Meier tries
to find out why the "carry-over" from the export sector

[7]Myrdal, Gunnar, Development and Underdevelopment,
National Bank of Egypt Fiftieth Anniversary Commemoration
Lectures, Cairo, 1956, pp. 49-51.

[8]Nurkse, Ragnar, "Trade Theory and Development Policy" in
H.S. Ellis (ed.), Economic Development for Latin America,
New York: St. Martin's Press, 1961, pp. 236-40.

[9]Haberler, Gottfried, International Trade and Economic
Development, National Bank of Egypt, Fiftieth Anniversary
Commemoration Lectures, Cairo, 1959, pp. 7-9.

has not had a more pronounced effect on the economy
internally. He first rejects the notion that foreign
trade is a cause of international inequality and then
finds the answer to his question in the secondary effects
of the expansion in the export base, when as a result of
this expansion the production functions of the goods exported change. Changes in the input coefficients lead
to backward linkages effects: as exports grow, new industries supplying inputs for the export sector are developed when conditions within the country make this
possible. Other benefits from the change of the production function would include a change in the distribu-
tive shares of income leading to a rise in consumption
and/or investment; the promotion of skilled labor and
entrepreneurial ability, the realization of externalities
and a rise in employment.[10]

The developing countries' imports have shown
the same tendency to grow at a slower rate than world
imports, though not as slow as their exports, with a
consequent deterioration in their balance of trade.

The lag in the growth of exports is due to
several causes: inadequate policies, overvalued rates
of exchange, misallocation of resources, and last but not
least, the customs barriers imposed by the industrialized
countries. Hence the argument of the poorer nations
urging the richer ones to institute a system of trade
preferences in their favor. Looking at table IX/1
above, if the poor countries' percentage share of world
exports had been the same in 1966 as it was in 1960,
their export earnings would have amounted to $42.7

---

[10]Meier, Gerald M., Leading Issues in Economic
Development, 2nd. ed., 1970, pp. 511-14.

billion instead of $38.4 billion. An analysis of export
price indexes of primary commodities[11] for the period
1961-66 shows that it was foodstuffs which exerted the
strongest downward pull (of the magnitude of 18 per cent
in 1961 and 1962, with 1958 as a base year). On the
other hand, nonferrous base metals exerted an upward push
which culminated in an index price of 216 for the year
1966, but they carry a weight of only 5 per cent in the
primary commodities price index, while the weight for
foodstuffs is 41 per cent.

International Solutions

Of the various measures designed to provide
either temporary or long-term assistance to the developing nations, some are old and have been tried out over a
number of years with varying degrees of success and
others are new or still in the planning process.
Strangely enough, little attention has been given to
ways of increasing their trade compared to the drive for
increased aid. The reasons for this apparent oversight
may be summed up as follows:

    1. Aid to the poorer nations, though not
too popular, is not a political issue while
the opening up of markets to cheap imports
which would cause prejudice to a rich section
of the community or to some vested interests,
would be one.

    2. Giving preferences to a group of countries
would constitute discriminatory practices in

---

[11]U.N. Monthly Bulletin of Statistics, March, June and
December 1967.

international trade which would be contrary to
the obligations of the contracting parties
under the General Agreement on Tariffs and
Trade (GATT).

3.   The terms of trade have been moving against
the producers of primary commodities for more
than 15 years: to encourage them to increase
the volume of these products might cause the
prices of primary commodities to decline still
further.

Dr. Raul Prebisch, the secretary general of
UNCTAD, who has for many years been pleading the case of
the developing countries, has repeatedly said that existing international trade is tilted in favor of the developed nations.   This argument is not quite accepted by
the rich countries, but it has drawn their attention to
the fact that deliberate policy can switch trade to new
channels and can thus alter the terms of trade.

The United Nations Conference on Trade and Development

The first conference of UNCTAD met in Geneva in
1964 to study the trade problems of the developing nations, called during that conference the "Group of 77."
The most important decision of the Geneva Conference was
that UNCTAD should be a continuing institution with a
permanent secretariat and study committees.   There was
a second conference in New Delhi in 1968.   The main
points which were the subject of discussion and recommendations at both meetings were the following:

1.   to institute commodity agreements in order
to keep the prices of primary commodities from
falling any lower.

2.   to grant tariff preferences to the

manufactures of the less developed nations.

3. to grant them supplementary finance to offset the adverse effects of unforeseen falls in export income.

So far the two meetings have produced a wider exchange of views and studies have been initiated by the United Nations and other international agencies to find out what can be done to help the developing nations.[12]

Overview

The trade and payments problems of the developing countries must be viewed against the background of their efforts to raise their standard of living, their high rate of population growth, and the need to protect their infant industries. On the basis of past experience and certain assumptions, it is possible that they will be facing a rising foreign exchange gap for many years to come. Faced with this problem, their policy makers have tried trade restrictions and exchange control, including multiple rates and tariffs. Meanwhile, greater attention is being given to the causes of the secular lag in world trade of primary commodities; a factor which is being closely looked into is the problem of the trade barriers of the major importing countries. These barriers include agricultural protective policies, import quotas, internal excise taxes, as well as measures to protect their own industries from low-wage competition products. In the final analysis, the industrialized nations will realize that by helping the developing nations, they can open new outlets for their own products.

---

[12] a third meeting (UNCTAD III) is scheduled in Santiago, Chile, mid-April 1972.

173

REFERENCES

1. de Vries, Margaret G., "Trade and Exchange Policies for Economic Development," Finance and Development, The Fund and Bank Review, Vol. IV, No. 2, 1967.

2. Haberler, Gottfried, A Survey of International Trade Theory. Princeton, N.J.: Princeton University Special Papers in International Economics, No. 1, July 1961.

3. Haberler, Gottfried, International Trade and Economic Development, National Bank of Egypt, Fiftieth Anniversary Commemoration Lectures, Cairo, 1959.

4. Host-Madsen, Poul, "Balance of Payments Problems of Developing Countries," Finance and Development, The Fund and Bank Review, Vol. IV, No. 2, June 1967.

5. Meier, Gerald M., Leading Issues in Economic Development: Studies in International Poverty, 2nd. ed., Oxford: Oxford University Press, 1970, Chapter VIII.

6. Meier, Gerald M., The International Economics of Development. New York: Harper & Row, Publishers, 1968, Ch. 3.

7. Morgan, Betz, Choudhry, eds., Readings in Economic Development. Belmont, Cal.: Wadsworth Publishing Company, Inc., 1963, selections 22, 23, 24 and 25.

8. Myrdal, Gunnar, Development and Underdevelopment, National Bank of Egypt Fiftieth Anniversary Commemoration Lectures, Cairo, 1956.

9. Nurkse, Ragnar, "Trade Theory and Development Policy" in H. S. Ellis (ed.), Economic Development for Latin America. New York: St. Martin's Press, 1961.

10. Ohlin, Bertil G., International and Interregional Trade. Cambridge, Mass.: Harvard University Press, 1933.

11. Prebisch, Raul, Towards a New Trade Policy for Development, UNCTAD, Report of the Secretary General, United Nations, Geneva, 1964.

12. United Nations, "Towards a New Trade Policy for Development." New York: Report by the Secretary General to the U.N. Conference on Trade and Development.

REVIEW QUESTIONS

Terms

balance of trade

the import coefficient

"peripheral" countries

the theory of comparative cost

direct costs and "real" cost
of production

export-expansion

productive factors endowment

balance of payments

industrial centers

the pattern of exchange

international division of
labor

import-substitution

factor-scarcity

primary commodities

Questions

1. Does the adoption of an entirely free trade policy between industrialized and non-industrialized nations work to their mutual advantage?

2. How does structural change affect the pattern of foreign trade?

3. Comment upon the causes which widen the gap between the developed and the developing nations.

4. Discuss the main disadvantages to the application of the theory of comparative cost to developing countries.

5. Comment on the principle of protecting infant industries.

6. Discuss the effect of the decline in the prices of primary commodities on world markets, on the economies of the peripheral countries.

7. Describe the different aspects of the terms of trade.

8. What is the contribution of international trade to development?

9. Why do richer nations prefer to give aid rather than trade preferences to the poorer ones?

10. Explain the reasons for and comment on the two meetings of UNCTAD.

175

CHAPTER X

THE VARIOUS FORMS OF FOREIGN AID

"The question is not whether
development will happen. It will.
Rather, the choice is between slow,
halting growth in an environment of
desperation with declining levels of
assistance and embittered international relations, or growth as part
of a positive, concerted campaign to
accelerate and smooth the absorption
of the technological revolution in the
poorer countries, with a reasonable
chance that the spirit of shared concern
and effort will reduce the frictions and
the dangers, and facilitate and ex-
pedite positive results."

Mr. Lester Pearson at the 1969
Annual Meeting of the World Bank

This chapter will study the flow of foreign
aid to the developing countries, including both public
and private, and financial as well as technical forms of
aid.   Private foreign investments, bilateral and multilateral technical assistance and the sources of direct
foreign economic aid will be successively covered.

The contribution of private foreign investment
to the economic development of the host countries has
several beneficial aspects; the most important of these
is the net increase in output resulting just as much
from the additional capital funds as from the better
techniques of production and marketing. One should also
mention the employment opportunities as well as on-the-
job training for the local labor force and prospective
managers, increased public revenue and new contacts with
foreign markets.   On the other hand, although the

transfer of new technology almost inevitably accompanies
private foreign investment, the extension of technical
assistance per se, irrespective of profit-ability to the
promoter, has a big role to play in planning and select-
ing the projects for investment.

The Facts about Private Foreign Investment

Private investment in developing countries can
take many forms: new direct investment, reinvested earnings, portfolio investment and export credit. The first
two involve outlays of a long-term nature, the fourth
requires medium term credit and the third, short-term
capital movements. It is with the first two that we
are concerned here, i.e. with the type of investment
which leads to capital formation and increased output.

Private investments are profit-motivated,
whether they are domestic or foreign and, for the latter,
certain conditions must be present to justify them.
First, the estimated net rate of return from the projects
involved must at least equal - or exceed - the return
from alternative competing uses of the funds. Secondly,
and this point follows from the first, the planning of
the outlays must take into account the higher risks involved and yet allow for competitive pricing.

The criteria used in judging the productivity
of a foreign investment are two-fold: a) its capacity
to produce goods and services which will make the outlay
self-liquidating, and b) its ability to provide enough
foreign exchange to offset the amount lost through the
repatriation of profits to the investor's country. As
regards the economics of foreign investments, these depend on whether the investments involve an export of

capital funds, or merely an investment of capital equipment and services. The assumption in the latter instance is that local costs are financed from domestic sources, such, for instance, as in the case of a partnership with local participation.

When an export of capital is made, there is a transfer of purchasing power which will appear as a debit on the balance of payments of the host country. On the other hand, when capital equipment (bought and paid for by the foreign investor in his own country of residence) is exported, the host country's imports will increase by the value of the capital equipment without a concomitant increase in its foreign indebtedness and the balance of payments of the investor's country of residence will show unrequited exports. Both entries, then, will be bookkeeping ones and in the latter case will be a lesser evil for the investor's country than an export of capital. Exports of services will be paid for, generally in local currency, by the enterprises who benefit from them.

The flow of direct private investment from the developed to the developing countries for the years 1956 to 1968 inclusive, added up to $27,863 million, (averaging $2,143 million per year), out of a total of $44,995 million, the balance being accounted for by bilateral and multilateral portfolio investments.[1]

Creditor Nations and Recipient Nations

To the host country, foreign investments represent the acquisition of productive capacity it could

---

[1] see Pearson, Lester B. (ed.), Partners in Development, 1969, table 15, p. 378.

not otherwise have been able to afford and hence a more
rapid pace in its economic development.   To the country
of the investors, the foreign outlays generally achieve
either one, or both, of two purposes, namely: a) the
development of needed commodities which it does not
produce domestically, and b) new markets for its output
in the recipient countries.   Although most developing
countries appreciate the economic benefits of foreign
investment, many fear the resulting domination of their
economy by foreigners;   the welcome they extend to foreign investors is not, therefore, completely unqualified
and often involves various controls accompanied in some
instances by heavy taxation and the blocking of profits
by means of exchange control restrictions.

Cases of litigation are taken care of by the
World Bank's Convention on the Settlement of Investment
Disputes which has a panel of arbitrators to improve
relations between states and nationals of other states.
Adherence to the Convention is voluntary but it can be
used as a clause in an agreement and the Convention's
decisions are final and binding.   Moreover, bilateral
agreements for the protection of investments as well as
national guarantee schemes, are in practice in most developed and developing countries to provide coverage
against expropriation, inconvertibility and war or
insurrection.[2]

Early in 1969, a meeting in Amsterdam brought
together businessmen from the industrialized countries
and government representatives from the less developed
nations, for "a dialogue between the developing world

---

[2]Barclays Bank, Overseas Review, May 1967, p. 1-2.

and private enterprise".[3]   Some points of interest came
to light at that meeting: it was found, for instance,
that the recently rising trend in the flow of private
foreign capital to the developing countries seems to
have coincided with a decrease in the flow of public
funds to them; so that in 1968, total private investment and lending accounted for almost 45 per cent -
compared with 29 per cent in 1962 and 47 per cent in
1956 - of all aid and investment funds to the less developed countries.   The rise in the flow of private
investment funds is at least partly accounted for by
the relatively high average yearly net rate of return
of 9.5 per cent on foreign capital invested in all but
the extraction industries, in both developed and developing countries.   Finally, the transfer of managerial know-how was found to be at least as important to
economic development as that of capital, if not more.

United Nations Technical Assistance

        Technical assistance is one of the basic tools
for promoting development.   As extended by the United
Nations, it is conceived as a long-term continuing
activity designed to help in new projects to the point
where developing countries can take over.   In so doing,
it has focused mainly on spotting out sound development
opportunities to aid-giving countries, after having
thoroughly studied them to avoid misallocation of resources.   In January 1959, a new type of institution,
the U.N. Special Fund was created to define the standards
for, and carry out pre-investment studies to assess the

---

[3]Ibid., May 1969, p. 1-2.

feasibility of specific development projects.[4] In so
doing it was coordinating and in some cases upgrading,
the work of private consultants and other international
agencies. The Special Fund handled four types of projects: 1) large scale surveys of resources and capital
funds needed for major projects; 2) the creation of
training institutions for technical manpower and key
personnel; 3) research into the potential for industrialization in developing countries and the means to
adapt modern technology to their needs, and 4) assistance
in planning economic development.[5]

In 1965 the Special Fund was merged with the
United Nations Technical Assistance Board and is now
called the United Nations Development Program (UNDP).
Contributions to the Fund had risen from $25.8 million
in 1959 to $85.5 million in 1964.[6] They came mainly
from the industrialized countries but also from developing countries and the Soviet bloc. The amount pledged
for 1970 was $238 million up almost 21 per cent from the
$197.5 million pledged for 1969.[7] Pre-investment pro-
jects approved up to the end of 1968 added up to 1,025,
averaging four and a half years in duration, and were

---

[4]the creation of the Special Fund was an outgrowth of a
proposal by a group of underdeveloped countries for a
Special U.N. Fund for Economic Development (SUNFED) which
did not come into existence because it was not supported
by the U.S. who suggested instead a smaller substitute,
the Special Projects Fund (see U.N., Report on a Special
United Nations Fund for Economic Development, N.Y., 1953).

[5]Gordon, D. L., "Charting the Channels for Development
Capital", Finance and Development, Vol. II, No. 2, June
1965, p. 79-83.

[6]Ibid., p. 82.

[7]UNDP, "Pre-Investment News", N.Y., Nov. 1969.

estimated to cost on completion $2,441 million of which
the UNDP will provide $1,003 million and the recipient
governments $1,438 million.[8]

The World Bank, a specialized agency of the
U.N., also provides technical assistance to the governments of country members. The most important is in
the identification and preparation of projects and is
carried out by the Bank's permanent missions in Eastern
and Western Africa. There is also the Economic Development Institute, a staff college for senior government officials of the developing countries, a special
study on multilateral investment insurance, and the International Centre for Settlement of Investment Disputes
mentioned above.

The United States Point-Four Program

The only concerted effort by the United States
to extend technical assistance as such was embodied in
the Point Four program which was announced by President
Truman in his inaugural address in 1949, as a bold new
program of "making the benefits of our scientific ad-
vances and industrial progress available for the improvement and growth of underdeveloped areas."[9]
Although in the following year the Korean War put a
heavy claim on U.S. military assistance, expenditures
on technical aid rose from $30 million to $150 million
a year and a number of new but non-recurring programs
were included in the federal budget under the heading

[8]United Nations, Press Release DEV/316, N.Y., Jan. 10th
1969.

[9]Ohlin, Goran, "The Evolution of United States Aid
Doctrine" in American Foreign Policy: Essays and
Comments, B. J. Cohen (ed.), 1968.

of "assistance to economic development". However, the
objectives of the program do not seem to have been understood or appreciated and objections were raised
against the program by some of the recipient countries
who suspected it of ulterior motives, and at home, mainly
by legislators and businessmen. In 1956-57, after a
series of foreign policy setbacks, the whole scheme was
reappraised and it was decided to concentrate on an enlarged long-term assistance program, rather than one
geared to short-term foreign policy.

In recent years, United States assistance for
technical cooperation has been included in the general
program of the Agency for International Development (AID)
and has accounted for about thirty per cent of total expenditure under the Foreign Assistance Act and for about
seventy-five per cent of the U.S. personnel paid from
AID funds: 8,000 government technicians plus 10,000
volunteers, mostly Peace Corps, were working overseas in
1967.[10] One third of the technicians and half of the
expenditure were devoted to Vietnam. Agriculture,
education and health and family planning were the three
main fields in which assistance was extended.

Other Technical Assistance

France, West Germany, the U.S.S.R. and Japan
also extended technical assistance to the developing
world; the list is not exhaustive, inasmuch as such
assistance is often part and parcel of economic aid for
specific projects. France's contribution lays emphasis
on education and is directed primarily to her former

[10]Committee for Economic Development, Assisting
Development in Low-Income Countries: Priorities for
U.S. Government Policy, 1969, part 4.

colonies in Africa, but other areas benefit as well.
West Germany's contribution is mainly concerned with
infrastructure, some scholarships and cultural projects;
the recipients are for the most part African nations.
The U.S.S.R.'s technical assistance is mostly a part of
its economic aid and will be discussed in the next chapter.   It does send missions occasionally and upon request to carry out geological surveys and mineral prospection.   The beneficiaries are mainly African and Asian
countries.   Japanese aid has been increasing rapidly in
recent years and is directed mainly to Asian countries;
technical assistance goes with economic aid.

Facts about Economic Aid

Foreign funds for financing development, from
both public and private sources, during the period 1956
through 1968, added up to $116,561 million,[11] or a yearly
average of $8,966 million.   Great as these contributions
may seem, they nevertheless represented a small percentage
of the recipient countries' national income and a still
smaller percentage of that of the donor countries.
However, the advantage of this flow of funds was primarily
in its contribution to capital formation by financing
either domestic investment, or imports of machinery and
other equipment, or the building of roads and railways,
ports and communication media.   Of no less importance
was the increase in agricultural production brought about
by imports of fertilizers, hybrid seeds, irrigation pumps
and other modern methods of cultivation.

_____

[11] see Pearson, L.B., op. cit., table 15, p. 378.

184

Another less tangible advantage of the foreign
aid flow has been the mobilization of local potential
skills and resources providing initiative and direction
to transform these skills into goods and services for
production, consumption, or export. In other words,
the technical know-how and the ability to plan and to
organize which accompany the transfer of aid are almost
just as important in sparking the take-off.

Notwithstanding the above advantages, views
about foreign aid have changed with the years and in
the light of experience some of the developing nations
have come to express some reservations about it. Not
the least factor affecting their views are the considerable amounts which the LDC's have to pay in debt service: for the period 1961-68 for instance, such debt
service added up to $25,873 million - on an accumulated
debt of $282,269 million,[12] i.e. a rate of return of
about 9 per cent which goes to the donor countries.
These payments which use up a large chunk of the LDC's
meager kitty of foreign reserves, do not include repatriation of earnings on foreign investments. It is no
wonder that the majority of developing countries now
prefer trade to aid. The latter view is corroborated
by the argument that investment financed by domestic
saving is not sufficient to sustain economic growth and
that it must be complemented by goods and services obtained from abroad through international exchange and
trade.

Another aspect of the flow of foreign development capital is the necessity that it be applied to the
most economic use. A study prepared for the U.S. Agency

---

[12]Pearson, op. cit., tables 9 and 10, pp. 371-72.

for International Development (AID), on the evaluation
of capital requirements for development, adopted a three
phase approach designed to measure quantitatively the
constraints on development.[13]   In the first stage, the
savings constraint relates the propensity to save of
the economy to its investment needs.   In the second
stage, the economy's propensity for increasing its foreign exchange earnings is measured against its development needs for imports.   In the third stage, and this
is the most important of the three, shifts in the limitations imposed by the economy's absorptive capacity
of development capital are taken as a measure of economic
performance.   In other words, the more capital the
economy can absorb effectively, the better its chances
of progress.   The model can be applied on a country by
country basis and has room for a variety of assumptions.
However, experience has shown that the model can only be
an approximation of real life because the three constraints often coexist at the same time and affect each
other.[14]   Moreover, the model applies only to aggregates
and capital, as explained in the earlier chapters, and
is not homogeneous in underdeveloped countries.

Bilateral and Multilateral Aid

Of the total flow of aid funds mentioned
above, only just under five per cent was channelled
through multilateral agencies and the balance of over
95 per cent consisted of bilateral aid, of which 56 per

---

[13]Chenery, H. B., and Strout, A. M., "Foreign Assistance
and Economic Development", American Economic Review,
September 1966.
[14]see Hawkins, E. K., "Measuring Capital Requirements",
Finance and Development, No. 2, 1968, pp. 2-7.

cent were public grants and loans and 39 per cent,
private direct portfolio and other investments.   It
is obvious from these data that the largest proportion
of aid comes from official sources and a question which
has fueled debate over the years is whether some of this
capital would not be more efficiently used if channelled
through multilateral agencies.   The main argument has
centered on the difficulty of managing a large multilateral aid program on the basis of one vote each of
over 100 member governments when the bulk of the funds
comes from only a few sources.

In this connection, it is interesting to review briefly some of the other arguments which have been
advanced for and against multilateral aid.   The first
concerns the coordination of efforts and assistance
which can best be achieved by international agencies
and there is no doubt that some of them (the United
Nations, the World Bank) have been doing a good job in
this respect.   Second, it is considered that multilateral
aid, because of its non-political, no-strings-attached
character, is more acceptable to developing countries.
However, some of the LDC's who have no compunction on
the political aspect find that the international agencies are more exacting as regards economic performance
in the recipient countries, less generous with funds and
altogether less flexible than donor countries.   Still
another argument is concerned with efficiency and relative cost of the projects carried out.   Whether an
individual country or an international organization is
more efficient depends on the selection of the experts
either one employs and the effectiveness of the experts
will determine also the relative cost.   The latter argument, therefore, does not hold water.   Generally

speaking, it is difficult to see how a country which
contributes large amounts of aid can be expected to
give up all its rights about the destination and the
use of the aid; as a matter of fact, this would be
considered by some legislative bodies as a loss of
sovereignty.[15]

United States Aid

Official U.S. aid to the less developed
countries consists of grants and loans and is channelled through the U.S. Agency for International
Development. Total expenditures by the AID and its
predecessors, for the period April 3rd 1948 to June
30th 1967, amounted to $40,688 million.[16] This sum
includes amounts expended on loans (about 30 per cent),
grants (about 70 per cent) and excludes military
assistance, Food for Freedom program (Public Law 480)
and Export-Import Bank loans. This total was distributed as follows: Europe $15,227 million, Near
East and South Asia $8,852 million, East Asia $6,507
million, Latin America $2,942 million (plus $350
million administered by the Inter-American Development
Bank through the Social Progress Trust Fund), Vietnam
$2,645 million, and Africa $1,595 million.

Up to the year 1959, under the policy of
"world-wide procurement", the aid-recipient countries
were free to use the funds granted or loaned to them
for purchase of commodities in the cheapest market.
However, in October 1959 this policy was changed to

---

[15]for a more detailed discussion, see Asher, Robert E.,
"Multilateral versus Bilateral Aid: An Old Controversy
Revisited" in Cohen, B. J., op. cit.
[16]Agency for International Development, U.S. Economic
Assistance Programs, April 3, 1948 - June 30, 1967.

one whereby the use of U.S. loan funds was limited to
U.S. goods, and in December 1960 the use of grant funds
for world-wide procurement was barred in 19 industrialized countries.

Other Bilateral Aid

On December 19th 1961, the General Assembly
of the United Nations designated the 1960's as "the
United Nations Development Decade, in which Member
States and their peoples will intensify their efforts...
to accelerate progress" and "to attain in each underdeveloped country a substantial increase in the rate of
growth... taking as the objective a minimum annual rate
of growth of aggregate national income of 5 per cent at
the end of the Decade".[17]   To achieve this rate of
growth in the developing countries, it was recommended
that the advanced countries devote 1 per cent of their
own national incomes, to them during the decade.   As
these incomes themselves were expected to grow at an
annual rate of 4 to 5 per cent, capital assistance was
expected to increase by about $4-5 billion yearly and to
more than double during the decade.   This expectation
did not sound unreasonable then because the flow of aid
during the decade of the 1950's had been increasing at
a very high rate.   However, what actually happened during the 1960's was a slight but steady decline in the
absolute amount of aid given up to and including 1963,
a slight rise in 1964, a bigger one in 1965 and a decline in 1966.   These figures are shown in table X/1
which lists the ten top countries by order of importance

---

[17]United Nations, The United Nations Development Decade:
Proposals for Action, New York, 1962.

of aid given for the developed market economies. As
regards the 1 per cent of national income which was to
be devoted to aid, although some countries exceeded this
ceiling, most of the others did not even reach it.   It
is here interesting to note that of the countries which
have been devoting a relatively large percentage of
their national income to aid, all except Switzerland,
are nations which had, or have still, large colonial
empires.   These data are shown in table X/2.

Table X/1

Net Flow of Resources to Developing Countries
from Developed Market Economies

(millions of $'s)

Country	1961	1962	1963	1964	1965	1966
United States	4,050	3,953	4,192	4,459	5,156	4,928
France	1,341	1,364	1,216	1,308	1,247	1,214
United Kingdom	829	708	629	841	929	896
West Germany	753	622	548	592	634	615
Japan	298	214	228	274	422	422
Italy	182	322	282	189	229	468
Netherlands	219	144	128	114	222	239
Canada	101	109	114	141	172	264
Belgium	170	128	178	159	190	180
Switzerland	198	152	150	84	121	138
Total for 22 countries	8,423	7,905	7,848	8,452	9,655	9,087

Source: United Nations, The External Financing of
Economic Development, Compiled from Table 4,
p. 10.

As regards trends after 1966, the flow of
capital assistance from the top donor nations, continued
to register a decline as far as the United States and
the United Kingdom were concerned, but moved upwards for
the other countries, particularly in the case of France.

Table X/2

Net Flow of Resources to Developing Countries
as Ratio of G.N.P. of Donor Countries

(percentages)

Country	1961	1962	1963	1964	1965	1966
France	2.07	1.89	1.52	1.48	1.33	1.20
Switzerland	2.05	1.42	1.28	0.65	0.87	0.93
Netherlands	1.77	1.08	0.87	0.66	1.16	1.15
Portugal	1.63	1.42	1.65	1.58	0.74	0.74
Belgium	1.40	0.99	1.28	1.02	1.12	0.99
United Kingdom	1.08	0.88	0.74	0.91	0.94	0.86
United States	0.77	0.69	0.70	0.69	0.74	0.57
West Germany	0.92	0.70	0.58	0.57	0.56	0.51
Average for 16 countries	0.87	0.76	0.71	0.70	0.74	0.64

Source: compiled from United Nations, op. cit., table 5,
          p. 12.

It should be mentioned here that the amounts
shown in table X/1 include multilateral aid, i.e. aid
channelled through international agencies, which as seen
earlier, is a very small percentage of total aid.   In
the aggregate, the net amounts transferred in 1966 constituted just over 0.6 per cent of the combined gross
national product of the developed market economies.

Table X/3

Commitments of Economic Aid to Developing Countries
from Centrally Planned Economies

(millions of $'s)[*]

Country	Total before 1954-1962	1963	1964	1965	1966[a]
Bulgaria	20	6	-	-	30
China (mainland)	365	88	305	77	6
Czechoslovakia	468	20	118	43	192
Eastern Germany	108	-	71	132	-
Hungary	151	14	10	42	52
Poland	332	8	54	22	-
Romania	112	-	70	-	-
U.S.S.R.	2,898	205	618	279	867
Total Commitments	4,454	341	1,246	595	1,147

Source: United Nations, op. cit., table 7, p. 16.

[*]national currencies converted into dollars at official
rates of exchange.

[a]preliminary data.

Looking at the contribution of the centrally
planned economies from available data, we find that the
trend is set by the largest contributor, i.e. the Soviet
Union from whom the flow of aid has differed with the
years.   Details of this contribution are given in table
X/3.   Regionally, the biggest recipient was Africa
where the largest share went to the United Arab Republic,
followed by southern and south-eastern Asia where the
largest amount of aid went to India, West Asia where Iraq
and Syria shared the biggest contribution, and finally

Table X/4

Net Flow of Resources to Developing Regions

from Multilateral Agencies

(million $'s)

Recipient Region	Medium of Transfer	1961	1962	1963	1964	1965	1966[a]
Latin America[b]		-49	69	286	316	160	265
	U.N.	12	25	30	39	38	39
	Other	-61	44	256	277	122	226
Africa[b]		122	146	118	189	230	246
	U.N.	55	45	55	78	74	86
	Other	68	101	62	110	156	160
Asia[b]		125	194	211	217	423	352
	U.N.	56	84	91	86	86	96
	Other	69					
All Developing Countries[c]		224	415	644	734	826	876
	U.N.	148	157	203	215	211	234
	Other	76	258	441	519	614	642

Source: United Nations, op. cit., table 6, p. 13.

[a] preliminary data, partly estimated.

[b] French Overseas Territories are all included in Africa and French Overseas Departments all in Latin America; Portuguese Overseas Provinces are all included in Africa.

[c] including net disbursements in developing countries in the Pacific and all unallocated flows.

Latin America where only Argentina and Brazil received aid.[18]

---

[18] United Nations, The External Financing of Economic Development, pp. 16-17.

Multilateral Aid

Table X/4 shows the net flow of resources to developing regions from multilateral agencies. This aid is net and therefore includes all grants and loans less subscriptions, contributions, participations and repayments. Only United Nations activities and expenditures are gross.

The United Nations extends aid through its specialized agencies some of which have become prestigious with the years. Such are the United Nations Educational, Scientific and Cultural Organization,better known as UNESCO, the World Health Organization (WHO), the Food and Agricultural Organization (FAO), the International Labour Organization (ILO), the International Monetary Fund (IMF) and the International Bank for Reconstruction and Development (IBRD) also known as the World Bank. All these organizations have become very important in their own right and in the case of some, like the World Bank, the fact that they are specialized agencies of the U.N. is sometimes overlooked. They, therefore, have their own separate budgets or subscriptions contributed directly to them by the member states. The United Nations agencies whose disbursements figure in table X/4 are the U.N. Development Programme, the U.N. Fund for the Congo, the U.N. High Commissioner for Refugees, the U.N. Children's Fund, the U.N. Korean Reconstruction Agency, the U.N. Relief and Works Agency and the U.N. Temporary Executive Authority (West Irian). The mention of some of these agencies is somewhat reminiscent of some of the acute political crises the world has gone through since World War II and to which the United Nations has managed to bring some relief, if not a final solution.

The International bodies whose aid to the developing countries figures under the word 'other' are the following: the African Development Bank, the Asian Development Bank, the European Development Fund, the European Investment Bank, the World Bank and its subsidiaries the International Development Association and the International Finance Corporation, the Inter-American Development Bank and the Organization of American States.

All the organizations named above have been formed specifically to finance development and their performance will be examined more closely in part III in assessing their contribution to the development of the third world. They are all of recent creation, the oldest being the World Bank which together with the IMF, came into being in 1946 as a result of the Bretton Woods Conference.

REFERENCES

1. Chenery, H. B. and Strout, A. M., "Foreign Assistance and Economic Development", American Economic Review, September 1966.

2. Cohen, B. J. (ed.), American Foreign Policy: Essays and Comments. New York: Harper and Row, 1968.

3. Committee for Economic Development, Assisting Development in Low Income Countries: Priorities for U.S. Government Policy. New York, 1969.

4. Federal Reserve Bank of Boston, "The Buy-American Policy of the United States Government: Its Balance-of-Payments and Welfare Effects", New England Economic Review, July/August 1969.

5. Gordon, D. L., "Charting the Channels for Development Capital", Finance and Development, The Fund Bank Review, Vol. II, No. 2, June 1965.

6. Hawkins, E. K., "Measuring Capital Requirements", Finance and Development, The Fund Bank Review, Vol. V, No. 2, 1968.

7. Krause, Walter, International Economics. Boston: Houghton Mifflin Company, 1965.

8. Pearson, Lester B. (ed.), Partners in Development. New York: Praeger, 1969.

9. United Nations, Report on a Special United Nations Fund for Economic Development. New York, 1953.

10. United Nations, The United Nations Development Decade: Proposals for Action. New York, 1962.

11. United Nations, The External Financing of Economic Development: International Flow of Long-Term Capital and Official Donations, 1962-66. New York, 1968.

12. United States Agency for International Development, The Foreign Assistance Program, Fiscal 1968, Annual Report to the Congress. Washington, D.C., January 1969.

13. United States Agency for International Development, U.S. Economic Assistance Programs: April 3, 1948 - June 30, 1967. Washington, D.C., February 1968.

REVIEW QUESTIONS

Terms

a feasibility study

managerial know-how

a pre-investment project

technical assistance

savings constraint

bilateral assistance

the U.N. Special Fund

the U.S. Point-Four Program

the Economic Development Institute

capital assistance

absorptive capacity constraint

multilateral assistance

Questions

1. Name some of the criteria used for assessing the profitability of a foreign investment.

2. What is the difference, from the point of view of the balance of payments of a donor country, between aid extended by means of an export of capital funds and that given in capital goods?

3. Is the extension of aid by an advanced country purely a philanthropic action or does any benefit accrue from such action to the donor country?

4. What trend has the flow of aid to the LDC's taken in the decade of the 1950's and in that of the 1960's? Was it different and why?

5. What is meant by the U.N. Development Decade? Has it fulfilled its expectations?

6. Was the benefit from aid to the developing nations purely financial or was it the result of what this aid could accomplish?

7. Is there more than one approach to assess capital assistance requirements and what particular factor do these requirements mainly depend on?

8. Give some of the arguments in favor of economic aid being channelled through an international agency.

9. Name the region in the world which has been the biggest recipient of U.S. aid.

10. Discuss the argument that advanced nations should devote no less than 1 per cent of their respective G.N.P.'s to foreign aid.

PART II

DEVELOPING REGIONS: COMPARATIVE ANALYSES

This part includes comparative studies of the
developing regions of the world: four different areas are
covered and two chapters are devoted to each area; they
are Latin America, the Middle East and North Africa,
Africa South of the Sahara, and Southeast Asia. Basic
data such as area, population, national accounts and foreign trade, are given for every country within each area,
so that intraregional and interregional comparisons can
be made. The data are compiled from recognized international sources such as the publications of the United
Nations, the International Monetary Fund and the World
Bank. The various statistical tables acquaint the student with the large array of sources of information available and the use of which can be easily mastered.

In the course of these studies, each country's
potential for progress is assessed in the light of its
resources and degree of development, against the background of the area of which it is a part, using the parameters and techniques developed in Part I of the text.
As in Part I, a large selection of references is given
for each area, to provide scope for more reading and
research.

CHAPTER XI

LATIN AMERICA

The countries of Latin America differ from
other developing nations in two main respects: the first
is that most of them have been independent for a long
period of time; the second is that they have a comparatively high per capita income (an average of about
$400.); they also have a higher rate of literacy.
Nineteen nations will be covered in this and the following
chapter: Argentina, Bolivia, Brazil, Chile, Colombia,
Costa Rica, Dominican Republic, Ecuador, El Salvador,
Guatemala, Honduras, Jamaica, Mexico, Nicaragua, Panama,
Paraguay, Peru, Uruguay, and Venezuela.[1] Although the
nations studied differ from each other in their resources
and economic structure, they share a common history and
culture and also the conditions of their environment
which have to a large extent affected their development.

Before 1930, growth in Latin America was the
result of external forces, i.e., events in the world
economy, such as fluctuations in international trade,
etc., rather than internal ones. This kind of development did not generate enough stimulus internally to overcome archaic institutions and practices which had their
source in the remote colonial past. Practices and acquired rights which were started originally by the white
settlers to assert their supremacy over the indigenous
natives, have in modern times obstructed the implementation of reforms more consistent with modern world conditions.

---

[1]Cuba is not included because of lack of data.

Two growth rates are important to watch and to
compare in studying the countries of Latin America, just
as for other developing nations: the growth of population
and that of output. For the continent as a whole, the
rate of growth of the population is estimated at an average of about 3.5 per cent a year and the rate of economic
growth at 6.0 per cent, which leaves a net per capita rate
of growth of about 2.5 per cent per annum although these
rates differ between countries. It should be noted that
the rise in output is just keeping ahead of the rise in
population, because of the very high rate of population
increase, and thus not providing enough of the amount of
capital accumulation required for development. In this
necessarily brief study of the 19 Latin American nations,
a look will first be taken at their resources in order to
assess the potential for expansion; then a comparison
will be made of the various countries' stage of development. Finally, four basic issues which, it is considered, are common to all Latin American countries and
closely connected with their development, will be covered;
these issues are: inflation, land reform, industrialization and economic integration. The first two issues
are studied in this chapter. The last two will be
covered in chapter XII, within an assessment of the
Alliance for Progress.

Resources and Potential for Development

Table XI/1 shows that the rate of population
growth varies for individual countries over a range which
goes from 1.3 per cent for Uruguay to 4.3 per cent for the
Dominican Republic and Venezuela. Total population which
added up in 1969 to over 256 millions, is expected to

double every 24 years and reach 625 millions by the year
2000 - that is if the present trend continues. It is a
young population: over forty per cent of the total inhabitants are below the age of 15 years. To meet this
expansion without reducing the present standard of living,
it is estimated that agricultural production will have to
increase by 6 per cent yearly, which is double the present
rate; at least 140 million new jobs will have to be
created before the end of the century; over a million new
homes built annually; more than 200,000 additional phys-
icians made available by 1980, to maintain the present
ratio of doctors to people - which in itself is not quite
adequate. Finally, hundreds of thousands new classrooms
will have to be created to meet minimum standards.

Resources. Some resources have been exploited
for many years, others have recently become economically
exploitable because of better technology, greater demand
and the resulting higher prices on world markets, and/or
the availability of foreign investment. Examples of the
latter type of resource are: the rich pampa region of
Argentina where transportation problems precluded meat
exports until the introduction of the refrigerator in
ships in the last quarter of the 19th century; the rich
but for long inaccessible Cerro Bolivar iron ore deposits
in eastern Venezuela which are part of the Guiana high-
lands. Still other resources such as the large areas of
land in Brazil, for instance - unoccupied and unexploited - could be transformed into producing areas if they
became more easily accessible to markets.

Land use in Latin America adds up to a very
small percentage of its 7.7 million square miles; generally, it includes land which receives enough rainfall

Table XI/1

LATIN AMERICA: AREA AND POPULATION

Country	Area in sq. miles	Population (000) 1958	Population (000) 1969	Av. rate of growth per annum %
Argentina	1,072,748	20,086	23,980	1.8
Bolivia	424,163	3,360	4,800	3.9
Brazil	3,287,204	65,750	92,280	3.6
Chile	286,397	7,316	9,570	2.8
Colombia	439,813	14,458	20,460	3.8
Costa Rica	19,575	1,153	1,680	4.1
Dominican Rep.	18,816	2,826	4,170	4.3
Ecuador	104,506	4,105	5,890	3.9
El Salvador	8,164	2,321	3,390	4.2
Guatemala	42,042	3,584	5,010	3.6
Honduras	43,277	1,823	2,500	3.4
Jamaica	4,411	1,566	1,950	2.2
Mexico	760,375	33,704	48,930	4.1
Nicaragua	57,143	1,330	1,920	4.0
Panama	28,753	1,002	1,420	3.8
Paraguay	157,047	1,687	2,310	3.3
Peru	496,223	9,483	13,170	3.5
Uruguay	72,172	2,471	2,850	1.3
Venezuela	352,143	6,830	10,040	4.3
	7,674,872	184,855	256,320	

Source: United Nations Statistical Yearbook.

and does not need an expensive irrigation network, although such a network exists in a few countries such as
Mexico, for instance. Lack of cultivation is due in
some areas to dryness or the poor quality of the soil;
in others which are potentially cultivable, the long dis-
tances to markets, the need to build highways, high

freight rates, etc. are the reasons which have delayed exploitation.

Agricultural output includes such temperate zone commodities as grain, wool and meat produced mainly in Argentina and Uruguay, as well as tropical zone commodities such as coffee in Brazil, Colombia, Costa Rica, Ecuador, El Salvador, Guatemala, Honduras and Nicaragua; bananas grown in Costa Rica, Ecuador, Guatemala, Honduras and Panama, sugar in the Dominican Republic, cotton in Nicaragua and Paraguay, and timber in Paraguay. Agriculture makes its biggest contribution to the national product in Honduras (43%), Paraguay (36.5%), Nicaragua (35%), Ecuador (34.2%), Costa Rica (31.2%), Brazil (30.7%), and Colombia (30.3%). Agriculture is the backbone of most of the Latin American economies and the main emphasis is on the transition from subsistence to commercial agricultural production as well as on diversification.

Mineral resources are substantial although probably not as abundant as in other developing regions. They include oil in Venezuela which accounts for 25 per cent of all Latin American exports but for only 7 per cent of the world proven reserves; copper, iron and nitrates in Chile which produces 15 per cent of the world's total copper production and holds 30 per cent of the world reserves; oil and tin in Bolivia; lead, copper, silver, zinc and iron in Peru; lead, silver, copper and iron in Mexico; iron and manganese in Brazil, and coal in Venezuela, Mexico, Colombia, Argentina, Peru and Brazil. Mining contributes a very small percentage to the national product of the respective countries, except for Venezuela (27.8%), Bolivia (12.1%), Chile (6.9%) and Peru (5.9%). The contribution of mining will increase when these countries start using their mineral products in manufacturing.

Comparative Basic Data

Any attempt to convert national output data of
the Latin American countries, from national currencies
into dollars, can be very frustrating.   Multiple exchange
rates, currency devaluation or revaluation and/or changes
in statistical accounting methods, are just as many ob-
structions to accurate results.   Such an attempt was made
in table XI/2 where each country's gross domestic product
for the years 1958 and 1969 was converted into current
dollars, at the appropriate (official or prevailing) rate
of exchange.[2]   Then, the 1969 dollar values were deflated
into 1958 dollars to get the real rate of growth for the
period 1958/1969.

The results show great disparities between the
various countries in total gross domestic product, disparities which appear also on the per capita level.   The decade of the 1950's was a prosperous one which witnessed
high rates of economic growth for almost all the countries
studied;   the factors behind this expansion were repercussions of external events: recovery of the world from
the Great Depression of the 1930's, World War II, the
Korean War and the boom of the post-war years.   Growth
in per capita G.D.P. during the decade of the 1960's was
at a lower rate than during the 1950's.   This trend is
particularly evident in several countries which, owing to
inflation and high rates of population increase, had negative rates of change.   On the other hand, economies
which had made a slow start continued to grow rapidly.
Such was the case in Peru where the development of the
fishing industry has been very successful, in Bolivia
where per capita G.D.P. was the lowest in Latin America

---

[2]rates of exchange are given in table XI/4.

Table XI/2

LATIN AMERICA: NATIONAL ACCOUNTS

Country	GDP in mn. $'s[a] 1958	1969	1969 GDP[b] in 1958 $'s	Av. rate of change p.a. in 1958 $'s %
Argentina	17,770	22,977	18,381	0.3
Bolivia	324	932	746	11.0
Brazil	16,960	29,550[c]	23,640	3.9
Chile	3,016	6,341	5,072	6.1
Colombia	2,867	6,188	4,951	6.5
Costa Rica	461	813	650	3.7
Dominican Rep.	714	1,181[c]	950	3.3
Ecuador	818	1,667	1,333	5.7
El Salvador	555	953	762	3.3
Guatemala	971	1,679	1,343	3.4
Honduras	362	663	530	4.1
Jamaica	594	1,112	889	4.5
Mexico	10,328	27,200[c]	21,760	11.0
Nicaragua	340	749	599	7.0
Panama	383	917	733	8.2
Paraguay	235	554	443	8.0
Peru	1,645	5,242	4,193	14.0
Uruguay	894	1,964	1,571	6.9
Venezuela	7,343	9,933[c]	7,946	0.8

Sources: United Nations Statistical Yearbook and International Monetary Fund, International Financial
Statistics.
Note: data are in dollars of the years indicated, i.e.
pre-devaluation dollars.

[a]for exchange rates at which the G.D.P. was converted into
$'s see table XI/4.

[b]deflated on the basis of a price index of 123.

[c]1968.

in 1958, and in Mexico where the rise in industrial production is ahead of the rest of the economy.

In terms of sheer magnitude of gross domestic
product, table XI/2, column 4, shows that, by order of
importance, Brazil, Mexico, Argentina, Venezuela, Chile,
Colombia and Peru had the highest G.D.P.'s.   Looking
rather at per capita G.D.P. (table XI/3, column 4) we
find that Venezuela, Argentina, Uruguay, Chile, Panama,
Mexico, Jamaica and Costa Rica, all had per capita
G.D.P.'s above $350.   As regards the rate of growth in
per capita G.D.P. for the same period (table XI/3, column 5), we find that Peru, Bolivia, Mexico, Uruguay and
Panama, averaged a rate of growth above 3 per cent per
annum during the 11-year period covered.   The negative
average registered by Costa Rica, Venezuela, Argentina,
the Dominican Republic, Guatemala and El Salvador, was
the result of one or two bad years, rather than a steady
decline.   As a matter of fact, Argentina, Costa Rica,
the Dominican Republic, as well as Brazil and Mexico,
recorded in 1969 rates higher than the regional average.

Though the period covered may not be long
enough for assessment of long-term trends, it is important for several reasons: it includes the transition from
unusual world economic conditions causing both external
and internal cyclical fluctuations, to more normal economic world conditions.   Moreover, this period also marks
the change in emphasis from external stimuli such as foreign trade, to internal ones such as industrialization
and land reform, for the realization of economic development.   Finally, it is the period which saw the beginning
of interstate cooperation in the form of the much-abused
Alliance for Progress and also the various efforts for
economic integration.

Table XI/3

LATIN AMERICA: PER CAPITA G.D.P.^{a}

Country	Per/cap. GDP in $'s 1958	1969	1969 GDP^{b} in 1958 $'s	Av. rate of change p.a. (1958 $'s)
Argentina	884	959	766	1.1
Bolivia	97^{c}	194	155	5.9
Brazil	257	330^{d}	264^{d}	0.2
Chile	412	662	530	2.8
Colombia	198	302	261	1.9
Costa Rica	399	483	386	-3.2
Dominican Rep.	252	293^{d}	235^{d}	-0.67
Ecuador	199	283	226	1.1
El Salvador	239	281	224	-0.5
Guatemala	270	335	268	-0.6
Honduras	198	265	212	0.6
Jamaica	379	570	456	1.8
Mexico	308	575^{d}	460^{d}	4.9
Nicaragua	256	390	312	1.9
Panama	382	645	516	3.1
Paraguay	139	239	191	3.3
Peru	173	398	318	7.5
Uruguay	361	687	551	4.7
Venezuela	1,075	989^{d}	791^{d}	-2.6

Sources: United Nations Statistical Yearbook and International Monetary Fund, International Financial
Statistics.

^{a}computed from table XI/2.

^{b}deflated on the basis of a price index for the dollar
of 123.

^{c}1959. ^{d}1968.

N.B.: Data are in pre-devaluation dollars.

In view of the foregoing, any study of the
Latin American economies should first take into account
the differentials in economic structure and development
which are evident from a preliminary look at their basic
data and which indicate the initial stage from which they
started their progress: the lower the base, the higher
the rate of growth at the beginning.   Secondly, it is
also essential to find out the degree of complementarity
in resources, production and exchange which is possible
on the inter-regional level, as a preliminary step con-
ducive to economic integration.

Inflation

Table XI/4 shows the evolution in the rates of
exchange, in relation to the U.S. dollar, in the countries of Latin America, for the period 1958/1969, while
table XI/5 shows changes in the cost of living index and
the money supply for the same period.   It will be seen
that Argentina, Brazil, Chile and Uruguay, where a rate
of inflation of between 40 and 80 per cent a year is not
uncommon - in 1964 it was around 100 per cent in Brazil -
suffered large declines in the value of their national
currencies, during the early 1960's, although the situation is now being brought under control.   Others, such
as Colombia and Peru, have had a milder rate of inflation, while for some the rate of exchange has remained
stable over the whole period.   Such serious inflation
has had numerous effects: a) it has slowed down economic
growth; b) it has accentuated the disequilibrium in the
balance of payments; c) it has forced governments to resort to 'stop-gap' policies such as diverting potential
exports to home markets allowing an unhealthy increase in
imports; d) it has discouraged savings and this in turn

Table XI/4

LATIN AMERICA: RATES OF EXCHANGE

Country	National Currency	National Currency per U.S. $ 1958	1967	1969
Argentina	peso	18.0	350.0	3.50
Bolivia	boliviano	11.9	11.9	11.88
Brazil	cruzeiro[a]	37.1	2.715	4.35
Chile	escudo[b]	993.0	5.79	9.98
Colombia	peso	7.22	15.82	17.93
Costa Rica	colon	5.60	6.62	6.95
Dominican Rep.	peso	1.0	1.0	1.0
Ecuador	sucre	15.15	18.18	18.18
El Salvador	colon	2.50	2.50	2.50
Guatemala	quetzal	1.0	1.0	1.0
Honduras	lempira	2.0	2.0	2.0
Jamaica	Jam. pound[c]	.36	.41	
	Jam. dollar			.833
Mexico	peso	12.49	12.49	12.49
Nicaragua	cordoba	7.05	7.05	7.05
Panama	balboa	1.0	1.0	1.0
Paraguay	guarani	111.3	126.0	126.0
Peru	sol	24.50	38.70	38.70
Uruguay	peso	10.20	200.0	250.0
Venezuela	bolivar	3.35	4.50	4.50

Source: Exchange rates taken from International
Financial Statistics.

[a] new cruzeiro as from 1967 equals 1,000 of the old
cruzeiro.

[b] new escudo as from 1959 equals 1,000 of the old escudo.

[c] on Sept. 8, 1969, Jamaican pound was changed to Jam. $
which equals U.S. $1.20.

has affected the pattern of domestic investment.

Before looking into the causes of inflation, two points need to be made clear: the first regards the method of calculating the rise in prices which may not be a true reflection of conditions in the marketplace because information regarding prices differs largely between urban centers and rural areas; moreover, the price index is often based on a sample too small for it to be entirely relevant and it is, therefore, not always quite accurate.[3] The second point is that most of the countries suffering from acute inflation are, comparatively, the most highly industrialized in Latin America - with the exception of Mexico which has had relative price stability, though highly industrialized.

Causes of Inflation

The causes of inflation in Latin America are so complex that any attempt at pinpointing them runs the risk of being too simplistic. However, certain factors stand out by themselves. The first is the suddenness of the process of structural change, more specifically industrialization, which seems to have been undertaken when the economies of the respective countries were not quite prepared for it; i.e. they failed to adopt the measures necessary to make the transition from an agrarian to an industrial society painless and effective. Such, for instance, was their neglect to provide for the expansion of the agricultural sector to meet the need for feeding an

---

[3] see Mikesell, R. F., "Inflation in Latin America" in Nisbet, Charles T., ed., Latin America: Problems in Economic Development, 1969, pp. 143-189.

Table XI/5

LATIN AMERICA: CHANGES IN PRICES AND MONEY SUPPLY

Country	Consumer Prices Dec. 1963 = 100		Money Supply Dec. 1963 = 100	
	1962	1969	1962	1969
Argentina	78	316	78	468
Bolivia	102	147	84	205
Brazil	55	739	61	1,027
Chile	69	411	74	812
Colombia	69	170	90	273
Costa Rica	98	112	89	190
Dominican Rep.	91	103	92	118
Ecuador	95	130	89	194
El Salvador	98	105	83	130
Guatemala	99	106	89	134
Honduras	98	118	92	199
Jamaica	97	128	104	189
Mexico	100	121	86	199
Nicaragua	97	109[a]	89	135
Paraguay	98	113	90	161
Peru	91	193	90	184[a]
Uruguay	69	1,713	78	2,100
Venezuela	99	110	93	170

Source: International Financial Statistics, I.M.F.

[a]1967.

increasing urban labor force.   They also neglected to reform the fiscal system so that it would provide the additional revenue needed to finance social overhead capital projects.   The result was an undue expansion of the money supply caused mainly by large budgetary deficits.

Secondly, the imperfection of input markets, more specifically the labor market - or the inefficient utilization of some land holdings - led to bottlenecks causing rises in wages and prices not matched by rises in productivity.   Finally, the declining receipts from exports of primary commodities, and uncertainty regarding world markets, aggravated the financial burden of the industrialization program.

Remedies for Inflation

Price stability had been emphasized not only at
the Punta del Este meeting, but also by various international agencies who put pressure on individual countries; some of the stabilization programs were successful, in others the results were not up to expectations.
Argentina and Peru seem to have been able to reduce inflation, Brazil and Uruguay have only somewhat reduced
its intensity, but it would seem that in Chile inflation
was still out of control in 1970.[4] The stabilization
programs consist mainly of price controls, wage freezes,
credit curbs on the private sector's activities, and
mainly a reduction in budgetary deficits. Notwithstanding the impact of these programs on inflation, their
short-term effects are understandably unpalatable and
politically unpopular; hence, the policy makers of the
countries concerned have been faced with the usual conflict between promoting economic growth and maintaining
price stability.

Land Reform

The generalization of the institution of land
reform in the Latin American states was one of the main
objectives set for the Alliance for Progress during the
discussions which took place at the Punta del Este meeting. It was also a controversial topic which brought
forth strong arguments for and against: the contrast between the great wealth of the landowners and the extreme
poverty of a large number of landless farmers; the unused
large areas of productive land, and the fear that agricul-

---

[4]see Chemical Bank, International Notes, "South American
Highlights: 1969-70", # 169, May 1970.

tural output would suffer from the process of redistribution. The charter of the Alliance stressed a dual objective, namely: 1) to change the unjust distribution of wealth and income in the rural sector, and at the same time, 2) to accelerate growth of output, improve economic conditions in rural areas, and thus widen the domestic market for local industrial production. In order to assess the progress achieved in recent years, one should cast a brief glance at the system of land tenure in the Latin American states.

System of Land Tenure

The pattern of land tenure in Latin America shows to a large extent the same features as those present in most of the less developed countries: wealthy landowners of very large estates, a number of very small farmers, and masses of landless peasants and agricultural workers, almost all at the subsistence level. For instance, in 1950, in Argentina, 5 per cent of the farms included 75 per cent of the land under cultivation; in Paraguay, 5.2 per cent of the farms covered 94 per cent of the land and so on. The main forms of land ownership in the countries studied, are the following: 1) the latifundia, or plantation-type farm, organized for large-scale production on a commercial basis; 2) the hacienda - or estancia - which is the large estate giving the owner political power as well as wealth and purchased as a prestige symbol or as a hedge against inflation, rather than for efficient economic exploitation; 3) the minifundia, or small family-sized holding, characterized by low yield and subsistence-type farming, too small to provide full time work and adequate income to its owners. In terms of numbers, the latter type is the most commonly found.

The origin of the large agricultural estates

can be traced to three main sources, all condoned by the
government; they were: 1) the expropriation of the land
holdings of Indian communities; 2) the confiscation of
Church property; 3) the distribution of public domain
to large and medium-sized farms. The latter were given
away by the government in return for either military service, loans to government, or for political reasons; in
no case was there any distribution of small plots. Some
of the land was donated by the government with the pro-
viso that it be devoted to cash crop plantations, such as
coffee, in Colombia, parts of Venezuela and Costa Rica,
Guatemala and Peru. Thus, by the middle of the nineteenth century there emerged a class of wealthy landowners of plantation estates, or latifundia, some of them
foreign. Part of the purpose of creating these plantations was to promote exports and these started coming
out of Argentina as early as 1830. The owners, although
not averse to progress per se, were generally against the
parcelling-out of the land. In any case they seem to
have felt no particular urge to make their estates produce to capacity, while the high rate of population
growth was creating an ever increasing demand for food
production.

Prerequisites, Goals and Actual Achievements

As mentioned in Chapter VI above, there are
certain prerequisites for a land reform program to
achieve economic success, the three most important ones
being productive land, a regular supply of water, so
that the newly parcelled-out holding can get its needs
for cultivation, and the availability of cheap credit to
enable the new landowners to obtain their requirements

of seeds, fertilizers and implements. The mere distribution of public domain to landless peasants would,
therefore, be useless unless the land were productive
and the farmers were given the means to cultivate it.
Hence the failure of some programs of indirect tenure
reform which did not succeed in either changing the
pattern of land holdings or in alleviating poverty in
the rural sector. Moreover, to carry out land reform,
extensive funds are needed. The main objective of the
Punta del Este meeting in connection with land reform
was to give land to about one half of the landless
farmers, or campesinos, inclusive of demographic growth,
within a period of about 15 years.[5] The following
pages look briefly at some of the reforms which have
been realized with a measure of success.

Land reform was brought to _Mexico_ in 1917 by
a peasant revolution, at a time when 90 per cent of the
cultivable land was owned by 3 to 4 per cent of the
farmers and when almost all enterprises outside the agricultural sector were foreign-owned. After the revolution, all land holdings in excess of 100 hectares[6]
were granted to communal farms called 'ejidos'. By

------

[5]The Inter-American Committee for Agricultural Development
(ICAD) which includes representatives of the United
Nations Food and Agricultural Organization, the United
Nations Economic Commission for Latin America, the Organization of American States, the Inter-American Institute
for Agricultural Sciences and the Inter-American Development Bank, has carried out extensive studies on land
reform in various countries.

[6]1 hectare (ha) is a metric measure of area = 10,000 sq.
meters = 2.4711 acres.

1965, 120 million acres of land had been granted to 2.2 million peasants[7] and though the landowners were given bonds in compensation for the expropriated land, it is estimated that a very small percentage of the total value was actually paid. Agricultural production dropped sharply after the redistribution and remained low until large investments made possible commercial plantations with big-scale irrigation and mechanization schemes. The development of the latter generated exports of industrial fibers and provided food supplies to the cities - as well as making Mexico the first Latin American country to diversify its exports. The proceeds from agricultural exports led in turn to a high rate of capital formation.

In 1958, eighty per cent of the productive land in Venezuela was owned by two per cent of the farms. Land reform legislation was passed in 1958 and there followed a wave of invasions of the haciendas, led at first by communist peasant organizers and then by the government's Accion Democratica party: the party leaders received the best plots.[8] The initial objective of the government was to settle 350,000 new small landowners over a period of ten years, but the process was delayed by the high cost of the reform: compensation to the landowners is calculated at current market prices and is paid in cash up to an amount equivalent to about $6,000. - the balance being paid in government bonds. By 1966, 125,000 families had been resettled; in some cases the

---

[7] see Flores, Edmundo, Latin America "Land Reform: Meaning and Experience", pp. 139-40, in Nisbet, ed., op. cit.
[8] see The Economist, "More Law than Land for Latins", p. 1008, 4-10 June 1966.

peasants were already on the land and their squatters'
rights were confirmed. Agricultural production has increased since the inception of the reform, but Venezuela
still has to import food. This land reform program is
so far the one most in line with the directives of the
charter of the Alliance for Progress, but it has also
been a very costly one to implement and other countries
do not have a source of income similar to that which
Venezuela gets from its oil industry.

Of all the Latin American countries, Chile was
the one most in need of land reform, the reason being
that about 75 per cent of the cultivable land in the
Central Valley which is the only source of food for the
country's nine million inhabitants, is owned by three
per cent of the farmers. The latter look upon their
estates as prestige symbols and a hedge against inflation;
they do not consider it necessary to exploit them in full.
The result is that a sizable percentage of Chile's imports
consists of food, at least part of which could be grown
domestically. Yet a land reform legislation passed in
1963 remained still-born because of its too generous
stipulations regarding compensation and lack of funds to
implement it. In 1967, a new law provided for the expropriation of farms covering more than 200 acres of land
suitable for cultivation and of all abandoned land. The
landowners are left with a maximum of 200 acres and the
more efficiently run farms have been spared from expropriation so far.[9]

---

[9] see Northrup, Bowen, "Chile Seeks to Uplift its
Benighted Peasants through Agrarian Plan" in The Wall
Street Journal, November 14, 1968, p. 1.

The ambitious objective of resettling 100,000 families by 1970 was delayed by a very severe drought and the economic problems which the country has been facing. By the end of 1968, over three million acres had been expropriated from about 690 farms (out of just under 6,000 large estates) and an estimated 10,000 families had been resettled.   The new beneficiaries have to go through a transition period of three years during which they are trained in managing their farms, before they get their title to the land.   Compensation to landowners is paid on the basis of the assessed value of the land, rather than market price which is higher.   Chile's land reform is too recent for an appraisal of its results.

In Bolivia, in 1952, the Indian serfs chased the landowners from their haciendas and divided the land and possessions between them.   Only later was land reform legislation enacted.   The taking over of the land was part of a general upheaval which did not start bearing fruit until more than a decade later and its cost seems to have been heavy.

Up to 1963, 73 per cent of the arable land in Peru was held by a small group which constituted less than half of one per cent of the farmers and who 'owned' a quarter million rural families.   In 1969, with the change of regime, a comprehensive land reform program was decreed into law by the military dictatorship, which is meant to eradicate feudalism.   Not enough is known yet about this reform, except that the vast sugar and cotton plantations owned by U.S. firms have been nationalized.

Most other Latin American nations have paid lip service to the goals of the Alliance by enacting land reform legislations, implementation of which seems to be dragging. Instead, the landowner class has adopted such other measures as the use of hybrid seeds, cultivation of marginal lands, irrigation projects and the resettlement of farmers on acquired land. Though essential when accompanied by land reform, these measures do not provide the social and economic benefits, or the change in the pattern of tenure which have become associated with land reform.

REFERENCES

1. Anderson, Charles W., Politics and Economic Change in Latin America. Princeton, N.J.: Van Nostrand, 1967.

2. Bailey, Norman A., Latin America: Politics, Economics and Hemispheric Security. New York: Praeger, 1965.

3. Chemical Bank, New York, International Notes, Nos. 169, 170, 171.

4. Committee for Economic Development, Latin America. New York, 1966.

5. The Economist, "More Law than Land for Latins". London, 4-10 June 1966.

6. Flores, Edmundo, "Latin American Land Reform" in Latin American Problems in Economic Development, Nisbet, C. T. ed., pp. 132-140.

7. Glade, Wm., The Latin American Economies. Princeton, N.J.: Van Nostrand, 1969.

8. Gordon, Wendell C., The Political Economy of Latin America. New York: Columbia University Press, 1965.

9. Nisbet, Charles T., ed., Latin America: Problems in Economic Development. New York: The Free Press, 1969.

10. Pearson, Lester B., Partners in Development. New York: Praeger, 1969.

11. Warriner, Doreen, Land Reform in Principle and Practice. London: Oxford University Press, 1969.

CHAPTER XII

THE ALLIANCE FOR PROGRESS:

ECONOMIC DEVELOPMENT AND INTEGRATION

In appraising the Alliance and its realizations, it is important to place it in its chronological - or historical - context, in the change of attitude and policy of the United States towards its Latin American neighbors. To do so, one should look at the various steps which preceded it. This chapter will also cover the scope of economic assistance extended to Latin America, the progress of the industrialization program, foreign trade patterns and the stake of the United States in Latin America.

Setting the Stage

In 1958, Mr. Nixon, then Vice-President, began to point out the need for a change in U.S. policy toward Latin America, after his rather stormy visit to that continent in the spring of the same year. His opinion was shared by Dr. Milton Eisenhower in the U.S. and by Mr. Kubitschek, then President of Brazil. The latter called for an "Operation Pan-America". At the same time, it was also agreed to establish a regional institution to provide the capital necessary to finance development. Thus, by 1959, the Inter-American Development Bank came into being with a capital of $850 million, of which the U.S. contributed $350 million. Within the Bank, a Fund for Special Operations, to which the United States contributed $150 million, was to provide "soft" (interest-free) loans for development projects.

At the third annual meeting of the Committee of Twenty-one, in Bogota, Columbia, in September 1960, the U.S. announced the establishment of a $500 million Social Progress Trust Fund for investment in Latin America in structural social reforms of such institutions as the taxation system and the system of land tenure, as well as low-cost housing, public primary education, health services and other social programs which had never before qualified for U.S. public loans. Comparatively small as these commitments were,[1] they marked a complete reversal from previous U.S. policy which had shown resistance and opposed a negative attitude to Latin American pleas for development assistance since the end of World War II. The commitments also stressed the United States' recognition of the urgent need for social reforms, a need felt by most of the Latin American republics and urged by some of their more progressive policy makers, although the rulers of the biggest two countries among them seemed to think otherwise: Argentina and Brazil preferred that priority be given to aid for economic development and only accepted the assistance for social reform because it would free funds for other projects.

Thus, the stage was set for a more dramatic, if not more realistic, undertaking.

"Alianza para el Progreso"

In March 1961, the late President Kennedy presented to the U.S. Congress the basis of his "alliance for

---

[1] a delegate at the Bogota meeting asked for a development fund of $3 bn. a year for a period of ten years. One year earlier, at the second meeting of the Committee of Twenty-one in May 1959, in Buenos Aires, Castro had asked that the U.S. provide $30 bn. over a ten-year period for economic development in Latin America.

progress" to assist the Latin American republics in their
social development, saying that

>"economic growth without social progress lets
>the great majority of the people remain in
>poverty while a privileged few reap the benefits
>of rising abundance."

Later, in a speech to Latin American diplomats at the
White House, President Kennedy said

>"...I have called on all the people of the
>Hemisphere to join in a new Alliance for
>Progress - Alianza para Progreso - a vast
>cooperative effort....to satisfy the basic
>needs of the American people for homes, work
>and land, health and schools." [2]

A ten year development program showing the potential and
needs of each of the various countries and the scope of
the financial and technical aid that the U.S. could give,
was to be drawn up. A meeting of the Inter-American
Economic and Social Council of the Organization of
American States was scheduled for August 1961 at Punta
del Este in Uruguay, to draft an agreement that would be
agreed upon by all the nations.

The Charter of Punta del Este was signed on
August 17th, 1961. The Charter stressed the need to:
a) raise the standard of living of the people of Latin
America by setting a target rate of economic growth of
no less than 2.5 per cent per annum; b) provide urban
and rural housing programs; c) wipe out illiteracy and
extend primary education; d) improve health conditions;
e) assure price stability; f) encourage agrarian and
tax reforms; g) find a solution to the problem of the
fluctuations in the prices of primary commodities;
h) accelerate industrialization and economic integration;

---

[2] U.S. Dept. of State Bulletin 44, April 3rd 1961.

i) support and strengthen democratic institutions. The latter was the basic political principle of the Alliance, stating that "free men working through the institution of representative democracy can best satisfy man's aspirations."

Economic and technical aid was to come mainly from the United States, but also from multilateral agencies. Two conditions were necessary for any of the countries involved to qualify for U.S. aid, namely: i) that the ruling class in the recipient country show willingness to give up some of their wealth and privileges, and ii) that the country's government show readiness to make institutional improvements leading to social progress. It should be noted that at this stage the promoters of the Alliance on both sides had shown great imagination but little practical sense: apart from the difficulties inherent in achieving so many major objectives at the same time, no working framework was provided to help carry out and supervise the implementation of these objectives. With planning being the economic basis of the Alliance, the United States had suggested that each nation prepare a long-term plan providing for the social projects and reforms stipulated in the Charter, as well as its urgent need for funds which would be met partly out of the $1 billion of U.S. aid. It was also suggested that a committee of seven experts be set up to study these reports and submit them to the Inter-American Economic and Social Council. The first of these suggestions met with objections from the smaller nations who stated that it was not within their possibilities to prepare a report of the caliber required, while the second suggestion met with the objection of

some of the bigger nations who found the creation of the
committee an infringement to their sovereignty.
Finally, it appears in the light of subsequent events,
that the United States had made commitments which were
not quite substantiated because either of political
developments in Latin America and/or resistance from
Congress.

Only three years after the declaration of the
Alliance, early in 1964, was a committee created with
the mandate of all the members and the power to make
recommendations for distribution of Alliance funds;
this was CIAP (Comité Interamericana de la Alianza para
el Progreso), a committee of seven members plus a chair-
man.   Apart from the member representing the U.S. each
of the other members represented a group of countries,
whose respective representatives took turns at membership.   All members had to have technical as well as
political qualifications.   The function of the committee was to receive yearly reports from each Latin American country and to prepare its own report accordingly.
The committee's headquarters were established in Washington, D.C.; it was decided that its meetings should
be attended by representatives of the country whose report was being discussed, plus delegates from the U.S.
Agency for International Development, the Inter-American
Development Bank, the World Bank, and the International
Monetary Fund.   The year 1964 then marks the beginning
of the functioning of the Alliance on a practical and
efficient basis.   Its progress - or lack of it - is
assessed briefly at the end of this chapter.   Meanwhile,
a review of economic assistance to Latin America since
the Alliance follows.

Economic Assistance

In spite of the emphasis on social programs, evidence shows that a large part of U.S. assistance to Latin America in the early years of the Alliance went to cover debt repayments to bankers, including the Export-Import Bank. Table XII/1 gives the various sources of economic assistance to Latin America and the note at the foot of the table shows the big gap between total and net U.S. public assistance; this gap represents servicing and repayment of loans. In net terms, the amount of $2,119 million shown as long-term loans extended by the Bank in table XII/1 was matched by repayments of loans to an amount exceeding the above figure by $437 million.[3] Public indebtedness to foreign creditors in Latin America was of the order of $10 billion in 1960 and a sizable percentage of all economic assistance was absorbed by debt service.[4]

U.S. Private Investment

From 1950 to 1963, the flow of U.S. private investment to Latin America amounted to $5.8 billion of which $3.2 billion was new investment and $2.6 billion re-invested earnings. However, total earnings repatriated to the United States from Latin America for the same period added up to $11.5 billion, which meant a net gain for the U.S. of $5.7 billion.[5] Moreover, most of these investments were in industries producing goods for the local market rather than for export and

[3] Levinson and de Onis, The Alliance that Lost its Way, 1970, p. 134.

[4] Ibid., p. 135.

[5] Perloff, H. S., Alliance for Progress, 1969, pp. 136-7.

Table XII/1

LATIN AMERICA: ECONOMIC ASSISTANCE, 1961-69

(Private, Public, Multilateral and Bilateral)

	(in mn. $'s)
Total U.S. direct private investment	4,381
of which: re-invested earnings	(2,353)
direct outflow from U.S.	(2,028)
less: repatriated earnings and profits	8,141
Net outflow from Latin America	-6,113
U.S. private aid[a]	388
Total U.S. public assistance (F.Y.'s 1961-69)	6,389[b]
of which: A.I.D. net total	(3,258)
to Social Progress Trust Fund (IDB)	(458)
Food for Peace (P.L. 480) net	(1,355)
Exp-Imp Bank long-term loans, less repayments	(-437)[c]
Other U.S. economic programs, net	(1,755)[d]
Total International Aid	5,800
of which: IDB Fund for Special Operations	(2,457)
World Bank	(2,601)
International Finance Corporation	(117)
International Development Association	(132)
Other United Nations agencies	(420)
European Economic Community	(73)
Bilateral Aid (other than U.S.)	
Development Assistance Committee	3,215
Net economic assistance, grand total	9,679

Sources: Levison & de Onis, op. cit., pp. 137-8, and U.S.
Department of Commerce, Survey of Current
Business, Oct. 1969 and previous issues.

[a] includes Ford, Kellog and Rockefeller Foundation grants,
U.S. Partners Program and other agencies.

[b] total authorizations and gross disbursements were $10,287
mn.:   difference represents loan repayments and interest.

[c] total long-term loans for the period, irrespective of
repayments, were $2,119 mn.

[d] includes U.S. subscriptions to the IDB Ordinary Capital
Fund and to the Fund for Special Operations totalling
$1.57 mn.

when production was for export, the investments were in
the exploitation of natural resources, rather than in
the production of new manufactured goods which would
provide diversification of exports. Early in the
1960's, U.S. investment somewhat tapered off but later
in the decade, because of the loans extended by means
of the Alliance to Brazil, Chile and Colombia and more
particularly the many stabilization programs initiated
with the help of the International Monetary Fund to reduce inflation, investment has been on a larger scale.
By 1969, direct U.S. investment in Latin America
amounted to $12 billion;[6] the magnitude of this amount
explains the problems created by the repatriation of
the returns from capital.

The Inter-American Development Bank (IDB)

Most foreign economic aid has been channelled
through the Inter-American Development Bank (IDB).
The Bank also administers the Social Progress Trust Fund
for the United States Government under the Alliance, as
well as the Fund for Special Operations. For its working capital, the IDB, like the World Bank, raises funds
on international capital markets by selling bonds and
by raising loans. This is in addition to the $1 billion
in callable capital subscribed by its members and contributions from members and other sources, of which the
$1.8 billion it received from the United States Govern-
ment is the most important. By the end of 1970, the
IDB had accumulated about $6 billion in assets, its loans
outstanding amounted to over $4 billion and new loans
were being given at the rate of between $600 and $700

---

[6]Levinson and de Onis, op. cit., p. 136.

million a year.

The IDB's loans finance all kinds of projects, but one third of the funds available are earmarked for agriculture, aid to education and health programs, all of which are channelled through the Special Fund. The IDB's earnings from all its loans in 1970, amounted to about $44 million. However, notwithstanding its increasing activity, the Bank has to cope with the usual problems associated with fast growth: criticism was levelled at its selection of loan recipients, since not all requests for loans could be satisfied; financial support from its largest contributor was shrinking owing to the reservations of the U.S. Congress. At the same time, as the IDB's operations became more spread-out internationally, so did its sources of finance, with Japan, Canada, the United Kingdom and the member nations of the European Economic Community increasing their contributions to its working capital. Thus, funds raised in 1970 amounted to $187 million, compared with $177 million in 1969.

The Inter-American Development Bank has also been active in carrying out research and statistical surveys for its members in an effort to compare resources and fields of activity and help them integrate their economies. According to its Ninth Annual Report,[7] net capital inflows during the decade of the 1960's into Latin America were far below the outflows from the area, and this was reflected in an unfavorable balance of payments. However, the international reserve position of the Central Banks in the various countries increased by

---

[7]IDB, "Socio-Economic Progress in Latin America", Social Progress Trust Fund, Ninth Annual Report, 1969, April 1970.

a yearly average of about 5.7 per cent. (See table
XII/2 for changes in international reserve positions).
To maintain that favorable position, said the report,
annual gross capital inflows would have to increase to
$5 billion during the decade of the 1970's from about
$4.5 billion during the 1960's. The Tenth Annual
Report of the IDB[8] shows that the average rate of
economic growth for the period 1968-70 for Latin America was above 6 per cent; that in 1969 the average investment coefficient for the area rose to 21 per cent
of gross domestic product from 19 per cent in 1967;
with domestic savings providing 91 per cent of total
investment, the average saving coefficient was 18.6 per
cent of G.D.P. in 1969 rising from 17.7 per cent in
1966. The per capita G.D.P. for the whole area averaged
only 1.9 per cent during the first half of the 1960's,
2.7 per cent for the period 1966-69 and rose to 3.5 per
cent in 1969. On the domestic front, the biggest gains
were in the industrial sector.

Industrialization

During the 19th century, there had been no
significant move to initiate industrial development in
Latin America, or to emulate the European industrial
revolution. Following the principle of the international division of labor, these countries just produced the primary commodities in which they specialized
and exported them to the industrialized countries of
the Western world. The failure to build new manufacturing enterprises may also have been due to the inability to shift resources and productive services from

---

[8] Ibid., Tenth Annual Report, 1970, April 1971.

Table XII/2

LATIN AMERICA: INTERNATIONAL RESERVE POSITION

Country	(End of per. mn. $'s)[c]		Ratio of Reserves to Money Supply	
	1960	1969[a]	1960	1969
Argentina	525	538	55	122
Bolivia	6.7	42	19	37
Brazil	345	657	10	0.45
Chile	111	344	29	65
Colombia	178	221	34	21
Costa Rica	41	65	18	20
Dominican Rep.	25.7	40	25	25
Ecuador	40.8	65	35	31
El Salvador	33	63.8	40	52
Guatemala	54	71.6	49	42
Honduras	13.3	31	41	14
Jamaica	69	141		
Mexico	442	662	32	17
Nicaragua	11.7	44.2	18	57
Panama	34.6	182.3	82	19
Peru	76	167	29	28[b]
Uruguay	187	184	85	59
Venezuela	609	933	57	63

Source: Data compiled from International Financial
          Statistics, I.M.F.

[a] including SDR's.   [b] 1967.

[c] data are in pre-devaluation dollars.

the agrarian to the industrial sector.   This state of
affairs continued up to the 1930's, during which time,
with few exceptions, proceeds from exports were sufficient
to cover Latin America's needs of manufactured products.
Near the end of the 1930's, as a result of depression in
the industrialized countries, the prices of primary commodities on world markets started declining.   This factor, together with the consumption demand of a rising population, provided the impetus to industrialize, first in
Mexico and then in Brazil, Argentina, Chile, as well as in
other countries of Latin America.

Import Substitution

The process of import substitution started with consumer goods industries and was followed, through the backward linkages effect, by steel, electric power, petroleum by-products, chemicals, pulp and paper industries, all built with both public and private funds. During the decade of the 1960's, manufacturing, electric power and construction have shown the highest growth rates in terms of value added. In 1968, manufacturing production grew by 8.6 per cent compared to an average of 5.4 per cent during 1961-68; it also contributed 23.4 per cent of the region's gross domestic product, but provided employment to 14 per cent of its labor force.

These achievements were hailed at first by experts and economists concerned with Latin American affairs as a step in the right direction to promote economic development. Their enthusiasm subsided when it was found out how small a percentage of the labor force the new industries had absorbed - a fact not surprising in itself, since modern industry is capital-intensive rather than labor-absorbing. More particularly, it was found that the new industries had been selected on the basis of feasibility, rather than economic rationality.[9] To protect the infant industries, tariff barriers were raised too high and kept too long, so that these enterprises had no compelling reason to become more efficient; with production costs high, their goods were non-competitive on world markets and they were thus unable to expand and realize economies of scale.

---

[9] see Prebisch, Raul, Towards a Dynamic Development Policy for Latin America, 1963, p. 71.

Other factors responsible for the problems facing the new industries also include: a) the shortage of
entrepreneurial ability and of skilled labor; b) the
limited size of the market; the latter factor makes the
production of capital goods involving a heavy financial
outlay practically impossible in the smaller countries,
unless their quality is very high; c) the restrictions
recently put on production, especially by foreign firms
exporting to Latin America to help in the industrialization effort by setting up assembly plants which would use
every year an increasing number of their components from
domestic production; such is the automobile industry in
Chile.

Examples of industries which are suffering from
the effects of too much protection in that they have not
been able to reduce their costs, are the car and steel industries in Chile and Brazil, the fertilizers industry in
Argentina, and the textiles and cement industries in
Venezuela.[10]

Export Diversification

The advice most readily given to developing
countries suffering from the decline in prices of primary
commodities on world markets is to diversify their exports
by processing some of their excess raw materials. Brazil
is the country in Latin America which has carried export
diversification to a larger extent than the others: during the 1960's, the share of manufacturing has increased
in Brazil's gross domestic product from 20 to 30 per cent.
Next come Mexico, Chile, Argentina and Colombia.

_____

[10] for a discussion of the problems of import substitution
in Latin America, see Nisbet, C.T., _op. cit._, Part six,
pp. 237-287.

Brazil has a capital goods sector which
supports its consumer goods industries; in the latter,
food processing and textiles are the most important and
the textile industry provides the largest number of jobs.
Metal processing, chemicals and transportation are also
important and, together with food and textiles, account
for almost two thirds of total production. Other manufacturing includes machinery, non-metallic minerals, electrical and communications equipment, wood, furniture,
paper, clothing, rubber and leather. Not all the new industries produce yet for export but they are being expanded for that purpose.

In Mexico, where manufacturing and construction
contribute about 30 per cent of the gross domestic product, the share of manufactured goods in total exports has
risen from 26 to 33 per cent in the decades of the 1950's
and 1960's. Textiles and processed foodstuffs account
for a large part of the increase. Argentina has concentrated on processing more of its agricultural products for
export, such as wool, linseed, hides and skins, in addition to the traditional ones of meat and cereals.

Colombia and Chile have initiated a large number
of new industries for the purpose of diversifying their
exports. In this connection it should be mentioned that
import substitution industries and export diversification
ones are not necessarily self-exclusive, although they
may tend to become so in practice, if protection is carried on for too long.

Trade Patterns and Economic Integration

Table XII/3 gives comparative data on the value
of foreign trade of the Latin American countries, for the
years 1958 and 1969, in both constant and current dollars,

Table XII/3

LATIN AMERICA: FOREIGN TRADE

(in mn. dollars)*

Country	Exports f.o.b.			Imports c.i.f.		
	1958	1969	Adj'69[a]	1958	1969	Adj '69[b]
L. A. total:	9,000	12,977	11,284	9,813	12,642	11,288
Argentina	994	1,612	1,400	1,233	1,576	1,407
Bolivia	50	182	158	80	167	149
Brazil	1,243	2,311	2,009	1,353	2,242	2,002
Chile	386	1,069	929	415	902	805
Colombia	461	608	528	400	686	612
Costa Rica	92	190	165	99	245	219
Domin. Rep.	128	184	160	149	243	217
Ecuador	133	183	159	105	262	234
El Salvador	116	202	175	108	209	187
Guatemala	108	262	229	150	250	223
Honduras	70	169	147	67	184	164
Jamaica	133	257	223	181	442	395
Mexico	736	1,430	1,243	1,129	2,078	1,855
Nicaragua	64	155	135	78	177	158
Panama	53	120	104	110	294	262
Paraguay	34	51	44	38	82	73
Peru	281	864	751	382	604	539
Uruguay	139	200	174	143	197	176
Venezuela	2,321	2,892	2,515	1,599	1,752	1,564

Source: International Monetary Fund, International
Financial Statistics, 'Trade' pages,
relevant numbers. * pre-devaluation dollars.

[a] adjusted to constant dollars (1958=100) at an export
price index of 115.

[b] adjusted to constant dollars (1958=100) at an import
price index of 112.

[c] in current dollars; the absence of a sign means a surplus.

234

Table XII/4

L.A.: FOREIGN TRADE RATES OF GROWTH

(in real terms)

| Country | Average rate of growth p.a., 1958-1969 | |
	Exports f.o.b. %	Imports c.i.f. %
L.A. total:	2.3	1.3
Argentina	3.6	1.2
Bolivia	19.6	7.8
Brazil	5.5	4.3
Chile	12.7	8.5
Colombia	1.3	4.8
Costa Rica	7.2	11.0
Dominican Republic	2.0	4.1
Ecuador	1.8	11.0
El Salvador	4.5	6.6
Guatemala	10.0	4.4
Honduras	10.0	10.5
Jamaica	6.1	10.7
Mexico	6.2	5.8
Nicaragua	10.0	9.3
Panama	8.7	12.5
Paraguay	2.6	8.3
Peru	15.2	3.7
Uruguay	2.2	2.0
Venezuela	0.75	-2.0

Source: based on Table XII/3.

and the deficit or surplus on merchandise account, in current dollars, for both years. Based on table XII/3, table XII/4 shows the rate of growth, in real terms, of both exports and imports, for the same period. Several points of interest emerge from the two tables: the first is the contrast between the large surpluses registered by Venezuela for both years - due to petroleum exports - and the rate of growth which is less than one per cent a year for exports, and a minus two per cent for imports. This indicates a relatively decreasing contribution of foreign trade to the national product in Venezuela. Sizable surpluses were also registered by Peru and Chile in 1969 which contrast with the deficits both countries registered

in 1958 and in these two cases reflect high rates of
growth of exports which are not offset by a similar expansion of imports.

The largest deficits for both periods were incurred by Mexico: these reflect expenditures on industrialization and capital formation. For all of Latin
America, the yearly rate of increase in merchandise exports in real terms for the period 1958-69 was about 2.3
per cent, and just over four per cent in terms of current
dollars. Progress was uneven and most of the advance
took place in the late 1960's, although for all Latin
American countries the average was pulled down by the poor
performance of Venezuela. Finally, the rise in the volume of exports was not matched by an equal rise in their
purchasing power. Diversification is generally still
limited and primary commodities account for the larger
percentage of exports, with petroleum, coffee and copper
contributing about half the export earnings.

Economic Integration

The most important markets for Latin American
exports during the period studied were primarily the
United States and the European Economic Community, with
the former slightly losing ground to the latter toward the
end of the period; these two markets accounted for roughly 55 per cent of total exports. Intra-regional exports
did not absorb more than ten per cent of the total during
the 1950's, but this percentage has slightly increased
in the 1960's. This fact raises the question of complementarity and the success of the various trade groupings. There were originally two such groupings formed
in the early 1960's: the Latin American Free Trade
Association and the Central American Common Market, but

a splinter group from the former, the Andean Group, was
formed in 1969.

   The Latin American Free Trade Association
(LAFTA) is a group of eleven countries which account between them for 85 per cent of the area's trade.   Seven
of these countries, Argentina, Brazil, Chile, Mexico,
Paraguay, Peru and Uruguay were founder members and four
others, Bolivia, Colombia, Ecuador and Venezuela, joined
later.   LAFTA was established in 1960, with headquarters
in Montevideo.   From 1960 to 1965, trade within it
almost doubled, with exports reaching $635 million and
imports $769 million.   The objectives of the group were
to gradually remove tariff restrictions between members
on most articles and to achieve free trade by 1972.
The negotiations on this issue have been very slow and
by the end of 1971 the members were far from achieving
their objectives within the stated deadline.   Mexico's
trade with the group expanded at a faster rate than that
of the other members, with exports rising from $5.7
million in 1960 to $62.2 million in 1968 and imports
from $3.6 million to $42.9 million.   In 1966 and in
1967, trade between LAFTA members reached $1.4 billion,
or about 11 per cent of their total trade.

   In May 1969, five countries from the LAFTA
group, Bolivia, Chile, Colombia, Ecuador and Peru,
feeling that progress within LAFTA was too slow and
also that, being smaller countries, they wished to coun-
terbalance the influence of the three bigger ones within
the group, formed, with the approval of LAFTA, the
Andean Common Market.   The main objective of this
splinter group is to make a bigger effort at integration
which is to be achieved within a period of eleven years

when all intra-regional trade barriers will have been
eliminated and a common external tariff agreed upon.
Other objectives include joint industrial program planning in order to achieve complementarity in output, the
acceleration of agrarian development and the use of
domestic and foreign investments to promote economic
integration.   The Andean Common Market countries cover
two million square miles, had in 1969 a combined gross
domestic product of $20,370 million and a total popu-
lation of about 51.9 million;   trade within the group
was about 5 p.c. of their total trade and expected to
increase fivefold by 1975.[11]   Venezuela was to join
the group but after attending their more than 30 months
of preliminary negotiations, the Venezuelan government
decided not to sign the agreement.

The Central American Common Market (CACM)
including Costa Rica, El Salvador, Guatemala, Honduras
and Nicaragua, came into existence in 1960 with the
financial support of the United States.   These five
small countries have a total population of about 14.5
million and an aggregate gross domestic product of
$4,857 million.   This group was able to increase trade
between its members from $12 million in 1960 to $20
million in 1968, mainly because of the unexpected inflow of large foreign investments which came after the
group was formed.   The CACM countries have been able
to free from tariff restrictions 90 per cent of their
non-agricultural products.[12]   A $30 million loan was

---

[11] see Chemical Bank, International Notes, No. 171,
December 1970.
[12] Levinson and de Onis, op. cit., pp. 180-182.

extended to the group in 1969 by the United States for
the purpose of improving their means of communication
and transportation.

Finally, the proposed Latin American Common
Market which is still in the planning stage is to bring
together the members of the Latin American Free Trade
Association and those of the Central American Common
Market but that is very much of a long range project.
Several reasons at present dim the chances of economic
integration within the Latin American continent: the
most important reason resides in their physical terrain
which has rendered inland communications and exploitation almost nil and which makes the "opening of the
South American heartland" an imperative prerequisite
to the success of their economic development.[13]
Other reasons are inequalities in the economic structures of the various countries, high costs of production which need the protection of high tariff barriers
and the resistance of vested interest groups, to mention only a few.

Complementarity

Table XII/5 shows the main commodities exported
by the countries of Latin America. It is evident at
first sight that these exports are all primary products -
agricultural or mineral - and include no manufactured
articles. A second point which strikes the observer is
that several commodities are produced and exported by
more than one country. Such, for instance, is coffee
which is exported by 11 out of the 19 countries studied,

[13] see Lippman, Walter, "Toward the Making of a Continent"
N. Y. Herald Tribune, Dec. 16, 1965, p. 24.

Table XII/5

LATIN AMERICA: COMMODITIES EXPORTED*

Argentina	beef, corn, wheat, hides, wool, linseed, quebracho
Bolivia	tin, antimony, tungsten, silver
Brazil	coffee, cotton, cocoa, iron ore
Chile	copper, iron ore, nitrates
Colombia	coffee, petroleum
Costa Rica	coffee, bananas, cocoa
Dominican Rep.	sugar, coffee, cocoa, bauxite, tobacco
Ecuador	bananas, coffee, cocoa
El Salvador	coffee, cotton
Guatemala	coffee, cotton, bananas, sugar
Honduras	bananas, coffee, wool, silver
Jamaica	aluminum, bauxite, sugar, bananas
Mexico	cotton, sugar, coffee, zinc, shrimp, lead, copper
Nicaragua	cotton, coffee, meat, sugar, gold, cotton seed
Panama	bananas, refined petroleum, shrimp
Paraguay	meat, timber, oilseeds, tobacco, cotton, quebracho, hides
Peru	copper, fishmeal, sugar, iron ore, silver, zinc, coffee, lead
Uruguay	wool, meat, hides, linseed oil, wheat
Venezuela	petroleum, iron ore

Source: International Monetary Fund, International Financial Statistics, October 1971.

*listed by order of importance of their value to total value of exports in 1969.

bananas (six countries), cotton (5), beef, cocoa and
iron ore (4 each), copper and bauxite (3 and 2 countries
respectively).   This raises the question of degree of
complementarity between the various countries' output,
which is a prerequisite for economic integration.
Petroleum products, copper and other minerals, as well
as cereals, would find ready markets within the area;
manufactured exports resulting from rational planning
and progress in industrialization would eventually
provide the necessary complementarity.

The Stake of the United States in Latin America

From the end of World War II through the decade
of the 1960's, U.S. corporations provided 75 per cent of
foreign private investment in Latin America;   by 1971
these investments were worth approximately $13 billion.
With the major emphasis on manufacturing since 1950, a
large variety of consumers goods, from assembled cars
to cosmetics, are produced, providing jobs for more
than a million local employees, not to mention the cadres
of second rank technicians and service personnel.   Although the output from these enterprises goes to meet
domestic needs which could not have been met by local
capital, labor and know-how, it not only does not provide
a surplus for export but relies on imports costing scarce
foreign exchange for most of its raw materials.   Moreover, repatriated profits and dividends of U.S. enterprises in Latin America amount to between 12 and 15 per
cent of investment and to more than 12 p.c. of Latin
America's annual export earnings.[14]   Up to the end of
the 1960's, investments by U.S. corporations in Latin

---

[14]Levinson and de Onis, op. cit., p. 136.

America have mainly been concentrated on the exploitation
of natural resources, rather than finding ways of using
industrially the primary commodities produced locally.

As the most important external economic and
political influence in Latin America, the United States
has tried to promote the objectives of political stability
and economic growth.   The latter objective was of primary
importance in providing markets for U.S. exports and attractive investment opportunities for U.S. capital.
Consequently, too often is U.S. aid to the Latin American
countries considered, both at home and in the countries
concerned, as a means of protecting U.S. interests.   Far
too often, the more far-reaching objectives, human and
practical, connected with aid are lost sight of, although
they were a primary consideration of the original decision
to extend such aid.

The countries of Latin America suffer from
weaknesses in their social, economic and political institutions; they lack the financial set-up, as well as
able entrepreneurs, trained technicians and skilled workers on which to base a rational development program which
would afford them rapid and sustained growth.[15]   Although
some of them have achieved commendable progress during the
decades of the 1950's and 1960's, this progress has often
been at the cost of a high rate of inflation and restrictions on trade and exchange.

In sponsoring the Alliance for Progress, the
United States embarked on a colossal attempt to promote
socio-economic as well as political progress in Latin
America.   The Alliance represents a new concept by means

---

[15] see The Rockefeller Report on the Americas, 1969.

of which the nations of a continent can be helped to
achieve their own development. Its apparatus is still
imperfect and needs strengthening and improving, but
there is no doubt that the concept in itself has great
potential. Ten years after the formation of the
Alliance, these goals still seem far ahead, although
some effective progress has been achieved. As this
kind of undertaking is necessarily a long range one,
it is really too early to attempt to pass any judgment
on it. More particularly, the Alliance should not be
blamed for shortcomings that only the responsible policy
makers in the various countries can correct.

REFERENCES

1. Alba, Victor, Alliance without Allies. Praeger,
    New York, 1965.

2. Baerresen, Donald W., Latin American Trade Patterns.
    Washington, D.C.: Brookings Institution, 1965.

3. Frank, Andrew G., Capitalism and Underdevelopment in
    Latin America. New York: Monthly Review Press,
    1967.

4. Dell, Sidney S., A Latin American Common Market?
    London: Oxford University Press, 1966.

5. Inter-American Development Bank, Social Progress
    Trust Fund, Annual Reports, Washington, D.C.,
    1968-1970.

6. Levinson and de Onis, The Alliance that Lost its Way.
    New York: Twentieth Century Fund, 1970.

7. Lieuwen, Edwin, U.S. Policy in Latin America.
    New York: Praeger, 1965.

8. London Conference on Obstacles to Change in Latin
    America. London: Oxford University Press, 1965.

9. May, Herbert K., Problems and Prospects of the
    Alliance for Progress. New York: Praeger, 1968.

10. Pan American Union. The Inter-American System.
    Washington, D.C.: Pan American Union, 1963.

11. Perlow, Harvey S., _Alliance for Progress_.
    Baltimore: The Johns Hopkins Press, 1969.

12. Prebisch, Raul, _Change and Development - Latin
    America's Great Task_. New York: Praeger, 1971.

13. United Nations Economic Commission for Latin
    America, _Economic Survey of Latin America_, 1967.

14. U.S. Congress, Senate, Sub-Committee on American
    Republics Affairs, _Survey of the Alliance for
    Progress_. Hearings, 90th Congress, 2nd Session,
    1968.

LATIN AMERICA

Topics for Reading and Research

1. _Inflation_: the effects of inflation over a period
   of ten years in the countries most affected by it;
   the measures taken to overcome inflation.

2. _Land Reform_: an up-to-date review of what most
   Latin American countries have achieved in the way
   of land reform.

3. _Industrialization_: its cost and realizations in any
   one or more of the countries of Latin America.

4. _The Oil Industry in L.A._: benefits to the countries
   concerned; importance to the United States from the
   point of view of: a) supply of petroleum products,
   and b) foreign investments.

5. _Foreign Trade_: Composition, scope and direction, by
   countries.

6. _U.S. Investments in L.A._: study of any five important ones: their contribution to the development of
   the host countries.

7. _Economic Integration in L.A._: the Latin American
   Free Trade Association (LAFTA) and the Andean Common
   Market.

8. _Economic Integration in L.A._: The Central American
   Common Market (CACM).

9. _The Alliance for Progress_: its philosophy and its
   assumed successes and failures.

PANAMA

VENEZUELA

GUYANA

SURINAM

FR. GUIANA

COLUMBIA

ECUADOR

Amazon R.

PERU

B R A Z I L

BOLIVIA

PARAGUAY

C H I L E

A R G E N T I N A

URUGUAY

LATIN
AMERICA

MEXICO

1 BR. HONDURAS
2 GUATEMALA
3 HONDURAS
4 EL SALVADOR
5 NICARAGUA
6 COSTA RICA
mjt

CHAPTER XIII

THE MIDDLE EAST AND NORTH AFRICA:

Basic Data and the Oil Industry

The term North Africa, or the Maghreb (sunset)
usually includes the four countries of Algeria, Libya,
Morocco and Tunisia.   The term Middle East differs
somewhat in its coverage between one author and another.
In this text, it will include Cyprus, Iran, Iraq, Israel,
Jordan, Kuwait, Lebanon, Saudi Arabia, Syria, Turkey and
the United Arab Republic.   Bahrein and Qatar on the
Persian Gulf, and some of the Trucial States, will be
mentioned in connection with oil production and when-
ever the data available permit.   The states of the
Middle East and North Africa have very much in common,
as a matter of fact, they are often studied together and
this is what will be done in this chapter unless otherwise indicated.

The area covered by the countries of the Middle
East and North Africa is bordered by the Mediterranean
sea on the north and west, the Black sea on the north,
the Caspian sea on the northeast, the Persian Gulf and
the Arabian sea of which it is an extension on the east,
and, on the southeast, by the Red sea which is connected
to the Mediterranean by the Suez canal.   Morocco on the
west has an extensive coast on the Atlantic ocean.
Access from the area to any of the seas surrounding it
is relatively unhampered and this accounts to a great
extent for its strategic importance.

This chapter will cover basic data and resources, the oil industry in the area and its importance
to the rest of the world, while the next chapter will

look into the various countries' efforts to develop by
means of industrialization and other realizations such
as solving the water problem, promoting and diversifying
their foreign trade and finding the means to finance
their progress.

Physical Features

The region is relatively flat except where it
is crossed by successive chains of mountains extending
from west to east, such as the Atlas chain in Morocco,
the Lebanon mountains, the Taurus chain in Turkey and
the Elburz mountains north of Iran.   The mountain chains
are broken in parts by fertile valleys watered by two
great river systems and by smaller streams, but more frequently by large desert areas which give the countries
under study one common characteristic.[1]   The deserts
are the Sahara in Algeria, the Libyan desert which
stretches from Libya into Egypt, and the Arabian desert
which constitutes most of the Arabian peninsula.   The
mountain chains and the plateaus which extend from them,
thus form in many parts a sort of screen which separates
rich coastal plains from the desert type of plantation
or no plantation at all.   Desert land in the Middle East
and North Africa may take any one of three forms: moving
sand dunes which may change the profile of an area from
day to day and are unsuitable for cultivation and human
habitation unless they are extensively changed by irrigation projects at very great cost.   Or, they may be
desert areas with stones and boulder, occasionally washed
by rivers and streams, and where water flows some kind of

_____

[1] approximately 90% to 95% of the land in these countries
is covered by deserts and cannot be used.

living can be obtained.   Finally, the desert steppes
where grass and bushes grow, are suitable for pastures,
given enough rainfall.

The two river systems are the Nile and the
Tigris-Euphrates;   they water a number of Middle East
countries and account to some extent for the early
emergence of the Middle East in history.   Egypt is
watered by the Nile and would probably not have existed
were it not for that river;[2]   Syria, Turkey and Iran
share the Tigris and Euphrates rivers;   smaller rivers
such as the Jordan and the Orontes have water basins
which though not dependent from, are contiguous to
that of the Euphrates river.

Resources and Basic Data

Roughly over 161 million inhabitants lived
in 1969 in the countries we are studying.   The majority
of them are Mediterranean in most of their aspects.
Racially and ethnically, there are mainly Semites - and
that includes both Arabs and those Israelis who are
originally from the area - some Eurasians in Lebanon
and Iran, Asiatics in Turkey, Greeks in Cyprus, and Kurd
minorities in Turkey, Syria, Iraq and Iran.[3]   (Some
factions among the Kurds have been agitating for the
creation of a Kurdish state by parcelling out parts of
their respective countries into one state, but others
fear that this new state might be tucked onto the Soviet
Republic of Kurdestan and prefer to belong to the country

---

[2] as a matter of fact, Egypt is often called a gift of
the Nile.

[3] there are approximately 9 million Kurds, of whom 4 ½
million in Turkey, 2 ½ million in Iran, 1 ½ million in
Iraq and ½ million in Syria.

in which they presently are).

The basic mineral resources of the area consist primarily of crude oil which accounts for over two
thirds of the world's proven reserves and 25 per cent
of its annual supply. Almost all the states under
study produce oil in varying quantities; those which
produce it in commercial proportions are Algeria,
Bahrein, Iran, Iraq, Kuwait, Libya, Qatar, Saudi Arabia
and Trucial Oman. Other mineral resources found in
limited supply are iron in Turkey and Egypt, chrome and
manganese in Turkey, cement in Turkey, Egypt and Lebanon, phosphates in Israel, Jordan and Cyprus. Main agricultural products include primarily cotton which constitutes Egypt's main export and is also produced in
Syria and Turkey; tobacco which is grown in Syria,
Lebanon and Turkey, and citrus fruit which is the most
important Israeli non-manufactured export.

The area studied is just over four million
square miles (see table XIII/1) and its inhabitants
added up to approximately 161,508,000 in 1969 - or an
average density of 42 persons per square mile. However, because of the vast stretches of uninhabited
desert, any measure of population density would be misleading. The four largest countries in size, are Algeria and Libya in North Africa, and Iran and Saudi
Arabia in the Middle East; the smallest three are
Lebanon, Kuwait and Israel. The most populated are
Turkey, Egypt and Iran, in the Middle East, and Morocco
and Algeria, in North Africa;[4] the least populated are
Kuwait and Cyprus. The average rate of population
growth is comparatively high for all these countries,

---

[4] note that those countries with the largest populations
are not those which are the largest in size.

Table XIII/1

MIDDLE EAST AND NORTH AFRICA: AREA AND POPULATION

Country	Area in sq. miles[a]	Population (000) 1958[b]	1969	Av. rate of growth per annum %
Cyprus	231	558	630	1.4
Iran	629,180	20,400	27,892	3.3
Iraq	171,556	6,510	9,350	3.6
Israel	7,993	1,997	2,822	3.7
Jordan	37,291	1,580	2,217	3.6
Kuwait	5,998	350	570	5.7
Lebanon	4,014	2,000	2,645	2.2
Saudi Arabia	617,600	n.a.	7,345	
Syria	71,209	4,300	5,866	3.3
Turkey	301,380	26,247	34,375	2.7
United Arab Rep.	386,198	24,655	32,501	2.8
Algeria	847,500	10,575[c]	13,349	2.6
Libya	679,358	1,255	1,869	4.4
Morocco	200,000	10,987	15,050	3.3
Tunisia	48,300	4,059	5,027	2.1
	4,007,808	115,473	161,508	

Sources: United Nations, Monthly Bulletin of Statistics, June 1968 and January 1970; also International Monetary Fund, International Financial Statistics, January 1971.

[a]area within boundaries existing before June 1967.

[b]estimates of mid-year population.

[c]1959.

with the possible exception of Cyprus; it is highest
in those countries where growth is due to immigration
as well as natural increase, such as Kuwait, Libya
and Israel.   In the first two the cause of population
inflow is economic, namely the prosperity brought about
by the oil industry; in the latter, it is due to a
non-economic reason, such as the creation of a new
state.

          National accounts data are given in table
XIII/2.   In 1969, Turkey and Iran seem to have had the
largest gross domestic product in absolute figures, and
Jordan and Cyprus, the lowest.   Taking the more meaningful measurement of per capita G.D.P. for the same year,
Kuwait is seen as having what is probably the highest
in the world, although its rate of growth on a per capita basis is low because of the heavy influx of population into the country; the two next in importance
for the area are Libya and Israel; the lowest G.D.P.
is found in Syria and in the United Arab Republic.
Both Israel and Cyprus have per capita G.D.P.'s which
compare very favorably with those of the oil producing
countries, in spite of their very limited natural resources.

          Table XIII/3 gives rates of exchange of these
countries, mainly to show the basis of conversion for
table XIII/2.   At the same time, the relative stability
of most of these countries' currencies should be noted.
The currencies of Cyprus, Iraq, Jordan, Kuwait and Libya
were pegged to the pound sterling and when the pound was
devalued in 1967 (from 1. = $2.80 to $2.60), only Cyprus
followed suit; the others felt that their economies were
strong enough to support the rate of exchange of $2.80
for their monetary units.   The Egyptian pound was pegged

251

Table XIII/2

MIDDLE EAST AND NORTH AFRICA: NATIONAL ACCOUNTS

Country	Total GDP in mn. $'s 1958	1969	Per. capita GDP in $'s 1958	1969	Av. rate of growth p.a. in p/cap. GDP %
Cyprus	281	487	503	776	4.9
Iran	4,026[a]	10,191	192[a]	365	10.0
Iraq	1,441	2,909	225	311	3.4
Israel	1,988	4,784	995	1,696	6.3
Jordan	260[a]	524[i]	159[a]	249[i]	6.2
Kuwait	1,828[d]	2,764	4,570[d]	4,848	0.85
Lebanon	1,039[f]	1,319[i]	444[f]	511[i]	3.5
Saudi Arabia	1,977[d]	3,566[i]	307[d]	502[i]	10.5
Syria	889[e]	1,014[g]	178[e]	194[g]	4.5
Turkey	4,300	14,166	164	412	13.0
United Arab Rep.	3,853	6,451	157	198	2.3
Algeria	2,714[f]	4,040	232[f]	302	6.0
Libya	1,116[f]	3,185[i]	715[f]	1,770[i]	36.0
Morocco	1,614	3,142	147	208	3.7
Tunisia	795[b]	1,100[i]	191[b]	223[i]	2.0

Sources: United Nations, Monthly Bulletin of Statistics and International Monetary Fund, International Financial Statistics, relevant numbers.

Note: data are in dollars of the years indicated, i.e. pre-devaluation dollars.

[a]1959. [b]1960. [c]1961. [d]1962. [e]1963. [f]1964. [g]1965. [h]1967. [i]1968.

Table XIII/3

MIDDLE EAST AND NORTH AFRICA: RATES OF EXCHANGE

Country	National Currency	National Currency per U.S. $ 1958	1967	1970
Cyprus	Cyp. Pound	.3571	.4167	.4167
Iran	Rial	75.75	75.75	75.75
Iraq	Ir. Dinar	.3571	.3571	.3571
Israel	Isr. Pound	1.80	3.0/3.50	3.50
Jordan	Jord. Dinar	.3571	.3571	.3571
Kuwait	Kuw. Dinar	.3571	.3571	.3571
Lebanon[a]	Leb. Pound	3.13	3.13	3.24
Saudi Arabia[b]	Saud. Riyal		4.50	4.50
Syria	Syr. Pound	3.82	3.82	3.82
Turkey	Turk. Lira	2.80	9.08	15.0
United Arab Rep.	Egyp. Pound	.3571	.4348	.4348
Algeria	Alg. Dinar		4.937	4.937
Libya	Lib. Pound	.3571	.3571	.3571
Morocco	Mor. Dirham	5.06	5.06	5.06
Tunisia	Tun. Dinar	.42	.525	.525

Source: International Monetary Fund, International Financial Statistics, 1959 and 1971.

[a] free market rate.

[b] par value of S.R. 4.50 = $1. as from January 1960.

to sterling up to 1962 when it was devalued to LE1 =
$2.30 instead of $2.86 prior to devaluation.   Israel
and Turkey are the two countries in this area which have
suffered from the acute sort of inflation which plagues
some of the Latin American countries and they have applied in the past the usual remedy of a stabilization
program, with concomitant successive devaluations of
their currencies.

The Oil Industry in the Middle East

It was mentioned earlier in this chapter that
about two thirds of the world's proven oil reserves (or
about 35 billion tons)[5] are located in the Middle East
which supplies 25 per cent of the world's needs.   The
discovery of oil in commercial quantities in these
countries is of fairly recent origin and has not failed
to make a strong impact on their economies.   In order
to better understand this impact, the facts about the
oil industry should first be examined.

Apart from its rich deposits, a factor which
makes the industry attractive to foreign investors, is
the very low cost of production (see table XIII/4, line
c).   While the cost of maintaining and expanding oil
production has averaged $1.67 per barrel in the United
States for the period 1951-65 it was $0.13 in the Middle
East and $0.38 in the Caribbean during the same period.[6]
There have been fluctuations up and down in both, in
the intermediate years, but the trend recently has been
downward.   This lower cost in the Middle East is due to
the cheaper labor and the cheaper price paid for the

---

[5] recent discoveries in Libya, Iraq and Saudi Arabia may
bring this figure higher yet.

[6] Stocking, G. W., Middle East Oil, 1970, pp. 423-4.

Table XIII/4

OIL INDUSTRY: WORLD COMPARISONS

	(1) World total	(2) United States	(3) Carib- bean	(4) USSR E.Eur. China	(5) Middle East
(a) Proven reserves, 1965					
mn. barrels:	357,300	39,400	32,900[a]	33,500	217,850
mn. tons:	47,900	5,100	4,500[a]	4,500	29,280
(b) Rate of increase in production 1960-65	8.6%	2.5%	4%	10.5%	9.5%
(c) Unit cost of production and expansion: $ per barrel, 1951-65 average		1.67	0.38	n.a.	0.13
(d) Production, mn. tons, 1965	1,550	427	200	248	415
(e) Net investments[b] in fixed assets (mn. $'s)	91,055[c]	43,125	7,305[d]	n.a.	3,140

Sources: for (a) Longrigg, S. H., *Oil in the Middle East*, 3rd. ed., 1968, Appendix III, p. 480.

for (b) *Ibid.*, p. 463. , for the years 1960-65.

for (c) Stocking, G. W., *Middle East Oil*, 1970, pp. 423-4.

for (d) Longrigg, *op. cit.*, Appendix II, p. 478 and other sources.

for (e) The Chase Manhattan Bank, *Capital In- vestments of the World Petroleum Industry*, 1967, pp. 18-19.

[a] includes all Western Hemisphere other than U.S.

[b] includes: total production, pipelines, refineries, marketing, etc.

[c] excluding U.S.S.R. and Eastern Europe, but including Canada, Western Europe, Africa and Far East.

[d] includes Venezuela (2,110) and other Western Hemisphere (5,195).

concessions. However, the latter point is oft belabored
by the governments of the host countries who have been
demanding - and obtaining - higher royalties from the
producers.[7] The greater part of oil production in the
world, outside North America and Eastern Europe, has been
developed under long-term concession agreements by a comparatively small number of American, British, British/
Dutch and French oil companies.[8]

The fact that these companies are internationally integrated has accounted for the effectiveness of
their operations. They have put up the initial capital
for pioneering oil ventures, started exploration and research and taken risks. Later they spread out their
operations, organized transport, refining and marketing,
to the exclusion of outsiders, the so-called independent
oil companies. The wide scope of their operations has
enabled them in the past to have almost full control of
production, refining, consumption and prices - that is
until such time as they started meeting stiff competition
from the independent newcomers. To go into the financial
details of oil production would take many pages and is
not the object of this chapter; but looking briefly at
the economics of it, the difference between the terms
of the big giants and those of the newcomers was not only
that the former gave 50 per cent of the profits to the
host countries and the latter gave them 75 per cent, but
also that while the former bore all the expenses of

-----

[7] in 1970-71, a dispute pitting 16 oil-producing firms
against their host countries made headlines and led to
some major changes in their respective agreements.
[8] Standard Oil (N.J.), Royal Dutch/Shell, Gulf, British
Petroleum, Texaco, Standard Oil of California, Socony,
Cie. Francaise des Petroles.

exploration and prospection, the latter asked the host
governments to bear part of the cost. This seems to
have been a more profitable arrangement for the countries concerned but one could wonder whether they would
have been able to bear their share of the cost of the
latter agreement had they not built up their reserves
during the early years of oil income. Be that as it
may, the more favorable terms offered by the so-called
independents have prompted the bigger firms, much to
their annoyance, to a re-appraisal of their conditions.

Profit sharing is not the only bone of conten-
tion; production targets is another. Here, the element
of competition between one producing country and another
comes into play: it is obvious that if they all increase
their production this is bound to result in a glut and,
therefore, lower prices. This was the situation before
the Middle East conflict of June 1967 when investment
returns on oil production outside North America and Venezuela, for the first time were lower than those inside.
Since then, the Arab oil embargo which lasted from June
until September 1967 and the closure of the Suez canal
have forced prices up. This is because there was no
decline in demand and the difference in supply was made
up from U.S. oil sources,[9] but the crisis emphasized the
dependence on Middle Eastern oil, particularly in Europe
and Japan.[10] Just after the lifting of the embargo,

---

[9] production in the U.S. was increased by 500,000 barrels
a day, but this cannot go on for long: U.S. reserves are
estimated to represent only 10 years supply, Chase Manhattan Bank, Petroleum Situation, January 1968.
[10] Europe depends on Middle East sources for 4/5 of its
supply, Japan for its total supply.

Libya's oil began flowing freely and shipments were increased by about 30 per cent because of new discoveries;
but the specific gravity of North African oil is lighter
than that of Middle Eastern oil and the latter is needed
for fuel oil.   Production also increased in Iran where
it reached nearly half a million barrels a day in 1967,
approaching the level of Saudi Arabia who in 1966 was the
leading Middle East producer.   Oil transported around
the Cape of Good Hope costs more and takes twice as much
time to reach its destination.

Table XIII/5 gives data for production, exports
and revenue from oil of the Middle Eastern countries.
Looking at columns (1) and (2), it can be seen that while
in 1964 Saudi Arabia, Kuwait and Iran were the biggest
producers, in 1969 Libya had caught up and occupied the
number one place.   Column (3) giving revenue from oil
should be kept in mind when looking at these countries'
development projects.

Refineries.   A few words should be said about
refineries: sale of petroleum by-products rather than
crude oil provides relatively bigger profits.   The Middle
Eastern countries between them have several refineries
with a capacity of approximately 95 million tons compared
with their production of about 615 million tons of crude
oil.   There is scope for building more refineries and
making up on by-products what they lose on the falling
price of crude, although their main customers, the European countries, already have the facilities for refining
and would rather buy the crude.

Transiting countries.   When discussing the
countries of the Middle East and also of North Africa,
it is customary for some writers to make the distinction
between the 'haves' and the 'have-nots', meaning those

Table XIII/5

MIDDLE EAST OIL PRODUCTION, EXPORTS AND REVENUE

Country	(1) Production[b] mn.metric tons			(2) Exports mn. U.S. $'s			(3) Revenue[d] mn. U.S. $'s		
	1961	1964	1969	1961	1964	1969	1961	1964	1969
Algeria	0.1	2.2	3.7	–	–	–	50[e]	59[e]	–
Bahrein	0.1	0.2	0.3	218[c]	202	–	11.3	12[e]	15
Iran	3.9	7.1	13.8	–	1,100	1,855	291	482	850
Iraq	3.5	5.1	6.2	625	789	973	265	353	500
Kuwait[a]	5.8	8.9	10.8	940	1,217	1,475	468	577	800
Libya	–	3.5	12.5	–	606	2,159	64	132	1,000
Qatar	0.7	0.8	1.4	128[c]	150	–	–	70	120
Saudi Arabia[a]	4.5	7.2	12.4	880	1,182	2,051	378	423	950
Trucial Oman	–	0.8	2.4	–	–	–	–	–	–

Note: Only producing countries which are net oil
exporters have been included.

Sources: Production data from "Crude Petroleum
Production" pages, United Nations Monthly
Bulletin of Statistics.   Exports data from
"Countries" pages, International Financial
Statistics, International Monetary Fund.
Data for revenue are estimates taken from
various sources.

[a] including Neutral Zone.

[b] monthly averages for respective years.

[c] amount is for 1962.

[d] includes royalties and taxes.

[e] estimate.

which produce oil and those which do not.   A better
distinction would be between producing and transiting
countries.   A large proportion of the oil produced in
Iraq and Saudi Arabia is carried by pipelines across
Syria, Jordan and Lebanon to the Mediterranean coast:
the pipelines were built and are operated by the producing companies and/or their subsidiaries who pay
royalties for the passage of the oil.   These royalties
were increased recently.[11]   The United Arab Republic
is also considered a transit country because of the Suez
canal through which (in normal times) tankers carrying
oil from the Persian Gulf and other points east of Suez,
reach the Mediterranean.   Tolls from the canal - up to
the time of its closure - had been increasing at a
fairly high rate: they amounted to over $200 million
in 1966.

      Israel has a 16-inch pipeline which runs from
Eilat on the Red Sea to Haifa on the Mediterranean.
It carries oil which comes from Iran on the Persian
Gulf, both for domestic use and for export; the crude
is refined at Haifa.   A larger (42 inch) 250 kms. long
pipeline was recently completed and has been in use since
1970: it runs from Eilat to Ashkelon on the Mediterranean
coast and has an estimated capacity of 15 million tons a
year.   Israel is hoping to induce the producers in Iran
to increase deliveries of oil in order to fully use the
bigger pipeline whose capacity could be increased to 60
million tons.   The crude is transported by third countries' shipping and the producers' decision on whether to
use steamers or pipeline will no doubt be affected by

---

[11]Lebanon now receives about $5.7 million annually.
Syria's share is much bigger (ab. $25 mn); Jordan
receives ab. $15 mn. (1970 data).

whichever is the lower alternative cost.

Economic Impact

The discovery of oil in commercial quantities
in the countries of the Middle East and North Africa has
marked the transition for these countries from a stage
of subsistence agrarian economies - or no economy at all
where only nomad life existed - to that of industrialized
nations. Springing from this transition, the forces of
change have had their repercussions in the social, economic and political spheres inside the countries concerned
and also beyond their boundaries. It is the economic
impact which will be examined here. Observing each
country individually, the economic impact of oil discovery and production is reflected in the scope of the
development it has been able to realize with the additional income thus obtained, and from its exposure to
the advanced technology brought in by the foreign investors. A factor which should be taken into consideration in evaluating this impact, is the relationship between the capital invested and the size of the nation's
population, i.e. per capita share of investment.
Political stability is another factor which greatly
affects the success of any development project.

In <u>Iran</u> where oil production and the beginning
of exports date back to 1908 and 1912 respectively, 90
per cent of the oil produced comes from a "Consortium",
the Iran Oil Operating Companies, a group of foreign-
owned companies with a majority of British interests.[12]
The balance is accounted for by four "partnership" com-

---

[12]including: British Petroleum (40%), Shell (14%),
Standard California (7%), Standard New Jersey (7%), Texaco
(7%), Mobil (7%), Gulf (7%), C.F.P. (6%), independents
(5%).

panies which operate on a 50-50 basis agreement with the
state-owned National Iranian Oil Company, in exchange
for the right of purchasing certain quantities of the
oil produced.   Since 1968, Iran has been the largest
producer in the Middle East and the fourth in the world:
total production in 1969 was 168 million tons, an increase of 18 per cent over 1968, and 92.6 million tons
for the first six months of 1970; which is an increase
of 16.3 per cent over the same period in 1969.   The
world rate of increase in production is about 10 per
cent for the same period.

Between 1961 and 1967, Iran spent $2,112
million on development projects, of which $1,500 million
came from oil revenue.   After a lengthy discussion with
the oil producing companies, the association of the Oil
Producing and Exporting Countries (OPEC) of which Iran
is a member, reached an agreement in February 1971
guaranteeing higher "posted" prices and hence an increase
in both royalties and taxes.[13]

Libya is the most recent major newcomer to oil
production: it started exporting crude oil in 1961 and
that was the first year it did not have a deficit in its
balance of payments.[14]   By 1970, it was second only to
Iran and registered in that year the highest rate of increase of all major producers (18%).   At the end of
1967, there were 40 companies of different nationalities

_____

[13] a "posted price", which usually does not relate much to
production cost, is a list price rather than the actual
price at which the oil will sell: actual sales are
usually subject to discounts.

[14] the deficit in previous years had been covered by
foreign aid and the expenditure of British and American
forces (see "Libya's Booming Oil Economy", in Viewpoints,
June-July 1963, by Garzouzi, Eva.

(but mainly British and American) operating 126 concessions and expansion was still in order.   In 1970 the government decided to cut back on production for conservation purposes.   As an oil producer, Libya shares two characteristics with Algeria: the first is that in both oil is pumped in pipelines from the oilfields directly to the Mediterranean coast, which makes it of easier access to European users.   The second characteristic is that the crude is lighter than Middle East crude, and natural gas occurs in association with it.

Oil was first discovered in <u>Kuwait</u> in 1938 and exports started in 1946.   Kuwait was then just a desert which did not even have drinking water; it is now available by pipelines from Iraq or from desalinated sea water.   The oil industry in Kuwait is owned by the Kuwait Oil Company which is shared in equal parts by Gulf and British Petroleum.   Of all the oil-producing countries, Kuwait is the one where the impact of oil discovery has been the most spectacular.   Its rulers have invested a comparatively large proportion of the revenue from oil in social overhead capital projects and manufacturing industries.

<u>Saudi Arabia</u> started exporting oil in 1934; the bulk of its petroleum industry is owned by the Arabian-American Oil Company (Aramco) which has a majority of American interests,[15] and which also owns the Trans-Arabian Pipeline (TAPLINE) which carries oil from the Persian Gulf to the Mediterranean coast.   Due to a shutdown of 112 days in 1969, of Tapline, the rate of

---

[15] including: Standard N.J. (30%), Standard Cal. (30%), Texaco (30%), and Mobil (10%).

increase in petroleum output was only 5.8 per cent in
that year, compared with a rate of 8.4 per cent in
1968 and 11.5 per cent over the period 1965-70. In
1970 the growth rate was about 17 per cent.

Iraq first discovered oil in 1927 and started
exporting it in 1934; its industry is owned mainly by
the Iraq Petroleum Company (I.P.C.) which includes
British, American, and French concerns.[16] Its production and exports suffered a decline of over 15 per cent
in 1967, but recovered the following year. Generally
speaking, it has fallen behind the other two early producers, Iran and Saudi Arabia, and has been overtaken
by both Libya and Kuwait.

Algeria is a relative newcomer to oil production; it also produces natural gas which is liquified
and bottled for shipment. The industry is owned by
French and American firms, the French having the larger
share.[17] Profits are split fifty-fifty between the
Algerian government and the oil companies, but the latter's investments out of profits are exempt from this
arrangement and such investment has been heavy. A
third of the crude produced in Algeria is processed in
French refineries. To promote sales of Algerian oil,
the French government decided in February 1968 to tie
the share of foreign oil companies in its retail market

---

[16] including: Shell (23 3/4%), British Petroleum (23 3/4%)
Compagnie Francaise des Petroles (23 3/4%), Standard N.J.
(11 7/8%), Mobil (11 7/8%) and Gulbekian (5%).

[17] a dispute between the Algerian government and French
producers arose in 1970 because the former raised prices
twice unilaterally without the consent of the latter
and was still pending at the end of 1971.

for petroleum by-products, to the proportion of their
crude requirements which they purchased from Franc zone
countries, mainly Algeria.[18]   Algeria receives grants-
in-aid from the French government for its development
budget.

The Sheikhdoms

So far little mention has been made of the
small Persian Gulf Sheikhdoms, namely Bahrein, Qatar
and the Trucial States, the reason being that information
on their subject is rather scanty.   However, an attempt
will be made here to give some idea about them.   The
Arabian Gulf area was best known, if at all, at the beginning of the century for its pearls: a multitude of
fishing boats were in the pearling business until the
Japanese developed the cultured pearl in the 1930's.
About two decades later, income from oil production was
to bring some of the small states in this area into the
twentieth century.

Qatar is a peninsula which extends 100 miles
northward in the Persian Gulf;   in the narrow strip of
water between its west coast and the Arabian mainland
is a cluster of small islands of which Bahrein is the
biggest.   To the southwest of the Qatar peninsula, is
the Trucial Coast where seven small states exist with
no defined boundaries between them.   They are commonly
known as the Trucial States, or Trucial Oman.   The
seven are: Abu Dhabi, Ajman, Dubai, Fajairah, Ras al-
Khaimah, Sharjah and Umm al-Qaiwain.   Two of these
states, Abu Dhabi and Dubai are now oil producers.

---

[18] see the Economist, 'French Petrol Market', February
24, 1968, p. 72.

Bahrein boasts the third largest oil refinery
in the Middle East, next to Dhahran in Saudi Arabia and
Abadan in Iran.   With a capacity of 10 million tons a
year, it processes mainly Saudi Arabian crude besides
its own.   This fact explains its relatively large exports in relation to its production (see table XIII/5).
Bahrein is an autonomous state under British protection;
the latter will end in 1972.   Its population is estimated at about 200,000.   Oil production is stabilized
at 3.5 - 4 million tons a year because of limited reserves, and revenue from oil was $15 million in 1969.
The oil concession is held by the Bahrein Petroleum
Company.[19]

Oil was discovered in Qatar in the 1930's but
production did not actually start until after World War
II, in 1949.   In 1969, output increased by 4.3 per cent
over 1968 and over 100 per cent over 1960.   Total production was estimated at 15 million metric tons in 1969,
and revenue at $120 million.[20]   Qatar's population is
estimated at 80,000, mostly concentrated in the town of
Doha on the east coast.

The Trucial States got their name from an
agreement signed with Britain in 1835 promising them
protection; as with Bahrein, the agreement will come
to an end in 1972 and the states have formed an alliance
with Bahrein and Qatar in anticipation of British with-
drawal.   Of the seven states, it is Abu Dhabi which has
achieved a spectacular growth and brought the whole group

---

[19] jointly owned by Standard Oil California and Texas Inc.
[20] oil industry is owned by Qatar Petroleum Co., which is
shared by Iraq Petroleum and Royal Dutch Shell.

of states into the focus of world attention. Production
in Abu Dhabi started in 1962 and by 1969 it was well over
700,000 barrels a day - or 36.5 million tons a year.
Revenue from oil rose from just over $100 million in
1966 to about $200 million in 1969. With a population
of about 25,000 this gives one of the highest per capita
incomes in the world.

Impact on the Non-Producing Countries

The effect of the oil-producing countries'
sudden rise to wealth on the other nations in the area,
has taken several forms. The first is that the countries
which have had little or no industrial activity outside
oil production, constitute a large and affluent market
for the goods and services of their neighbors. Raw and
semi-processed agricultural products, textiles and other
light manufactures, thus found both outlets and the
stimulus to expand output. Secondly, educators of all
levels, technicians and administrative personnel, have
also been attracted to the oil-producing countries studied
which , with the exception of Iran, are Arabic-speaking
and though the dialects may differ, the written language
is the same. Thirdly, individual fortunes rapidly
amassed sought investments in neighboring countries where
some industrial ventures and more particularly luxury
buildings,[21] have been financed by oil-rich potentates.
Fourth, visitors from the oil-producing countries account
for a sizable percentage of their neighbors' income from
tourism: to them, Cairo and Damascus have more attraction
than Paris and Rome, while the Lebanese mountains are
pleasanter than the Riviera, or even Swiss resorts.

---

[21] more especially in Beirut.

Last but not least, financial assistance in
the form of loans and grants, has been forthcoming in
recent years from the rich countries to their less
fortunate neighbors. Considering the needs of the
latter, such assistance has been so far no more than a
drop in the ocean, but it is a step in the right direction. The most effective form of it has come from
Kuwait which has instituted the Kuwait Fund for Arab
Economic Development.

REFERENCES

1. American Enterprise Institute, United States
   Interest in the Middle East: A Special Analysis,
   1968.

2. Baldwin, G. B., Planning and Development in Iran.
   Johns Hopkins Press, 1967.

3. Brown, L. C., State and Society in Independent
   North Africa, Middle East Institute, 1966.

4. Doherty, K.B., Jordan Waters Conflict, International
   Conciliation #553, Carnegie Endowment for International Peace, 1965.

5. El-Kammash, M. M., Economic Development and Planning
   in Egypt, Praeger, 1968.

6. El Mallakh, R., Economic Development and Regional
   Cooperation: Kuwait, University of Chicago Press,
   1968.

7. Europa Publications Ltd., The Middle East and North
   Africa, 15th. ed., London, 1968, and following years.

8. Gallagher, C.F., The United States and North Africa:
   Morocco, Algeria & Tunisia, Harvard University
   Press, 1963.

9. Grunwald, K. and Ronall, J. O., Industrialization
   in the Middle East, New York: Council for Middle
   Eastern Affairs, Inc., 1960.

10. Israel, Office of Economic Opportunity, Israel:
    Economic Development, Past Progress and Plans for
    the Future, 1967.

11. Kardouche, G. K., *The U.A.R. in Development.* Praeger, 1967.

12. Kazemian, Gholam H., *Impact of U.S. Technical Aid on the Rural Development of Iran.* Theodore Gaus' Sons, 1968.

13. Kermani, T. T., *Economic Development in Action: Theories, Problems and Procedures as Applied in the Middle East,* World Publications Company, 1967.

14. Longrigg, Stephen H., *Oil in the Middle East: Its Discovery and Development,* 3rd. edition, 1968.

15. Mead, Donald C., *Growth and Structural Change in the Egyptian Economy,* Homewood, Ill.: Richard D. Irwin, Inc., 1967.

16. Mikdashi, Z., *A Financial Analysis of Middle Eastern Oil Concessions, 1901-1965,* Praeger, 1966.

17. Nolte, R., *The Modern Middle East,* Atherton Press, 1963.

18. Ofer, G., *The Service Industries in a Developing Economy: Israel as a Case Study,* Praeger, 1967.

19. Robinson, R. D., *High-Level Manpower in Economic Development: The Turkish Case,* Harvard University Press, 1967.

20. Royal Institute of International Affairs, *Great Britain and Egypt, 1914-1951,* Royal Institute of International Affairs, Information Dept., Papers (London) no. 19, 1952.

21. Saab, G. S., *The Egyptian Agrarian Reform: 1952-1962,* Oxford University Press, 1967.

22. Shorter, F. C., *Four Studies in the Economic Development of Turkey,* Princeton Studies on the Near East, Kelley, 1967.

23. United Nations, *Economic Developments in the Middle East, 1959-1961,* New York, 1962.

24. U.S. Agency for International Development, *A.I.D. Economic Data Book: Near East and South Asia,* 1968.

25. U.S. Library of Congress, Legislative Reference Service, *A Select Chronology and Background Documents Relating to the Middle East,* U.S. Government Printing Office, Division of Public Documents, 1969.

330.1
L677 T
Lewis, William Arthur

330.01
WAHHC
Wann, Henry J

330.1
A229T
Adelman, Irma
Ec. Growth & Dev.

DAVIDSON COLLEGE LIBRARY
Circulation Desk
Daily Record Sheet

DESK/PEOPLE ON DUTY

Jiao

Time	
8:00 – 9:00	————
9:00 – 10:00	————
10:00 – 11:00	————
11:00 – 12:00	————
12:00 – 1:00	————
1:00 – 2:00	————
2:00 – 3:00	———— 0 hrs Mw
3:00 – 4:00	————
4:00 – 5:00	————
5:00 – 6:00	————
6:00 – 7:00	————

CHAPTER XIV

ECONOMIC DEVELOPMENT

IN THE

MIDDLE EAST AND NORTH AFRICA

The unsettled conditions which have characterized the countries of the Middle East and North Africa
almost ever since the end of World War II, overshadow
the fact that all these countries have, in varying degrees, devoted a sizable proportion of their resources
to economic development.   They have formulated plans
and implemented them, achieving for the most part fairly
high rates of growth, although the latter are often
somewhat reduced by the high rate of increase in population resulting from both natural growth and immigration.   In formulating their plans, the various nations
gave priority to the sectors of their economies which
were in need of it: over and above the usual prerequisites for development of social overhead capital
projects and productive industrial investments; a problem
which is shared by all the countries of the area is the
shortage of water.   This is usually accompanied by desert
soil, a low percentage of land which can be cultivated -
hence a low land/man ratio and the unsuitability of comparatively vast areas for human living.

The above conditions constitute something of a
vicious circle: there is not enough water to bring more
land under cultivation and the absence of adequate veg-
etation as well as of human habitation amplify the
aridity of the land.   Rainfall in North Africa and the
Middle East varies between 5 and 40 inches a year but most
of the countries we are studying lie in the middle or

lowest part of the range. They, therefore, have to rely on irrigation projects based on their river systems. Where agriculture gets its water supply from an irrigation system, intensive farming is practiced but when output depends on rainfall it is less abundant and more uncertain. Whatever the type of farming, the methods are traditional, the tools archaic and, except where a few cash crops are produced for export, agricultural output barely covers domestic needs.

To understand the nature of the problems in this area, one should remember that most of its population has been for centuries predominantly agrarian, both by inclination and as a result of economic conditions. The rich were always more inclined to invest in land than in the more risky industrial ventures and the poor preferred life and work in their villages to more exacting employment in factories and congested urban housing. Only when it was not possible for them to eke out a living in the village, did they trek to the city.

The discovery of oil was an accident of nature which disturbed the rural life of the population, whether it was of the nomadic or the settled type. Similarly, the urge to industrialize was first spurred by the disappearance of traditional foreign sources of imports during the two World Wars; it was next given impetus when sudden wealth created by the oil industry widened the scope of Middle Eastern markets. Thus, to the more common type of industrial activity such as mining, food processing and textiles have gradually been added heavier industries such as steel, petro-chemicals, fertilizers plants and the manufacture of some capital goods.

Another characteristic which is common to these
countries is that their exports still consist largely of
primary products. Even Israel which is the most industrialized among them, does not export a large volume of
manufactured articles; polished diamonds which are really
re-exports, classify as highly skilled handicrafts rather
than manufactured goods. Proceeds from exports are still
an important source of foreign exchange, as well as income
and these nations' reliance on primary products, whether
they be mineral or agricultural, puts them at the mercy
of price fluctuations on world markets. The normal
remedy to such a situation is to diversify exports by
using more of the raw materials in home production, i.e.,
more domestic industries. Hence to the initial need of
building up productive capacity is added that of export
diversification. This chapter will cover the water problem, industrialization, foreign trade and the means by
which these various developments were financed.

Planning Development

The early plans during the 1950's gave priority
in most countries to increasing water resources and expanding the area under cultivation, the construction of
grain silos, land reform and the resettlement of rural
families and supply of agricultural credit cheaply.
During the 1960's, more attention was given to the building of infrastructure and social overhead capital such as
highways, electric power plants, port improvement, oil
refineries, etc. At the beginning of the 1970's, Iran,
Israel, Lebanon, Turkey, the U.A.R. and Algeria were
concentrating mainly on industrial development, while
Cyprus, Iraq, Syria, Libya, Morocco and Tunisia were
still devoting the major part of their respective budgets

to the agricultural sector.   Jordan and Saudi Arabia
were concentrating on communications, highways, railways and ports.   Kuwait is converting a desert into
an economically livable country.

Table XIV/1 gives data on gross fixed capital
formation, in dollar value and as a percentage of gross
domestic product.   It is interesting to note that
Cyprus, Israel, Lebanon and Tunisia have been investing
a larger percentage of their g.d.p. than the oil producing countries, with the exception of Libya.   In absolute figures, Turkey and Iran have been putting more
resources in capital formation, but they are also the
largest two countries in the group, in terms of population.   Table XIV/2 shows the international reserve
positions of the countries under study for the period
1958 to 1970, i.e., every country's official holdings
of gold, foreign exchange, reserve position with the
International Monetary Fund and Special Drawing Rights
which were first distributed in 1970 and added up for
the countries of the Middle East to about $125.5 million.[1]
The last column in this table gives the overall change
for the period covered, a change which varies from 2,900
per cent for Libya to a minus 68 per cent for the United
Arab Republic and a minus 17 per cent for Iran.   Both
the latter countries have been industrializing on a large
scale.   So is Turkey who has however realized a 50 per
cent increase in her reserves over the twelve year period

-----

[1] of which:

Cyprus	$3.4 mn.	Jordan	$ 2.7 mn.	Algeria	$12.6 mn.
Iran	21.0	Syria	6.4	Morocco	15.1
Israel	15.1	Turkey	18.1	Tunisia	5.9
		U.A.R.	25.2		

I.M.F. Press Release, No. 1, 1971.

Table XIV/1

M.E. and N.A.:   GROSS FIXED CAPITAL FORMATION

(in million dollars and as percentage of GDP)*

	1961	1963	1964	1965	1966	1967	1968	1969
Cyprus	$ 47	$ 72	$ 50	$ 50	$ 80	$ 90	$115	$116
	15%	20%	16%	18%	19%	19%	23%	24%
Iran	729	652	788	1022	1184	1541	1817	2035
	16%	12%	13%	13%	16%	19%	20%	19%
Iraq	241	216	284	276				
	14%	10%	12%	12%				
Israel	807	742	916	978	829	668	823	1060
	26%	28%	29%	27%	20%	16%	19%	22%
Jordan	48	56	53	67	77	74	84	110
	14%	15%	12%	14%	15%	13%	16%	18%
Kuwait	218	269	271	266	378	456	440	417
	12%	13%	13%	13%	15%	19%	16%	15%
Lebanon			226	253	280	242	248	
			21%	22%	23%	19%	19%	
Saudi Arabia			344	442	518	517	565	594
			10%	12%	18%	17%	17%	17%
Syria[a]	154	167	166	380	189	214	238	
			16%	15%				
Turkey	871	1063	1174	1305	1683	1918	2316	2596
	14%	14%	14%	15%	16%	16%	18%	18%
United Arab Rep.				823	866	826	672	766
				16%	16%	14%	11%	12%
Algeria[b]			364	344	364	547	810	1094
			13%	11%	11%	16%	22%	27%
Libya			297	394	468	547	768	
			26%	26%	25%	24%	24%	
Morocco	207	278	272	286	301	375	388	429
	11%	11%	10%	10%	12%	13%	13%	13%
Tunisia	162	210	202	254	247	244	226	260
	18%	22%	24%	26%	25%	24%	20%	21%

Source: International Monetary Fund, International Financial Statistics, 'Country' pages, relevant nos.
*for rates at which national currencies have been converted into dollars, please see table XIII/3.

[a]gross investment.   [b]gross capital formation.

Table XIV/2

M.E. and N.A.:   INTERNATIONAL RESERVE POSITIONS[*]
(million $'s)

Country	1958	1961	1963	1965	1967	1969	1970	Change %
Cyprus	24	45	66	84	104	176	208	766
Iran	254	208	245	236	305	311	209	-17
Iraq	290	218	295	234	368	476	462	59
Israel	192	280	515	643	715	412	449	340
Jordan	46	51	63	140	244	262	257	454
Kuwait			872	929	1026	1282		47
Lebanon	108	161	206	251	281	347	386	257
Saudi Arabia		239	514	726	761	602	662	177
Syria		21	22	45	74	59		180
Turkey	286	194	178	141	119	245	431	50
United Arab Rep.	425	203	216	193	196	145	135	-68
Algeria				184	442	409	338	83
Libya	53	87	122	246	385	918	1590	2900
Morocco	129	185	110	99	76	114	141	9
Tunisia	47	74	62	36	40	37	58	23

Source: International Monetary Fund, International Financial Statistics

[*]including official holdings of gold, Special Drawing Rights as from 1970, Reserve Positions in the Fund and Foreign Exchange.   Amounts shown are for end of period.

with massive economic aid from the OECD countries. Of
note that Iran's reserves have been declining in spite
of the increasing revenue from the oil industry.

The Water Problem

Of the total area of over four million square
miles covered by the countries of the Middle East and
North Africa which are studied here, roughly about 14
per cent is cultivated. This percentage is small if
one considers that in most of them the agricultural sector makes a large, if not the largest, contribution to
national output. There is also a direct relationship
between the size of the cultivated area and the availability of water; as a matter of fact, about 20 per
cent of the farmland depends upon irrigation systems
for its water supply. The dearth of arable land because of insufficient water supply is, then, a problem
which affects the whole area. Irrigation and land
reclamation schemes, more rational planning as regards
acreage and crop rotation, efforts to develop institutional agricultural credit, to improve marketing conditions and to stabilize prices are measures which have
been taken to improve agricultural output.

Increasing water resources is undertaken in
several ways: storage dams, diversion weirs, pipelines
and covered ducts, desalinization plants and terracing.
Storage dams retain excess river flow during the flood
season and make it available through a network of canals
during the dry periods. The stored water also serves
to generate hydro-electric power. The most important
such project built in the Middle East so far is the
second Aswan dam spanning the Nile River in Egypt,

completed in 1970.[2]   Three major dams were built in
Iran: the Sefid Roud, Dez and Karadj.   Iraq built two
major storage dams: the Ramadi over the Euphrates River
and the Samarra over the Tigris River.   The Euphrates
dam in Syria was the last to be started and is expected
to be similar in size to the Aswan dam; it is due for
completion near the end of the 1970's.

Another form of dam is the kind which does not
store river flow but simply diverts it (hence the name
of diversion weir) to a man-made canal, for irrigation
purposes and for generating hydro-electric power.   The
East-Ghor project in Jordan and the Litani in Lebanon,
are examples of diversion dams.   A somewhat similar
project is the Jordan-Negev scheme in Israel which consists of a diversion weir, covered ducts and pipelines
which carry the water from the Jordan River to the Negev
desert, over a distance of 160 kilometers.

Still another way of obtaining water is by
means of the desalinization process which transforms sea
water and makes it potable.   It is a costly operation
in view of the volume of water involved.   Israel, Kuwait
and Saudi Arabia have built desalinization plants.   Finally, a method known as terracing which is applied to
hilly terrain, creates terrace-like indentations in the
flanks of the mountains which attract and retain a larger
share of rainfall than a slopy surface, thus making cultivation possible.   Terracing has been carried out in
Lebanon, Syria and Turkey.

---

[2] the first Aswan dam, first built in 1909 and expanded
several times since, is about 6 kilometers downstream
and has a smaller storage capacity.

Industrialization

Traditional industrial activity in the Middle
East has been mainly in food processing, cottage industries such as rug-making, pottery, etc., semi-manufac-
tured textile products, e.g., yarn, and mining. Apart
from oil, there are deposits of phosphates, iron, copper,
manganese, and chrome ore in most of the countries. In
the late 1960's very important copper deposits were found
in the Kerman area in Iran and are being exploited by the
Kerman Copper Industries;[3] these reserves are estimated
at 300-400 million tons. Large copper deposits were
also found in Saudi Arabia where the reserves are estimated at 8 million tons. Jordan is expanding its phosphate mining and Cyprus, its iron mining; in both countries mineral products contribute a large share of exports. Mineral deposits are rich but still not exploited
on a large scale in Morocco and Tunisia; they are more
varied in the former where they include iron phosphates,
manganese ore, copper, lead, coal, tin, cement and petroleum. In Tunisia, phosphates, iron ore, zinc and lead
contribute already more than 30 per cent of exports.

The following summary listing is to give an
idea of the progress of industrialization and new trends
during the 1960's, rather than a complete survey.[4]

In Cyprus where main industrial activity is
concentrated in mining of phosphates, copper and iron

[3]owned 70 per cent by Iranian interests and the balance
by British and African interests.

[4]the information in this summary is collected from
various sources; up-to-date facts are from various
periodicals, and the I.M.F.'s International Financial
News Survey.

ore, new developments center on the expansion of iron
ore mining and the new oil refinery at Larnaca, completed in 1971, at a cost of $20 million.

In Iran, existing industries include oil
mining, cement, sugar, cigarettes, tobacco and small
manufactured articles; the two most important developments are: a) the newly discovered copper fields from
which production is to start in 1974 with a yearly output of 150,000 tons, and b) the new steel mill, built
30 miles outside the city of Isfahan, with a capacity
of 2.5 million tons a year, which will eventually be
the center of a large industrial complex. The mill
was built by Russian technicians and with a Russian
credit of $286 million, in exchange for natural gas
exports. The 40-inch Trans National Gas pipeline is
to carry the gas from the Persian Gulf oilfields to the
Soviet border, while an extension of it will provide
energy to the steel mill complex. Other new industries
already producing and expanding, are electrical ap-
pliances, automobile assembly, textiles and refriger-
ators; petrochemical production is planned.

In Iraq, old established industries other than
oil mining and refining, include cement, beer, cigarettes and tobacco. New infrastructure projects include
a crude oil supply pipeline at Mosul refinery with a
projected capacity of 30,000 barrels a day, two hydro-
electric stations in the north, a power station at
Samarra and a chemical fertilizers plant. Phosphate
mining in the west and a paper mill at Basrah are other
new projects.

Israel has more diversified industries than
any of the other nations: phosphates, magnesia, hydro-
chloric acid, cement, fertilizers, sugar, beer,

cigarettes, tobacco, cotton yarn, textiles, artificial
fibers, chemical, electrical, rubber and plastic products. New industries consist of frozen foods, and the
Koor Steel foundry and rolling mill with a capacity of
80,000 tons of steel ingots a year. Infrastructure
projects include the oil refinery at Haifa with a capacity of 5 to 6 million tons a year, construction of
homes to meet the increase of population through immigration, desalinization of sea water, and the new
Eilat-Ashkelon pipeline which carried 11 million tons of
crude in 1970 from the Red Sea to the Mediterranean; it
was planned to increase its capacity to 20 million tons
in 1971.

In <u>Jordan</u>, the main activity is in mining
phosphates and the production of cement, cigarettes and
tobacco. New developments are in expanding phosphate
mining, production of petroleum products, detergents,
batteries and paper.

In <u>Kuwait</u>, apart from oil mining and refining,
the most important new domestic project has been the
construction of the world's largest desalinization
plant, by a French consortium; it will process 25 million
gallons of sea water, at Shuaiba near the city of Kuwait,
and will be entirely completed in 1972. Otherwise
Kuwait has undertaken a large domestic social overhead
capital formation program and, through the Kuwait Development Fund, has invested large amounts in low cost
loans to neighboring Arab countries; the loans are primarily to finance infrastructure projects.

In <u>Lebanon</u>, the banking and exchange sector
makes the largest contribution to national income: 91
commercial banks, most of them branches of foreign banks,
operate in Beirut which is one of the few free exchange

centres left in the world. Traditional industries include cement, sugar refining, beer, cigarettes, tobacco,
processed foodstuffs, cotton yarn and textiles.
Speeded-up construction, mainly for the hotel industry,
and the building of grain silos are the most important
new developments.

In Saudi Arabia, where industrial production
started recently from almost scratch, completed infrastructure projects include a new modern international
highway network, connecting the country's main cities
and linking it with Qatar and Jordan; expansion of the
ports of Jeddah and Damman and the creation of a new
port on the Red Sea; water distribution and sewage
systems for the cities of Riyadh, Jeddah and Mecca; a
large-scale irrigation and drainage project at Al-Hasa;
and a 7.5 million gallons a day desalinization plant at
Khobar, north of Jeddah. Other projects also completed are a fertilizers factory and petrochemical industries.

In Syria, whose manufacturing activity was
among the earliest to develop, existing industries produce cement, wool and cotton textiles, beer, cigarettes,
tobacco and milled flour. New developments are mainly
in oil production which began in 1968 when output was
one million tons; it rose to 2.6 million tons in 1969
and is to be increased still further. A new pipeline
connecting the oilfields with the Homs refinery, has a
capacity of 4 million tons a year. As infrastructure
projects, the port of Latakia was built in the late
1950's, and is still being gradually expanded; the Homs
oil refinery started operations in 1959 and the Euphrates
dam mentioned above, is expected to have a capacity of
800,000 KW of hydro-electric power in addition to the

increase in irrigation facilities and flood control. A
factory for the production of steel and steel products is
also planned.

In Turkey, established industries are varied
and mining contributes a large share to output: iron,
copper, manganese and chrome are mined and sugar, beer,
cigarettes, tobacco, cotton yarn are produced. New developments in infrastructure include a bridge spanning
the Bosphorus for which external financing of $75.5
million was obtained, from Japan ($30 mn.) and the bal-
ance from various Western European countries; a $263
million, 2-million ton capacity iron and steel plant at
Iskanderun on the Mediterranean and a one-million ton
oil refinery at Izmir, both financed by the U.S.S.R.;
an aluminum sheet and foil industry with a capacity of
9,000 and 11,550 tons respectively, financed partly by
Kuwait and an electric power project at Ambarli near
Istanbul, financed by a consortium of Swiss banks, at a
cost of $26.6 million.

In the United Arab Republic, the most important
long established industry which has been expanding and
improving its products over the years is cotton textiles.
Others are sugar refining, iron, manganese and phosphate
mining, beer, cigarettes and fertilizers. New developments in infrastructure include mainly the Aswan dam,
the expansion of the steel mill at Helwan, a suburb of
Cairo, and the new industrial complex adjoining it;
also an ambitious project, the building of a 207-mile
pipeline to carry crude oil, linking the Gulf of Suez
on the Red Sea with the Mediterranean, west of Alexan-
dria, and crossing the Nile south of Cairo. Other new
developments include expansion in oil production and in
refining facilities, and a new sugar mill, one of the

largest in the world, built at a cost of $69 million to process 150,000 tons of sugar a year.

In <u>North Africa</u>, the most important new infrastructure project shared jointly by all four countries is the new airline "Air Maghreb" created in 1969. Otherwise, both Algeria and Libya are using the income they receive from oil production in building up their infrastructure as well as modernizing the agricultural sector.   Tunisia is concentrating on the latter effort only, while Morocco is trying to diversify its output.

In <u>Algeria</u>, oil mining and refining and the production of natural gas, have long been and still are the most important established industries.   The most notable new development in this field is the agreement reached by the El Paso Natural Gas Company and the Algerian concern of Sonatrach for the export to the United States of 10 billion cubic meters a year of liquified gas, starting in 1973.   It is considered that to implement this agreement, an investment of about one billion dollars will be needed; this will involve the purchase of tankers, the construction of a pipeline, a gas liquefaction plant and other facilities.   Gas shipments will also be made to the United Kingdom and France. Other new investments include a paper factory with a starting capacity of 10,000 tons, a new refinery at Arzen in the east of Algeria by Japanese interests, and a 742 kilometers of pipelines from the Mesdar oilfields to the coast.   Steel, paper, chemicals, food and construction materials industries have also been created.

In <u>Libya</u>, transport and communications projects including a new highway linking Tripoli and Benghazi, new power plants, as well as consumers goods industries are

being implemented.   In <u>Morocco</u>, handicrafts such as
rugs, leather articles, food processing, woolen and
silk textiles, as well as mining of phosphates, lead,
zinc, iron ore, manganese, cobalt, copper and fertilizers were the old established industries.   New ones
include a projected iron and steel complex, the
S.A.M.I.R. oil refinery owned and controlled in equal
parts by the government and E.N.I. (Italy), a tire
plant as well as two factories for assembling trucks
and cars.   In <u>Tunisia</u>, food processing, mining of
phosphates and iron ore, wheat milling and production
of superphosphates, have been the major industries.
New developments include the sugar refinery at Beja,
a cellulose plant at Kasserine, a modern superphos-
phate plant, and a petroleum refinery at Bizerte.

Financing Development

Data were given earlier in this chapter on
the proportion of their gross domestic product that
the Middle Eastern and North African countries devote
to capital formation and also on their holdings of
international reserves (see tables XIV/1 and XIV/2).
In view of the magnitude of their development programs,
it is important to find out whether inflationary trends
were generated to any extent; this information is provided in table XIV/3 which gives changes in the consumer price index, as well as changes in the money
supply, for the period 1962 to 1970.   As mentioned
earlier, Turkey, Israel and the U.A.R. have registered
inflationary trends; the high average rate of yearly
increase for Libya in both prices and in the stock of
money is due to the fairly recent discovery of oil deposits and the fast expansion in oil production.   The

Table XIV/3

MIDDLE EAST AND NORTH AFRICA:

CHANGES IN PRICES AND MONEY SUPPLY

Country	Consumer Prices (1963 = 100)		Money Supply (mn. $'s)		Av.rate of incr. p.a. %
	1962	1970	1962	1970	
Cyprus	98	111	52	115	7.8
Iran	100	111	596	1,190	12.5
Iraq	96	119	358	602	8.5
Israel	94	142^a	419	896	17.0
Jordan		113	94^b	291	26.0
Kuwait	n.a.	n.a.	250	277	1.3
Lebanon	n.a.	n.a.	451	504	2.0
Saudi Arabia	n.a.	n.a.	240	527	15.0
Syria	98	117	246	487^c	14.0
Turkey	94	155	704	1,540	15.0
United Arab Rep.	99	143	1,019	1,706	8.3
Libya	104^d	139	86	608	76.0
Morocco	94	115	640	1,083	8.6
Tunisia	97	133	204	380	10.7

Source: I.M.F., International Financial Statistics,
         Country pages, relevant numbers.

[a] 1967.   [b] 1965.   [c] 1969.   [d] 1964.

other countries show relative stability compared with developing nations in other areas.

Following several economic measures to insure price stability, Turkey devalued its currency in August 1970, by changing the par value of the lira from 9 to 15 liras to the U.S. dollar; this step was also taken with a view to reduce the trade gap. Israel took several steps during 1970 to contain inflation: government reduced its borrowing, compulsory import deposits were imposed, and instruments of monetary management were used to reduce the availability of credit. The U.A.R. drastically reduced the controlled prices on essential consumer goods charged by government-owned corporations, in October, 1970; the resulting loss to the government was estimated at $10.4 million.

As regards the high rate of increase in the money supply for most of the countries studied, this may be due to other causes besides the intensified expenditure on development: revenue from royalties, the state of hostilities, the inflow of aid or, as in the case of Libya, the very high rate of growth of the G.D.P. Libya's annual increase of 76 per cent in its money supply contrasts sharply with the 1.3 per cent rate registered by Kuwait but one should remember in this case Kuwait's large investments abroad. Lebanon's low average rate of increase in its stock of money may be the result of the very large deficits in its balance of trade, or to the fact that it is the only country in the area which imposes no restrictions over movement of capital.

Foreign Aid

Foreign multilateral aid was extended by the World Bank and its two subsidiaries, the International Finance Corporation and the International Development Association. Cyprus received loans for port construction and the expansion of tourist facilities; Jordan, for irrigation projects; Morocco, for agricultural development, and the U.A.R. for the expansion of the Suez Canal. Recently, multilateral private aid was extended as mentioned earlier, in the form of joint financing by private banks from various European countries, and also from Japan, for a specific project.

Foreign bilateral aid came from various sources: Russia extended assistance to Iran for the construction of a pipeline and in exchange for natural gas exports; to

Iraq, Syria and the U.A.R. for industrial projects.   The
United States gave aid to Israel, Jordan and Turkey;
France gave financial assistance to Algeria, Morocco and
Tunisia; England to Cyprus and Jordan.   Kuwait, by means
of its Development Fund, extends interest-free loans for
economic development;   Iraq, Jordan, Lebanon, Syria and
the U.A.R. have received such loans.   Turkey has received
aid from the Organization for European Cooperation and Development (O.E.C.D.), mainly to help in its stabilization
program against inflation.

Internal Financing

Sources of internal financing were as follows:
(a) oil production which yielded royalties as well as
taxes levied from the producers; (b) receipts from tourism which most countries are making an effort to encourage
in its many forms, such as attracting sightseeing visitors
from various parts of the world, or Moslem pilgrims to
Mecca and Christian pilgrims to Jerusalem; (c) higher
public revenues due to either a reform of the taxation
system, or just an increase in the tax rate, or the normal
increase in the tax base resulting from growing investment
expenditures; (d) government borrowing through the sale
of long-term debt.

Foreign Trade

Several facts are evident from table XIV/4 which
gives foreign trade data: (a) with the exception of the
oil producing countries and more recently the U.A.R., all
the others had a deficit in their merchandise trade, for
the years shown, the assumption being that this was due to
their sizable imports of capital equipment for development; (b) apart from Libya - a relative newcomer to oil
production and exports - the countries which registered

Table XIV/4

MIDDLE EAST AND NORTH AFRICA: FOREIGN TRADE

(million $'s)

Country	Exports fob 1958	Exports fob 1969	Imports cif 1958	Imports cif 1969	Deficit (-) or Surplus 1958	Deficit (-) or Surplus 1969	Annual Rate of Growth of Exports %
Cyprus	49	98	103	206	- 54	-108	8.7
Iran	741	2,099	572	1,528	169	571	16.3
Iraq	567	1,045	307	440	260	605	7.7
Israel	141	729	423	1,331	-282	-602	37.4
Jordan	10	41	95	190	- 85	-149	28.2
Kuwait	930	1,476	190	646	740	830	5.4
Lebanon	31	161	213	527	-182	-366	26.0
Saudi Arabia	800	2,001	270	734	530	1,267	14.1
Syria	121	207	198	368	- 77	-161	6.4
Turkey	247	537	315	747	- 68	-210	10.7
United Arab Rep.	479	745	669	636	-190	109	5.1
Algeria	488	934	1,139	1,009	-651	- 75	8.3
Libya	14	2,168	97	676	- 83	1,487	140.0
Morocco	345	485	401	562	- 56	- 77	3.7
Tunisia	153	166	155	266	- 2	- 90	0.008

Source: I.M.F., International Financial Statistics, Trade pages, relevant numbers.

the highest average rate of growth in their exports, namely Israel, Lebanon and Jordan, are non-oil producing, though it should be mentioned that the high rate for the latter two is due to the fact that their exports were very low in the base year (1958); (c) in terms of total value of exports in 1969, Libya, Iran and Saudi Arabia are close front-runners, with Kuwait, Iraq and Algeria following; among the non-oil producing countries, the U.A.R. and Israel lead with Turkey and Morocco following and all the others trailing behind. Again it is seen that the order of importance of these countries' gross domestic product is not reflected in the value of their exports.

Composition of Exports

Apart from petroleum products which are exported
mainly to Europe, the composition of the main exports of
the countries of the M.E. and N.A. shows a certain degree
of complementarity. For instance, Syria and to a lesser
degree Turkey, export cereals which are needed by almost
all the other countries; hence the need for better irrigation methods to ensure a steady crop. These two countries also export tobacco and, together with Egypt, cotton
and textile products which have a ready market in neighboring countries. Cyprus, Jordan, Morocco and Tunisia
export phosphates as well as other non-ferrous minerals
which do not have much of a market in the area because
most other countries produce them also. Israel's main
exports are citrus fruit and diamonds for which the demand
in the area is not great, but, its many new budding industries of consumers goods would find a ready market in
neighboring countries - on the assumption that the hostilities in this area will not last forever. As regards
industrial production, the same could be said for the
U.A.R. and to a lesser extent for Syria and Turkey: they
all have a diversified output of manufactured goods which
go a long way to satisfy domestic needs but have not been
developed and improved enough yet to stand competition on
foreign markets. Finally, all the non-oil producing
countries export agricultural produce of various kinds for
which there is great need in the oil producing countries.
The various countries either produce and/or refine petroleum products in varying quantities, or are crossed by
pipelines carrying them and from which they can satisfy
their needs for industrialization.

As regards trading partners, the countries of
the European Economic Community seem to provide the biggest market for exports from the Middle East and North

Africa[5], whether they be petroleum products or other
goods; they are also the source from which the majority
of imports come.   As regards the destination of exports,
the E.E.C. countries are followed closely by Japan, the
United Kingdom, and the Soviet block, who is the main
trading partner of the U.A.R. and Syria.   The United
States buys comparatively little of these countries' exports but supplies a large part of the imports of Iran,
Jordan, Israel, Kuwait, Lebanon, Turkey, Morocco and
Tunisia.   Middle Eastern countries are the main destination of exports emanating from Jordan, Lebanon and
Syria and to a lesser extent, from Turkey and the U.A.R.
They supply imports to Iraq, Kuwait and Saudi Arabia and
also to Jordan, Lebanon and Syria.

* * * * * * *

It might be asked why a region which offers so
little in terms of land utilization and adequate living
conditions has had so much importance through history,
especially if one remembers that the discovery of oil in
it is of recent origin.   One answer to this question
might be that apart from being the crossroads of north
and south and east and west, the area was the birthplace
of the three most important religions in the world.
Another answer would be that in the past these countries
boasted a fertile crescent-shaped belt extending from
Baghdad to Beirut, via Turkey (hence the name of the
'Fertile Crescent').   With far less population then
than there is at present, the pressure on resources was
also less.   Past intestine wars, neglect and natural
soil erosion have reduced fertile land to arid deserts

---

[5]with the exception of those of Jordan, Lebanon and
Syria.

in many areas. Now, again, the attempt is to obtain,
by various means, more water in order to restore to these
lands their former fertility. Such is the course of
history.

In summary, three factors account for the
importance of this area to the outside world: the
first is its strategic position as the meeting point
of three continents; the second is its oil reserves;
the third is the Suez canal which shortens by over 40
per cent the distance between Europe and Asia.

THE MIDDLE EAST

Topics for Reading and Research

1. The water problem: the main projects which have
   been or are being carried out to remedy it.

2. Agricultural production: consumption needs and
   surplus for export.

3. Industrialization: traditional and modern projects;
   social overhead capital.

4. The oil industry: size, physical output and revenues;
   returns to the host countries.

5. The oil industry: oil pipelines and refineries;
   who owns them.

6. The oil industry: new concessions and changes in
   the pattern of investment.

7. Foreign trade: composition, scope and direction,
   by countries.

8. Impact of oil revenue on a selected country: Iran,
   Iraq, Kuwait, Saudi Arabia, Libya, from the point of
   view of a) development, b) holdings of foreign
   reserves.

9. Development plans: main emphasis and most important
   projects.

291

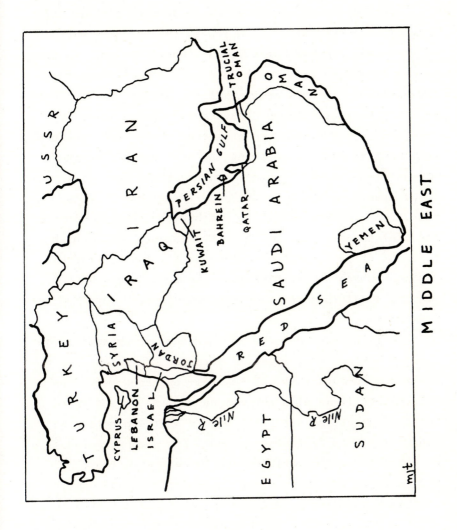

MIDDLE EAST

CHAPTER XV

AFRICA SOUTH OF THE SAHARA

The Facts Behind the Political Boundaries

Our study now takes us to an area rich in still
unexploited resources, but which is the least developed
of the areas covered, namely, sub-Sahara Africa. A few
points should be made clear in order to facilitate the
understanding of this area. First, Africa has two large
empty spaces: the large Sahara desert which is larger
than the United States and stretches across the continent
from west to east, separating the Arab north from the
diversified but mainly black south; the second of these
large spaces consists of the desert regions of the southwest. The Sahara desert is uninhabited, but running
parallel to the south of it is the expanse of the high
plateaus of pasture land - known as the former French
Soudan - which squats high over the Equator and where
grazing conditions and the presence of water have led to
the existence of nomadic life.

The second point is that the unevenness of the
terrain has not only rendered internal communications between the various parts of the sub-continent very difficult, but it is also the reason why the inland part
remained unsettled until the middle of the nineteenth
century. This fact also accounts for the backwardness
of the area. The earliest settlements were those of
the Arabs in the north along the Mediterranean coast;
then came the French, British and Portuguese settlements
along the west coast, the British and Dutch in the South,
and the British and Portuguese on the east coast, as well
as some Indian elements. This has produced a mixture of

people either wholly negroid or wholly caucasoid, except
for the smaller Asian and Arab segments.

The third point is that because of the high
rate of population growth, and the high incidence of
disease in the past, about fourty per cent of the population is under fifteen years of age.   Hence the very
large need for schools, teachers and educational material.
This pattern may change with time as, with the help of
the World Health Organization, disease and mortality will
take a lesser toll, and with the spreading of birth control methods, the birth rate will decline.   A fourth
point is that slave trading was a prominent fact in the
history of black Africa: it started before the coming
of the European settlers, but the latter stimulated it
by increasing the demand.   The Europeans remained on the
coast, buying the slaves from the Arabs and other raiders
who brought the slaves from inland.   The British were
the first to abolish slavery in 1807 and to resettle
freed slaves, using these settlements as bases for sur-
veillance against slave raiders first, and then as
colonies.

Finally, the arbitrary pattern of political
boundaries is the result of a fairly recent partition-
ing by the Great Powers.   Up to 1950, only Ethiopia
which got rid of Italian rule in 1941, and Liberia, a
small country made up of a settlement of freed slaves
from the United States,[1] were free from outside control.
In the early 1950's Egypt and Libya gained their independence and from then on the wave of independence swept

---

[1]these were settled on the west coast of Africa in the
middle of the nineteenth century and in 1947 Liberia's
sovereignty was recognized.

Africa. In 1956, it was the turn of the French posses-
sions in the Arab north - with the exception of Algeria
which did not become independent until 1962 - and of the
(Anglo/Egyptian) Sudan. In 1957, it was (British)
Ghana, in 1958 (French) Guinea and in 1960 (British)
Nigeria, (British and Italian) Somalia, Zaire (the former
Belgian Congo), as well as the 13 new states fashioned
out of former French West Africa,[2] capital Dakar, and
French Equatorial Africa,[3] capital Brazzaville. These
states, together with Madagascar island, now called
Malagasy, chose unlike Guinea, to remain within the
French Franc area and avail themselves later of associate
membership of the European Common Market. In 1961,
(British) Sierra Leone on the west coast, and (British)
Tanganyika on the east coast, became independent. The
latter was to unite in 1964 with the small island of
Zanzibar and become Tanzania. Zanzibar, settled by
Arabs from the Persian Gulf and once a thriving slave
market, is now famous for its cloves production.

Two small hilly states in the heart of Africa
and south of the Equator, Burundi and Rwanda, former
German colonies, under Belgian mandate after 1919 and
under United Nations Trusteeship since 1945, became independent in 1962; they have about five million people
who make a living out of a prosperous coffee trade.
Also in 1962, (British) Uganda, in 1963, (British) Kenya
and in 1964 the partitioned Rhodesias (British): northern Rhodesia became Zambia, western Rhodesia or Nyasaland

---

[2]Mauritania, Senegal, Mali, Niger, Ivory Coast, Upper
Volta, Togo, Dahomey and Cameroon.
[3]Gabon, Congo (Brazzaville), Chad and Central African
Republic.

became Malawi and Southern Rhodesia kept its name and its independence under white supremacy.   Colonial rule remains only in the Portuguese dependencies of Angola and Mozambique on the southwest and southeast coasts respectively, and in the British protectorates in southwest Africa of Bechuanaland, Basutoland and Swaziland. South Africa, a sovereign state strictly controlled by European settlers of British and Dutch origin, who now make up one fifth of the population, is a fully developed country which enjoys a high standard of living and thus is not included in this study.

<u>Basic Data and Resources</u>

<u>Population</u>

Table XV/1 gives area and population for almost all the countries on the sub-African continent: it will be seen from it that very often the size of the country has no relationship with the size of the population. Allowing for deserts and empty spaces, population density for all of Africa is of 11 inhabitants per square kilometer and compares favorably with that of 10 inhabitants per square kilometer in North America, 72 in Asia and 93 in Europe.   The country with the largest population is Nigeria, followed by Ethiopia, Zaire, the Sudan, Tanzania and Kenya, all having ten or more million inhabitants.   Looking at the area alone, we find that the largest is the Sudan, followed by Mali, the Zaire, Angola, Ethiopia, Niger and Mauritania.   Four out of the seven last countries mentioned have a very small-sized population.   As seen earlier, the boundaries between the various countries were dictated by political expediency rather than geographic or ethnic convenience.

Table XV/1

AFRICA SOUTH OF THE SAHARA: AREA AND POPULATION

Country	Area in sq.miles[a]	Population (000)[b] 1958	1969	Av. rate of growth p.a. %
1. Angola	481,350	4,667	5,430*	1.4
2. Cameroon	178,400	4,500	5,736	2.0
3. Cent. Afr. Rep.	238,000	1,161	1,518	2.6
4. Chad	495,000	2,980	3,510*	1.5
5. Congo [d]	175,600	750	915*	1.5
6. Zaire	902,300	13,474*	17,100*	2.4
7. Dahomey	44,695	1,940*	2,640*	3.2
8. Ethiopia	455,000	20,100	24,769*	1.8
9. Gabon	102,300	417	485*	1.4
10. Gambia	4,000	280	357	2.5
11. Ghana	91,800	6,420	8,600*	2.4
12. Guinea	95,000	2,896	3,890*	3.3
13. Ivory Coast	183,400	3,090	4,195	2.9
14. Kenya	225,000	7,652*	10,506*	2.9
15. Liberia	43,000	960*	1,150	1.7
16. Malagasy Rep.	228,000	5,131	6,600	2.1
17. Malawi	45,700	3,300	4,398	3.0
18. Mali	945,000	3,920*	4,881*	2.2
19. Mauritania	419,000	790	1,140*	4.0
20. Mauritius	720	610	799*	2.8
21. Mozambique	297,731	6,369	7,376	1.2
22. Niger	450,000	2,666	3,909	4.2
23. Nigeria	356,100	50,000	64,580	2.5
24. Reunion	969	318	426	2.9
25. Senegal	76,000	2,967*	3,780	2.4
26. Sierra-Leone	27,000	1,980*	2,512	2.4
27. Somalia	246,000	1,980	2,730	3.4
28. Southern Rhodesia	150,000	3,410	5,090	3.2
29. Sudan	967,500	11,146	15,186	2.8
30. Tanzania	363,700	10,014	12,926	2.2
31. Togo	20,700	1,360	1,815	2.6
32. Uganda	80,300	6,356*	9,500[c]	
33. Upper Volta	113,000	4,090*	5,278*	2.6
34. Zambia	290,300	3,040	4,208*	2.9

Source: for population, United Nations, Monthly Bulletin of Statistics, relevant issues.

[a] area within 1969 official boundaries. [b] estimates at mid-year; where the figure is followed by (*), the estimate is one made by the U.N. [c] basis of calculation not comparable with previous period. [d] former Belgian Congo.

Moreover, the cities were founded by the early European settlers wherever they found the climate favorable and these same cities now attract the Africans.   As mentioned earlier, the agglomeration of population is found along the coast; the coastal states have, therefore, thrived generally, while those which are inland and landlocked have remained poor, unless they have some already exploited rich resources, such as Zaire, for instance.

Income and Growth

Table XV/2 gives total and per capita gross domestic product for most of the African countries south of the Sahara, while table XV/3 gives the rates of exchange on the basis of which conversion into dollars for each country was made.   Looking at the more meaningful figure of gross domestic product per capita, it is seen that the small island of Reunion heads the list with a per capita g.d.p. of $725.0.   It is followed by Southern Rhodesia ($526.0), Gabon ($503.0), Zambia ($338.0), Ivory Coast ($322.0), Liberia ($318.0), Ghana ($261.0), and Mauritius ($256.0).   As far as the yearly rate of growth for the decade 1958-69 is concerned, Mauritania is first with a rate of 14 per cent and it is followed by the Ivory Coast (11.9 per cent), Gabon (10.7 per cent), Togo (9.5 per cent), Reunion (7.8 per cent) and Malawi (7.5 per cent).   Considering that France spends the equivalent of $200 million a year in aid to her former dependencies, it is not surprising to see them heading the list where income and economic growth are concerned.

It is interesting to note also from table XV/3 the relative stability, with few exceptions, of the various rates of exchange which fluctuate only when a change occurs to the mother currency with which they are pegged.

Table XV/2

AFRICA SOUTH OF THE SAHARA: NATIONAL ACCOUNTS

Country	Gross Domestic Product Total in mn.$'s		Per capita in $'s		Av. rate of growth p.a. in p/cap.GDP
	1958	1969	1958	1969[m]	%
2. Cameroon	460[a]	877[i]	100[a]	156[i]	6.2
3. Central Afr. Rep.	138[c]	156[e]	110[c]	116[e]	4.8
4. Chad	181[c]	213[d]	58[c]	66[d]	6.8
6. Zaire	962[b]	1,759	71[b]	103	4.0
7. Dahomey	148[b]	194[g]	72[b]	82[g]	2.9
8. Ethiopia	994[c]	1,486[h]	46[c]	62[h]	5.8
9. Gabon	128[b]	238[h]	287[b]	503[h]	10.7
11. Ghana	1,086	2,282	169	261[j]	4.9
13. Ivory Coast	455	1,322[i]	147	322[i]	11.9
14. Kenya	913[d]	1,431	103[d]	131	5.2
15. Liberia	222[b]	366[h]	231[b]	318[h]	4.2
16. Malagasy Rep.	543[b]	737[h]	100[b]	116[h]	2.3
17. Malawi	111[j]	283[j]	33	65[j]	8.8
19. Mauritania	59[a]	190[i]	73	169[i]	14.0
20. Mauritius	145[b]	202[i]	237[b]	256[i]	0.8
22. Niger	202[b]	318[g]	70[b]	88[g]	4.3
23. Nigeria	2,900[a]	4,127[h]	56[a]	80[h]	5.3
24. Reunion	231[f]	310[i]	587[f]	725[i]	7.8
25. Senegal	577[a]	713[j]	190[a]	188[j]	-0.9
26. Sierra Leone	259[d]	389[i]	112[d]	157[i]	5.0
28. Southern Rhodesia	728	2,674	213	524	13.1
29. Sudan	973	1,568[i]	87	104[i]	0.8
30. Tanzania[j]	493	1,182[j]	55	91[j]	3.2
31. Togo	102	215[g]	73	128[g]	9.5
32. Uganda	410	889[i]	65	108[i]	6.6
33. Upper Volta		244[g]		49[g]	
34. Zambia	792	1,370[i]	260	338[i]	3.3

Notes: 1) due to lack of data, not every country appearing in table XV/1 is included in this table, but the numbers of the respective countries have been kept the same for both tables, for easy reference. 2) Conversions into dollars are based on the exchange rates shown in table XV/3.

Sources: U.N. Monthly Bulletin of Statistics and International Monetary Fund International Financial

over

Table XV/3

AFRICA SOUTH OF THE SAHARA: EXCHANGE RATES

Country	National Currency	National Currency per U.S. $ 1958	1968	1969
French Franc Area:				
Cameroon)				
Cent. Afr. Rep.)				
Chad)				
Congo)				
Dahomey)				
Gabon)				
Ivory Coast)	CFA Franc	246.85	246.85	277.71
Malagasy Rep.)				
Mauritania)				
Niger)				
Reunion)				
Senegal)				
Togo)				
Upper Volta)				
Sterling Area:				
Gambia	Pound/Dalasi	.3571	.4167	.4167
Ghana	New Cedi	.3571	1.0204	1.0204
Kenya	Shilling	7.143	7.143	7.143
Malawi	Pound	.3571	.4167	.4167
Nigeria	Pound	.3571	.3571	.3571
Southern Rhodesia	Pound	.3571	.3571	.3571
Sierra Leone	Leone	.3571	.71	.83
Sudan	Pound	.3482	.3482	.3482
Tanzania	Shilling	7.143	7.143	7.143
Uganda	Shilling	7.143	7.143	7.143
Zambia	Kwacha	.3571	.7143	.7143
Portuguese Area:				
Angola)	Escudo	28.75	28.77	28.65
Mozambique)				
Others:				
Zaire	Congo Fr.	165.0		
	Zaire		.50	.50
Ethiopia	Eth. dollar	2.484	2.50	2.50
Liberia	U.S. dollar	1.0	1.0	1.0
Mauritius	Rupee	4.762	4.762	4.762

Source: I.M.F., International Financial Statistics, Country pages.

cont'd: Statistics;   relevant issues of both.
[a]1959. [b]1960. [c]1961. [d]1963. [e]1964. [f]1965. [g]1966.
[h]1967. [i]1968. [j]Tanganyika only. [k]g.n.p. [l]g.d.p. at factor cost. [m]data are in pre-devaluation dollars.

Resources

The continent of Africa covers approximately
one quarter of the world area and includes about eight
per cent of its population.   Compared with the countries
of industrial Europe, the land/man ratio, i.e. the per
capita area under cultivation, is three times higher in
Africa, livestock heads per capita are twice as high and
the grazing area per unit of livestock is nearly seven
times as high as in Europe.   Hence quite a few cash
crops are grown in larger volume in Africa than anywhere
else.

Cotton is grown in Egypt, the Sudan, Uganda,
Tanzania, Nigeria, Mozambique, the Central African Republic and Chad.   These countries produce between them
about half the quantity of cotton produced in the United
States.

Cocoa is grown in Ghana, Nigeria, the Ivory
Coast, Cameroon and Sierra Leone; these countries account
for seventy per cent of the world's output.

Coffee is produced in Uganda, Kenya, Sierra
Leone, Ivory Coast, Ethiopia and Nigeria, which account
for fourty per cent of total world production.

Timber comes from the equatorial forests of the
countries along the African west coast, such as Cameroon,
Ivory Coast and Nigeria.

Sugar is produced in South Africa, Mauritius,
Mozambique, Swaziland, Uganda, Kenya and Nigeria and tea
is exported in fairly large quantities from Kenya, Uganda,
Malawi and Mozambique.

Other products such as groundnuts (Senegal),
vanilla (Reunion) and cloves (Tanzania) come almost exclusively from these African sources.

When it comes to mineral resources, the African continent is still richer, not only in what it is producing but also for those resources which have yet to be exploited.

Starting with diamonds, except for a small production from Australia, the total world output comes from Africa, primarily from South Africa, but also from Sierra Leone, Ghana, Zaire and Angola. Two thirds of the world production of gold comes from South Africa, Ghana, Southern Rhodesia and Zaire.

Zambia comes third after the United States and the Sino-Soviet bloc, in its production of copper including smelter copper and refined copper; it is followed by Zaire. Seventy-nine per cent of the world cobalt exports come mainly from Zaire, while uranium comes from South Africa and Zaire.

Ghana is third in the world production of manganese, followed by South Africa and Zaire. Sixty per cent of the world exports of phosphates comes mainly from Togo. Nigeria has large petroleum deposits, although these do not compare with reserves in Middle Eastern countries.

Finally, large deposits of bauxite along the west coast, in Sierra Leone, Cameroon, Ghana and Guinea, has led these countries to promote, with the help of foreign investors and technicians, the construction of huge smelters, activated by hydro-electric power, for the production of aluminium. Cameroon and Ghana already have each a large smelter. Iron ore is also produced in large quantities in Sierra Leone and in South Africa.

Potential for Integration and Development

Soon after obtaining independence, several groupings emerged from among the African states: the earlier ones were predominantly political, the economic unions were to follow later. The first groupings had overlapping memberships: as a matter of fact, the third political group was merely an expansion of the first.

Political integration

Initially, the main purpose which led these countries into alliances was their concern over one or more political issues; economic cooperation seems to have occupied second rank. The first group was the African and Malagasy Union, otherwise called Brazzaville group. It included the following twelve independent African states: Cameroon, Central African Republic, Chad, Congo, Dahomey, Gabon, Ivory Coast, Malagasy, Mauritania, Niger, Senegal and Upper Volta. All of them former French colonies, they met for the first time early in 1961, at the invitation of the president of the Ivory Coast.

The second group was the Union of African States, or the so-called Casablanca group which first held a summit meeting of heads of states at Casablanca, in January 1961, at the invitation of the king of Morocco, for the purpose of co-ordinating their policy on the Congo and of considering a suggestion for the formation of an African high military command. The member states of this group were: Algeria, Ghana, Guinea, Mali, Morocco and the United Arab Republic; Ghana, Guinea and Mali left the group subsequently to form one of their own.

The third group includes the Brazzaville group states plus seven other states which are: Zaire, Ethiopia, Liberia, Nigeria, Sierra Leone, Somalia and Togo. With the exception of the first, they all met at Monrovia in May 1961; the meeting was sponsored by the

Presidents of Liberia, Senegal and Togo. The purpose of
the meeting was to consider the means of achieving African
unity, dealing with threats to peace and stability in
Africa, and the contribution of African states toward
world peace. This group was known as the Inter-African
and Malagasy States Organization, or the Monrovia group;
its more recent name is the 'Union Africaine et Malgache'.
Its charter concentrates more than that of the other
groups, on cooperation in economic and cultural matters,
as well as in the fields of health and scientific research. The creation of an African Common Market was
also implied. The group has also been successful since
its creation in mediating disputes between its member
states.

Economic Integration

As they consolidated their political entity,
the new African nations started looking towards economic
integration: regional customs unions which already
existed since colonial times were developed further,
others were created. The main objective was to pool
their utilities, e.g. means of communications, to get
access to areas of production and to ports, to eliminate
trade barriers, and to generally integrate their economic
policies.

The Central African Customs and Economic Union
was created as early as 1959 under the name of Equatorial
Customs Union and changed to its present name when its
terms of reference were enlarged to include free movement
of labor and the unification of investment legislation;
its members were the four equatorial states of the Central
African Republic, the Congo, Chad, Gabon, and also
Cameroon. They share a common monetary system and

central bank, common import duties and customs services, free movement of goods and capital between the member states, and coordinated fiscal policies. This union has two important features: the first is the "single tax", an overall tax on production levied from enterprises who market their output into two or more of the member states, and which has replaced all import duties and other indirect taxes; the other feature is the "Solidarity Fund" created to compensate the landlocked countries of Central African Republic and Chad for duty paid on goods cleared in the coast member states and re-exported to them.[4] Early in 1968, a parallel group, the Economic Union of Central African States including the Central African Republic, Chad and the Congo was created, but the first of these states withdrew eight months later.

The Customs Union of West African States was first formulated in 1959 but really established in 1966; its charter provided for a common external tariff and for uniformity in customs legislation and regulations between its seven members who were: Dahomey, Ivory Coast, Mali, Mauritania, Niger, Togo and Upper Volta. In May 1970, at a meeting attended by the rulers of the seven countries, it was decided to broaden the terms of reference of the customs union to include the improvement and coordination of infrastructure facilities and industrial projects, as well as the promotion of commercial exchange between its members. Its name was changed to the West African Economic Union.[5]

---

[4] I.M.F., International Financial News Survey, No. 2, Vol. XVIII, p. 9 and No. 17, Vol. XX, p. 140.

[5] I.M.F., International Financial News Survey, No. 36, Vol. XXII, p. 294.

The United States A.I.D. gave a 40-year $6 million loan to the Mutual Aid and Loan Guaranty Fund of the Union, to help establish a common market for meat and improve livestock production.[6] The loan is part of a 4-year coordinated effort by the European Development Fund and other donors for improved regional production, transportation and marketing of livestock in these countries.[7]

In December 1967, the East African Common Services Organization, a relic from the time of British rule, was replaced by the East African Economic Community and Common Market which came into being after signature of a 15-year treaty by the Heads of State of Kenya, Tanzania and Uganda. The headquarters of the Union were moved from Nairobi (Kenya) to Arusha (Tanzania) and it was decided to create an East African Development Bank. Railways, Harbors and Posts and Telecommunications for the three countries are handled jointly for the three countries by one separate corporation each.

The bases of the treaty were the following: 1) to maintain a common customs tariff against imports into East Africa; 2) to guarantee free movement of goods between the three countries, except for a "transfer tax" which may be imposed on specified manufactured goods, for a maximum period of 8 years, by a state which has a deficit in its total trade with the other two; 3) to prepare for the introduction of a common excise tariff.[8]

------

[6]A.I.D., Press Release, March 3, 1971, Washington, D.C.
[7]I.M.F., International Financial News Survey, No. 11, Vol. XXIII, p. 86.
[8]see I.M.F., International Financial News Survey, No. 23, Vol. XIX, p. 181 and Barclays Bank Overseas Survey, 1968, p. 76.

The East African Development Bank started operations in July 1968 with an authorized capital of $33.6
million and has been extending loans to finance industrial
projects in the three member countries.

At the request of the East African countries,
the World Bank constituted a Consultative Group on capital and technical assistance to East Africa, the first
of its kind, which met for the time in Paris in April
1968 and has had several meetings since. The group includes Canada, Denmark, Finland, France, Germany, Italy,
the Netherlands, Norway, Sweden, the United Kingdom and
the United States; it also includes representatives of
the International Monetary Fund, the United Nations Development Program, the African Development Bank, the three
countries concerned and the East African Community.[9]

The various customs and economic unions discussed above were dictated mainly by common boundaries
and the landlocked situation of some of the member
states, rather than by the needs of trade. As a matter
of fact, there is little in the way of commercial exchange between the various African countries, no doubt
because of the lack of complementarity and diversification
of their respective output.

Trade Conventions and Economic Development

The Convention signed in Yaoundé, Cameroon,
between the European Economic Community and eighteen
African nations in July 1963, is the most important
agreement of its kind with developing countries, not
only in Africa but also in other parts of the world.
The Convention which came into force in June 1964, for a

---

[9] I.M.F., International Financial News Survey, No. 18,
Vol. XX, p. 150.

period of five years, after ratification by all countries
concerned, granted duty free entry into the EEC countries
to such African commodities as coffee, cocoa, pineapples,
tea, pepper, vanilla, cloves, nutmeg and tropical woods
(timber).   In return, the African countries were first
to eliminate all discrimination in their tariffs, and to
abandon quantitative restrictions, on imports from the
EEC countries.   This was to lead gradually to a reciprocal duty free status granted to imports from the EEC
countries.   Exceptions from these privileges were provided in certain specified cases, such as the need for
protecting infant industries, to overcome balance of payments difficulties, or the need for additional revenue
for development.[10]

    Moreover, the African countries were to receive
during the five years of the agreement $230 million in
grants from the EEC Development Fund to partly compensate them for the loss of the privilege of support prices
in French markets which those of them who had been French
dependencies had enjoyed previously.   In addition, an
amount of $500 million, mostly in grants, was to be made
available by the European Development Fund, for social
and economic investment and technical assistance in the
African countries.   The states which thus became
associate members of the European Common Market were:
Burundi, Cameroon, Central African Republic, Chad, Congo,
Zaire, Dahomey, Gabon, Ivory Coast, the Malagasy
Republic, Mali, Mauritania, Niger, Rwanda, Senegal,
Somalia, Togo and Upper Volta.

---

[10] I.M.F., International Financial News Survey, No. 24,
Vol. XVI, p. 201.

The second Yaoundé Convention was signed in
July 1969 and became operative in January 1971, after
ratification by all parties; it will expire on January
31st 1975. This convention carries mutual exemption
from tariffs and quantitative restrictions on both sides,
with the previous exceptions favoring the African countries, plus cases of commodities coming under the regulation of an international commodity agreement, or of a
customs union or a free trade area agreement with other
developing countries. Likewise, the EEC states have retained the right to impose some restrictions on certain
processed agricultural products. The financial assistance to be granted under Yaoundé II has been fixed at
$918 million, during the period expiring on January 31st
1975, with particular emphasis this time on aid to industrial and infrastructure projects. In return, each
member state of the European Common Market has equal
rights of establishing business enterprises and of investing in the African countries. Movement of capital
between both sides is also to be free of restrictions.
Finally, access to the institutions of the EEC, such as
the International Court of Justice, has been made available to the African countries for solving any problems
which may arise and for airing their views.[11]

The Convention signed in Arusha, Tanzania, between the EEC member states and the countries of the East
African Union (Kenya, Tanzania and Uganda) also came into
force on January 1st 1971 and will expire on January 31st
1975. It provides for a free trade area between the EEC
and the three East African countries and while its

[11]Barclays Bank, Overseas Review "The EEC and Tropical
Africa", January 1971, pp. 3-4.

provisions are generally similar to those of the Yaoundé Convention, they are more limited in scope. First, this agreement does not carry financial aid, although the free movement of capital, the right to establish businesses and to invest, are retained. Second, quotas have been set by the European Common Market for some "sensitive" products such as coffee, cloves and preserved pineapples, from the East African countries.

Finally, the African Development Bank, created in 1965 and including about 30 African states among its members, has been active in promoting economic development among its members, by trying to solve some of the problems confronting them. More particularly, the Bank is giving emphasis to the problem of the declining prices of primary products on world markets for which the suggested solutions are the improvement and diversification of agricultural production as well as the promotion of import substituting industries. The Bank is also studying means to increase tourism to its member states.

REFERENCES

1. Barzanti, Sergio, The Underdeveloped Areas within the Common Market. Princeton University Press, 1968.

2. Benveniste, Guy, Handbook of African Development. Published for the Stanford Research Institute by Praeger, 1962.

3. Boyd, A. & Kirk, H., An Atlas of African Affairs. Praeger, 1965.

4. ECA/UNESCO, The Development of Higher Education in Africa. New York: UNESCO, 1962.

5. Ewing, A. F., Industry in Africa. London: Oxford University Press, 1968.

6. Ginzberg, Eli, Manpower Strategy for Developing Countries: Lessons from Ethiopia. Columbia University Press, 1967.

7. Hailey, Wm. M., An African Survey: a study of problems arising in Africa south of the Sahara. Oxford University Press, 1963.

8. Hance, Wm. A., African Economic Development. Praeger, 1967.

9. Harbinson and Myers, Manpower and Education. New York, 1965.

10. International Monetary Fund, Surveys of African Economies, Vol. 3, 1960.

11. Junod, Violaine (ed.), The Handbook of Africa. New York University Press, 1963.

12. Kamarck, Andrew M., The Economics of African Development. Praeger, 1967.

13. Legum, Colin, Africa: a Handbook to the Continent. Praeger, 1966.

14. Oser, Jacob, Promoting Economic Development: with illustrations from Kenya. Northwestern University Press, 1967.

15. Plessz, Nicholas G., Problems and Prospects of Economic Integration in West Africa. McGill University Press, 1966.

16. Robinson, E.A.G., Economic Development for Africa South of the Sahara. New York: St. Martin's Press, 1964.

17. U.N.E.S.C.O., An African Experiment in Radio Forums for Rural Development, 1968.

18. Whetham, Edith H., Readings in the Applied Economics of Africa. Cambridge University Press, 1967.

19. Woolf, Leonard S., Empire and Commerce in Africa: a study in economic imperialism. Fertig, 1968.

20. Yudelman, Montague, Africans on the Land. Harvard University Press, 1964.

Periodicals

1. Africa Report, Institute of African-American Relations, Washington, D. C.

2. African Affairs, Journal of the Royal African Society, London.

3. African Studies Bulletin, Royal African Society, London.

CHAPTER XVI

AFRICA SOUTH OF THE SAHARA:
TECHNICAL COOPERATION AND ECONOMIC DEVELOPMENT

In Chapter XV, the brief review of natural
resources in sub-Sahara Africa showed that it has a
sizable supply of them and that adequate exploitation
and development would bring forth more resources.   It
was also seen that means of communications between
various parts of the continent were either greatly inadequate or non-existent and that the efforts made to
develop highways and railroads are of recent origin.
Not least among the resources of the African continent,
are the various great rivers which, given adequate flood
control, form a potential network of waterways supplemen-
ted by lakes.   The water can be harnessed to bring more
land under cultivation by means of irrigation schemes,
and to provide cheap hydro-electric power for domestic
industries.   This chapter will study first the use which
is being made of water resources through the various
schemes initiated.   It will then cover the projects
under way to connect, by means of highways and roads,
various parts of the continent with each other.   Third,
the chapter will review the actual and expected impact
of the above realizations on economic development per se,
either in agricultural output or in the creation of new
industries.   Next, a very short review of the plan to
increase and improve education opportunities in Africa
will follow.   Thus, technical cooperation will be studied
through its extension and manifestations, rather than as
an end in itself.   Finally, the foreign trade data of the
countries studied will be briefly examined.

Harnessing Water Resources

Potential hydro-electric power resources in
Africa are considered to be equal to just slightly less
than half the world total.   While South Africa has large
supplies of coal to provide thermal power, and North
Africa - mainly Algeria and Libya - has sizable reserves
of natural gas, the other African states have to rely on
hydro-electric projects to provide cheap power for their
budding industries.

The largest scheme of its kind in Africa so
far, is the $450.0 million hydro-electric, irrigation
and navigation project on the Zambesi River in Cabora
Bassa in Western Mozambique, managed by the Commission
on Development and Settlement for the Zambesi, a body
somewhat similar to the U.S. Tennessee Valley Authority.
Apart from Mozambique, the mammoth project will also
benefit Rhodesia, Zambia, Malawi, Swaziland, Lesotho,
Botswana, Zaire and Angola.   It will bring an area of
about 3.5 million acres under irrigation; hydro-electric
power supply will start at 1,200 megawatts in 1975, and
will be developed to reach 18,000 megawatts in its final
stage.   Financing is provided by the ZAMCO Consortium
which includes German, French, Italian and South African,
as well as Portuguese investments - the latter accounting
for about 40 per cent of the total.

Spanning the same river, is the Kariba Dam
project, the first stage of which was completed in 1960:
a 705 megawatt power station provides power for both
Zambia and Southern Rhodesia by means of a 330 kilovolt
transmission system.   The second phase of the project
includes the construction of a 600 megawatt power station
on the north bank of the river.   A major part of the

financing was covered by loans from the World Bank which
gave $88 million for the first phase and $40.0 million
for the second.

In the same region but further to the east, is
the smaller Tedzani hydro-electric project in Malawi on
which work started in the middle of 1970.   Two Austrian
firms as well as British, Japanese and Swiss companies
are involved in it and it is expected to be completed by
early 1973, when it will provide 16,000 kilowatts of
additional power yearly.   The foreign exchange disbursements for the scheme, amounting to $8.25 million, are
financed by the International Development Association and
the African Development Bank.

Still further to the northeast, is the power
project at Kidatu on the Great Ruaha River in Tanzania:
a 25-year loan of $30 million from the World Bank at $7\frac{1}{4}$
per cent plus a 50-year loan from Sweden for $12 million
at a service charge of 3/4 per cent have been obtained
for the first stage of this project.

Further northwest, in the Sudan, two dams on
the Blue Nile, the Roseires dam and the Khashm el Girba
were completed in 1966 making it possible to bring an
area of more than one million acres under cultivation.
Most of the financing for foreign exchange came from the
World Bank, while the hydro-electric power works have
been carried out by British firms.   The Sudan government
is financing the development of the new land under the
Rahad Agricultural scheme, for which aid is also provided
by the U.S.S.R.

In West Africa, the oldest project is the Volta
River dam at Akosombo, Ghana, started in October 1960 and
completed in February 1966.   Electric power which began

to flow from the dam in September 1966 is to reach 580
megawatts at capacity and is to be developed ultimately
to 768 megawatts.   The main purpose of the dam was to
provide electric power for the Volta Aluminium Company
(VALCO), a smelter with a planned capacity of 145,000
tons per year, which consumes about 300,000 kilowatts of
electricity for which it pays the Ghana government around
$7 million yearly.   The estimated cost of the smelter is
$130 million; of this amount, Kaiser Aluminium and Chem-
ical Corporation and Reynolds Metals Company contributed
about $30 million and the balance came from the U.S. Ex-
port-Import Bank.   Otherwise, the Volta lake thus created
is also being used for transport between north and south
Ghana, especially for cargo.

In Liberia, the capacity of the hydro-electric
plant at Mt. Coffee was doubled in 1970 at a total cost
of $10 million of which a World Bank 20-year loan of $7.4
million at 7 per cent interest.   The consultants for the
project were financed by the U.S. Agency for International
Development.

In Cameroon, low cost hydro-electric power is
obtained from the Edea Falls to provide energy to the
ALUCAM aluminium smelter which was financed by an international group.

As regards navigable waterways, the Congo river
and its tributaries which account for about half the water
potential in Africa, provide about 8,000 miles of almost
entirely navigable waterways except where they are obstructed by rapids.   The Nile river, the longest in the
world, is navigable only in parts where the cataracts do
not interfere.   Finally, the Niger river in west Africa,
the great lakes in east Africa, lake Chad in the midst of

the Sahara desert, and the artificial lakes created by
the large irrigation schemes, also provide additional,
though limited means of communication.

Roads and Communications

As the developing countries in sub-Sahara Africa
come to grips with the problem of increasing their output,
either for export promotion or import substitution, they
find that their most pressing need is for means of communication to connect areas of production with markets
and ports.   This applies more particularly to the landlocked countries who lose as much as 35 per cent of the
proceeds from the sale of their exports in overland
freight charges.   Moreover, as these countries make more
use of the outlets provided by their neighbors on the
coast, the latter have to strengthen their communications
system to support the heavier traffic.   Consequently, it
is not surprising that the largest number of loans and
credits extended during the last ten years to African
countries by multilateral agencies or industrialized
countries - more particularly France and the United
States - has been for highway construction, road improvement and maintenance, or the building of railroad lines.
The multilateral agencies most involved in these projects
are the World Bank whose loans carry an interest charge
of 7 per cent, its subsidiary the International Development Association whose loans are interest free and carry
only a service charge of 3/4 per cent, and the European
Development Fund of the European Economic Community.

On the West Coast, probably the largest project
is the Trans-Cameroon Railroad connecting the coast in
the south with the northern part of the country and to be
extended eventually across the border into Chad.   There,

a <u>highway</u> project linking the capital Fort Lamy which is on the Cameroon border, with the lush Lake Chad agricultural area, is under construction, to stimulate its development by bringing it within reach of markets. The railroad which is Cameroon's largest social overhead capital project, will cost when completed about $100 million to which the largest single contribution is from the European Development Fund, followed by the World Bank, the IDA, the United States and France. Local expenditure on the project is borne by the Cameroon government. The cost of the Chad highway is about $10 million of which $4.1 million is lent by the IDA and the balance will come from the Chad government.

A new <u>railway line</u> in <u>Gabon</u> will connect the new port of Owendo in the south with Belinga in the northeast and the newly discovered deposits of high grade iron ore estimated at 850 million tons, as well as large timber resources. A number of various new industries will also be built along the railway line. The railway project will cost $133 million plus $29 million for rolling stock. About $13 million of this amount have come in a loan from the IDA and technical assistance in feasibility studies was furnished by the United Nations Development Fund. A parallel project for a <u>highway</u> will cost about $10 million in foreign exchange contributed by the European Development Fund, France and Germany.

<u>Nigeria</u> is carrying out a $35 million project for maintenance and improvement of <u>roads</u> connecting Port Harcourt on the coast with the inland part. A loan of $25 million from the World Bank will supply the larger part of the cost of this project, as well as the technical studies necessary. In the <u>Ivory Coast</u>, a <u>road network</u>

connecting the port of Abidjan with the hinterland which
will cost over $10 million, is financed partly by a loan
of $5.8 million by the World Bank.   Feasibility studies
for this project and others to improve the transport
sector have been carried out by the World Bank and the
United Nations Development Fund.   In Mali, 250 miles of
trunk roads are being built and 900 miles of existing
ones are being improved to connect the landlocked country
with Guinea and Senegal for the transport of foreign
trade, at a cost of over $10 million, of which an IDA
loan of $7.7 million and technical aid from Mainland
China.

Other countries who are carrying out similar
projects, with loans from the IDA are: Dahomey whose
highway extension is mainly to provide an outlet for
landlocked Niger; Senegal, a highway to improve access
to its groundnut production area; the Congo, to re-
inforce the road connecting Pointe Noire, the country's
seaport, and Brazzaville, the capital, and passing by
its potash mines, oil refinery and rich agricultural
area; the Central African Republic, to link its capital
Bangui with the Libreville port in Gabon and also with
Senegal for transport of its foreign trade; Mauritania,
to connect its capital Nouakchott, by means of a 250-kms.
road, with newly discovered copper deposits inland.
Finally, the Zaire has obtained a $2.2 million Eximbank
loan and a $2.5 million guaranteed loan from a United
States commercial bank, for the construction of a communications satellite earth station.

Trends and Achievements in Industrialization

Four trends in economic activity can be distinguished in the impact of the various efforts in harnessing

water resources, for irrigation and for the creation of
cheap power, and also in improving means of communication
and transport.   The four trends are the following:
1) the speeded-up exploitation of existing natural resources;   2) the creation of import substitution industries;   3) the diversification of output for both consumption and export, by processing the country's primary
commodities, and 4) the emphasis on expanding and improving productivity in the agricultural sector.   The
following brief survey will give an idea of how sub-
Sahara Africa is finally becoming conscious of its great
potential.

Exploitation of Natural Resources.   In the
speeded-up exploitation of existing natural resources a
distinction will be made between agricultural and mineral
resources.   Under the first, the most important is the
project for the exploitation of large forest areas in
eastern Gabon for which a survey by a French firm and
the United Nations Development Program has been carried
out at a cost of $1 million.   The project will be im-
plemented by the Food and Agriculture Organization; a 20-
year, $6 million loan was obtained from the World Bank
for building transport and communications facilities
across the area to be developed.   Another afforestation
project is being carried out in Zambia with the help of a
25-year, $5.3 million loan from the World Bank.   The IDA
is giving Uganda a $4 million dollar loan to expand pro-
duction of flue-cured tobacco which is grown by several
thousand small farmers, thus helping to raise their income.   In Upper Volta, an IDA 60-year loan of $6.2
million will help expand the area planted to cotton and
to improve yields.

Expansion of mineral resources includes copper production in <u>Zaire</u>, which is to reach 460,000 tons a year in 1974; the development of high grade bauxite, near Boké in northwest <u>Guinea</u>, with the help of the World Bank and the U.S. Agency for International Development. In <u>Niger</u>, uranium deposits estimated at 30,000 tons are being developed with the assistance of the French Atomic Energy Commission and a Japanese Consortium. The estimated annual yield is 1,500 tons of uranium concentrate which will be shared in equal parts by the two developers and the Niger government. Oil deposits off the <u>Gabon</u> shore are exploited by French, American and British firms in partnership with the government. In the <u>Malagasy Republic</u>, Tamatave the most important port, has been enlarged to cope with the increased exports of petroleum products and chrome ore from recently developed deposits, with an IDA credit of $9.6 million and technical assistance from the World Bank. Marble deposits in <u>Togo</u> are being extracted by an Italian firm after a survey by the U.N. Development Fund. In <u>Mozambique</u>, the Mirrote iron ore mines, believed to be among the most extensive in the world, are being developed by the Japanese Sumitomo group.

<u>New industries</u>. In the trend towards import substitution industries figure <u>Nigeria's</u> efforts towards industrial development: food, metal production, radios, footwear and paper industries are being encouraged with priority given to indigenous firms. <u>Uganda</u> expanded its cement industry at a cost of $10 million - a British firm was the main developer; newly created industries include a refrigeration assembly plant, meat canning, ceramics and printing. <u>Kenya</u> instituted its first steel rolling mill at a cost of about $3 million with a starting

capacity yearly of 36,000 tons of rolled steel bars; a new industrial steel complex is planned. The Ivory Coast built a sugar refinery of a yearly capacity of 40,000 tons. In the Congo, a government-owned textile factory was inaugurated in 1969; it was built at a cost of $5.4 million, with help from Mainland China. Cotton growing is planned to provide raw material for the factory which now relies on imported cotton.

In the category of export diversification industries, should be included the new spinning mill in Uganda, built with equipment and technicians from the U.S.S.R. at a cost of $12.6 million; Zambia's newly erected plant for the production of copper rods, at a cost of $3.5 million, which is to be the nucleus of a manufacturing group using copper as raw material; the new plant in Cameroon, producing 680 tons yearly of packed and cleaned-up shrimp with help from a U.S. concern, and Gabon's factory for the production of fertilizers and other chemical products, with the use of local natural gas resources, at a cost of $90 million.

Agricultural expansion. Finally, the emphasis on improving productivity in the agricultural sector is seen in Ghana's efforts to increase the yield of cocoa, its main cash crop, to realize an addition of 19,000 tons to total output by 1982 in the eastern region; Senegal's and Niger's farm credit programs to raise production of groundnuts, also their main cash crop; and the Malagasy Republic's irrigation program to increase rice production. In Ethiopia and Tanzania, the performance of the rural sector is being improved by means of village community projects providing infrastructure such as roads, water supply systems and the creation of agro-industrial economic units.

Education

With an illiteracy rate of about 80 per cent, Africa as a continent has the highest such rate compared to the other continents. As recently as the late 1950's the participation rates at the primary school level were comparatively low, mainly because of the insufficient number of such institutions. At the secondary school and higher education levels the participation rates were the lowest in the world. In May 1961, the Conference on the Development of Education in Africa called by the United Nations Educational, Scientific and Cultural Organization (UNESCO) and Economic Commission for Africa (ECA) in Addis Abeba, Ethiopia, was attended by delegates from North African countries. At this conference a 20-year (1960-1980) plan was adopted recommending to raise enrollment in the primary schools from 40 per cent of total children of primary school age in 1961, to 100 per cent in 1980; from 3 per cent in 1961 to 23 per cent in 1980 for secondary schools; and to attempt to keep college attendance at the 1961 level of 0.2 per cent through the period of the plan, notwithstanding the increase in population.[1]

Following the adoption of the Plan, a second conference was called in Paris by the ECA and UNESCO in March 1962 to discuss its implementation and means of financing. Implementing the plan had been estimated to gradually raise expenditure on education in African countries from $590 million in 1960 to over $2.6 billion in 1980. The expansion of secondary schools, the training

---

[1] ECA/UNESCO, The Development of Higher Education in Africa, New York: UNESCO, 1962.

of teachers for both primary and secondary schools, the
provision of textbooks in English, French and some
African languages, seemed to be the most important priorities then established. A permanent body, the Conference of Ministers of Education, was created; its terms
of reference were to study and recommend means of improving the educational system and to report at its bi-
yearly meetings on the progress achieved in implementing
the plan. Subsequent meetings were concerned with the
standardization of secondary education, adult literacy
and the means to promote higher education opportunities
and the training of adequate academic instructors.

The achievements of the Plan will, therefore,
have to be assessed from a dual angle: the availability
of teachers at every level of education and the additions
to the number of educated people in the countries concerned.

Foreign Trade

The foreign trade data appearing in table XVI/1
lend themselves to some observations. The first is the
low magnitude of the African countries' exports - with
the exception of Zambia, Nigeria, Zaire, Ivory Coast,
Angola, Southern Rhodesia, Sudan, Tanzania and Cameroon -
notwithstanding the large contribution that these exports
make to their G.D.P.; this is yet another indicator that
they have not yet reached their optimum production, or
consumption, that is, in the Western sense. The second
point is that although the rate of growth of most of
these nations' exports is above the world average, they
almost all continue to register deficits in their commodity trade balance, which means that their imports have
increased at a still higher rate than their exports.

Table XVI/1

AFRICA SOUTH OF THE SAHARA: FOREIGN TRADE

(Million dollars) Country	Exports fob 1958	Exports fob 1969	Imports cif 1958	Imports cif 1969	Surplus or Deficit 1958	Surplus or Deficit 1969	Export Growth % p.a.
Angola	128	327	130	322	− 2	5	14.1
Cameroon	115	230	107	207	8	23	9.0
Cent. Afr. Republic	16	34	20	36	− 4	− 2	10.2
Chad	25	29	28	50	− 3	−21	1.4
Congo	14	41	58	99	−44	−58	17.5
Zaire	406	644	362	410	44	234	5.3
Dahomey	15[a]	24	18[a]	50	− 3	−26	5.4
Ethiopia	63	119	75	155	−12	−36	8.1
Gabon	39	133	35	73[b]	4	60	21.9
Gambia	5	12[b]	8	17[b]	− 3	− 5	14.0
Ghana	263	302	237	347[b]	−26	−45	1.3
Guinea	23[c]	44[b]	47[c]	27[b]	−24	17	10.0
Ivory Coast	151	455	120	337	31	118	18.3
Kenya	93	191	120	327	−27	−136	9.0
Liberia	68	196	391	115	−323	81	17.0
Malagasy	96	114	126	180	−30	−66	1.7
Malawi		53		83		−30	
Mali	6[a]	16	15[a]	36	− 9	−20	16.6
Mauritius	61	66	63	68	− 2	− 2	.74
Mozambique	71	142	115	261	−41	−119	9.1
Niger	13[a]	23	14[a]	45	− 1	−22	8.7
Nigeria	380	891	467	696	−87	195	12.0
Reunion	32	46	48	144	−16	−98	4.3
Senegal	137	124	208	197	−71	−73	.8
Sierra Leone	55	106	67	112	−12	− 6	8.6
Somalia	16	32	12	52	4	−19	9.1
Southern Rhodesia		318		313		5	
Sudan	124	248	171	266	−47	−18	9.0
Tanzania	121	236	94	199	27	37	8.4
Togo	15	41	18	52	− 3	−11	15.7
Uganda	130	206	76	127	54	79	5.3
Upper Volta	7[a]	19	7[a]	46		−27	19.0
Zambia		1073		492		581	

Sources: International Monetary Fund, International Financial Statistics: Trade and Country Pages, and Direction of Trade, relevant issues.

[a]1960.   [b]1968.   [c]1959.

Third, because none of these countries owns any merchant marine, foreign trade data showing exports f.o.b. and imports c.i.f. minimize the value of the former and magnify that of the latter; in other words, the cost of freight works against the developing countries both ways.

As regards the <u>composition</u> of their exports, this reflects again the great variety of their resources. Items such as bauxite, manganese, petroleum, uranium and cobalt, are comparative newcomers as exports because, except for a fortunate few, most of these states depend each on one or two crops or minerals for a sizable proportion of their exports. As in the case of other developing countries, the tropical African states' ability to finance their imports with proceeds from their exports, to service and repay foreign loans and remit earnings on foreign investments, depends on increasing and diversifying their exports which up to now still reflect the pattern established under colonial rule.

AFRICA SOUTH OF THE SAHARA
Topics for Reading and Research

1. <u>Natural and mineral resources</u>: for export and for development.

2. <u>Investments in irrigation projects</u>: location, cost, and scope.

3. <u>Investments in industrial projects</u>: social overhead capital and manufacturing.

4. <u>Foreign private investments</u>: scope and magnitude.

5. <u>Electric power consumption</u>: needs for development.

6. <u>African states' affiliation with the European Economic Community</u>: its effect on development.

7. <u>Technical cooperation in Africa</u>: education and transportation.

8. <u>Foreign trade</u>: composition, direction, value and effect on development.

9. <u>Economic integration</u>: achievements and shortcomings.

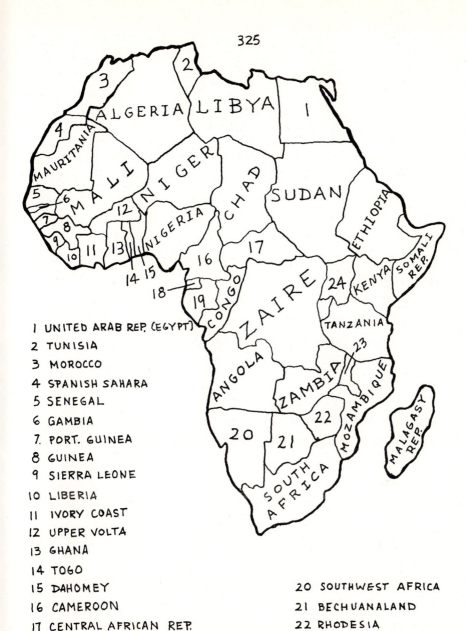

1 UNITED ARAB REP. (EGYPT)
2 TUNISIA
3 MOROCCO
4 SPANISH SAHARA
5 SENEGAL
6 GAMBIA
7. PORT. GUINEA
8 GUINEA
9 SIERRA LEONE
10 LIBERIA
11 IVORY COAST
12 UPPER VOLTA
13 GHANA
14 TOGO
15 DAHOMEY
16 CAMEROON
17 CENTRAL AFRICAN REP.
18 EQUATORIAL GUINEA
19 GABON

20 SOUTHWEST AFRICA
21 BECHUANALAND
22 RHODESIA
23 MALAWI
24 UGANDA

A F R I C A

mjt

CHAPTER XVII

SOUTHEAST ASIA:
RESOURCES AND DEVELOPMENT PATTERNS

The countries covered in this and the following
chapter are the following: Burma, Cambodia, China (Taiwan), Indonesia, Laos, Malaysia, the Philippines, Singapore, Thailand and Vietnam (South).   Information and
data will also be given, for purposes of comparison,
about Ceylon which is in South Asia, and Korea (South)
and Japan which are in East Asia.   The states of Southeast Asia present several characteristics as a group,
some of which have not been encountered yet in the foregoing studies made of developing countries: several of
these nations are not only islands, or groups of islands,
but one, Malaysia, is made up of parts of two islands;
at least three of them are, at the time of writing, involved in a devastating war which makes the availability
of up-to-date accurate data difficult; they vary greatly
in size and in economic structure: some have almost all
the productive capacity that they need, while others are
still in the early stages of capital formation; finally,
they present enormous differentials in per capita g.d.p.
levels which vary from $72.0 in Laos, to $774.0 in
Singapore.

Except for Thailand, most of the states of
Southeast Asia were, until about the middle of the twentieth century, under colonial rule; the latter, which
differed between one great power and another, generally
influenced their form of government and more especially
their outlook regarding the respective roles of the state
and of the market in their economies.   Besides the

colonial impact, there were the very strong influences
exerted by their two giant neighbors, namely India and
Mainland China, whose nationals make up a sizable proportion of the population in most of these countries.
These mixed influences, together with natural conditions,
have generated development strategies which greatly differ between one country and another in their attitude to
aid, trade, political institutions and the requirements
of technical assistance.

　　　　As regards aid, attitudes include Burma's
categorical refusal and Cambodia's sometime qualified
acceptance of it, as well as the all-out seeking of aid
by the others.　The various countries' trade comprises
either only one or two primary commodities, as in the
case of Burma, Cambodia and Indonesia, or diversified
exports in which manufactured goods constitute an increasingly larger proportion, as in the case of Singapore
primarily and to a lesser extent Thailand, Malaysia and
the Philippines.　Political institutions range, in their
bearing on economic development, from socialized planned
economies hemmed in with restrictions on trade and exchange, such as in Burma, Taiwan and South Vietnam, to a
completely free market center for exchange as in Singapore and to a lesser extent, Malaysia.　Finally, requirements for technical assistance follow the pattern of
economic development, and no common attitude to the rest
of the world can be detected in the countries studied;
nor is there yet any attempt at economic integration.
Future outlook is promising, though, because of the rising
demand for the natural resources of this region -
provided a much needed improvement and coordination of
administrative and fiscal systems can be achieved.　Such

a step would pave the way for more foreign capital investment in primary production.

Basic Data and Resources

The area for each country as well as comparative population data with respective rate of growth, are
given in table XVII/1.   The rate of population increase
tends to be more than 3 per cent for about half the
countries studied, and not much below it for the others,
which is very high for a developing economy.   If one
compares area and population data, it will be noticed
that population density differs a great deal between
Singapore where it is very high (over two thousand inhabitants per square mile) and Laos where it is barely
8 inhabitants per square mile.   It differs also within
countries such as in Indonesia where the key island of
Java is as densely populated as Singapore, while the
other islands are sparsely inhabited.   Indonesia is
almost as big, in area and population, as all the other
countries of Southeast Asia put together.   Because of
wars, migratory movements and changes of political boundaries, population statistics may not be absolutely reliable and should, therefore, be considered to indicate
trends rather than specific magnitudes.

Table XVII/2 gives data about total and per
capita gross domestic product and the rate of growth of
the latter, over a period of eleven years.   The data
are taken from United Nations sources and are, therefore,
as accurate as any could be under the circumstances.
However, here also the statistics are really more meaningful in showing comparative size and trends.   For instance, we find that Singapore has a per capita G.D.P.

Table XVII/1

SOUTHEAST ASIA: AREA AND POPULATION

Country	Area in sq. miles[a]	Population (000)[b] 1958	1969	Av.rate of growth p.a. %
Burma	261,789	21,529	26,980	2.2
Cambodia	69,898	5,140	6,701	2.7
China (Taiwan)	13,885	9,851	13,800	3.6
Indonesia	735,268	89,441	116,600	2.5
Laos	91,428	2,283	2,893	2.4
Malaysia	128,429	7,629	10,581	3.5
Philippines	115,830	25,795	37,178	4.0
Singapore	225	1,514	2,017	3.0
Thailand	198,455	24,873	34,738	3.5
Vietnam (South)	65,726	12,935	17,867	3.4
Ceylon	25,332	9,388	12,240	2.7
Korea (South)	38,004	23,330	31,130	3.0
Japan	143,000	91,540	102,321	1.0

Source: for population, United Nations, Monthly Bulletin
of Statistics, relevant issues; for area,
Agency for International Development, Economic
Growth Trends, Jan. 1971, pp. 10-11.

[a]area within recognized official boundaries.
[b]estimates at mid-year.

which places it almost at the line of demarcation between
development and underdevelopment; it is followed by
Malaysia, Taiwan and the Philippines, which stepped up
during the decades of the 1950's and the 1960's, their
rate of capital formation as well as their industrialization programs.   Laos and Burma, both with per capita
G.D.P.'s below $100.0 trail the group.

As regards average rates of growth of per
capita G.D.P., two contrasting points draw attention at
once and need to be explained. The first is the negative rate of economic growth appearing for Indonesia:
this rate reflects the phase of economic disorganization
and almost complete lack of capital formation that the
country went through after gaining its independence;
this trend was reversed in 1965 and recovery, under the
guidance of a consultative group including representatives
from the industrialized nations and the World Bank, is
slowly underway. The second point is the relatively
high rate (except of course for Japan, which is now a
highly developed nation) of 14 per cent appearing for
South Korea. The importance of this rate is magnified
when it is realized that it is mainly the result of the
very large gains in this country's gross domestic product
during the last three years of the period - the increase
for 1969 alone having been of the order of thirty per
cent. This rate is due partly to real growth resulting
from a vigorous program of capital formation (15 per cent
in 1965, 20 per cent in 1966, 21 per cent in 1967, 25 per
cent in 1968 and 27 per cent in 1969, of gross domestic
product), and partly to inflation. Apart from the two
extreme cases of Indonesia and South Korea, the differences in the rates of economic growth of the various
countries are just as wide as those in the level of per
capita G.D.P.: after South Korea, the highest rates were
registered by Taiwan, Thailand, Singapore and Cambodia;
the lowest, apart from Indonesia's negative rate, were in
South Vietnam, the Philippines, Ceylon and Burma.

Resources. The land/man ratio in East and
Southeast Asia is very low: agricultural land averages

Table XVII/2

SOUTHEAST ASIA: NATIONAL ACCOUNTS

Country	Gross Domestic Product Total in mn.$'s 1958	1969	Per capita in $'s 1958	1969	Av. rate of growth p.a. in p/cap.GDP %
Burma	1,317	1,790[a]	61	70[a]	1.6
Cambodia	660[b]	914[c]	115[b]	146[c]	6.7
China (Taiwan)	1,182	4,740	120	343	9.2
Indonesia	7,334	7,230[d]	82	64[d]	-2.8
Laos	168	208[d]	67	72[d]	0.75
Malaysia	1,602	3,660	210	346	5.9
Philippines	5,122	8,282	199	225	1.1
Singapore	668	1,564	441	774	6.8
Thailand	2,139	5,073[a]	86	150[a]	8.2
Vietnam (South)	2,360[e]	2,900[a]	167[e]	172[a]	0.6
Ceylon	1,234	1,830[d]	132	152[d]	1.5
Korea (South)	1,913	6,651	82	213	14.0
Japan	31,497	167,384	344	1,635	34.0

Sources: United Nations, Monthly Bulletin of Statistics,
          and International Monetary Fund, International
          Financial Statistics, relevant issues of both;
          data for Laos from U.S. Agency for International
          Development, Economic Growth Trends, 1967 and
          1971.

[a]1967. [b]1962. [c]1966. [d]1968. [e]1960.

Note: for the rates of exchange at which national cur-
       rencies were converted into U.S. dollars, please
       see table XVII/3. Data in pre-devaluation $'s.

0.5 acre per capita, compared with 5 acres in the United
States. As regards human resources, their overall literacy rate of 55 per cent for the whole area is comparatively high for developing countries; it is lowest in

Laos (15 per cent) and highest in Taiwan (78 per cent).[1]
Rubber and rice are the two most important primary commodities produced and exported: most of the former comes
from Malaysia and some from Thailand, Ceylon, Indonesia
and Vietnam; the latter is grown mainly in Indonesia,
Thailand and Burma.   Petroleum and natural gas products
from Indonesia, coal and tungsten from Korea, iron ore
from Malaysia, cement from China and Korea, and sugar
from the Philippines, are some of their most important
resources.

The industrial origin of the gross domestic
product differs to some extent between the countries
studied; however, except for Singapore, all of them are
still predominantly agrarian economies, in spite of the
efforts expanded by some countries for industrialization.

With such diversity in size, resource endowment, population density, degree of development and rate
of economic growth, plans and realizations between the
various countries are necessarily different.

Development Patterns

With the exception of Singapore, the agricultural sector in the countries studied provides employment
to between 60 and 90 per cent of the labor force and contributes between one third and one half of the gross domestic product.   In Burma, Cambodia, Indonesia and South
Vietnam, the transition from an agrarian economy to an
industrialized one has been slow and the contribution of
the manufacturing sector to total output has remained below twelve per cent.   However, the transition was faster

---

[1]Ceylon already had the second highest adult literacy
rate in 1950.

Table XVII/3

SOUTHEAST ASIA: RATES OF EXCHANGE

Country	National Currency	National Currency per U.S. $ 1958	1967	1969
Burma	Kyat	4.785	4.8	4.8
Cambodia	Riel	35.0	35.0	55.54
China (Taiwan)	T.Dollar	37.78	40.1	40.1
Indonesia	Rupiah	30.3	235.0	374.0
Laos	Kip	80.0	240.0	240.0
Malaysia	M.Dollar	3.06	3.07	3.09
Philippines	Peso	2.015	3.9	3.9
Singapore	S.Dollar	3.06	3.09	2.97
Thailand	Baht	21.10	20.8	21.0
Vietnam (South)	Piastre	35.0	117.5	117.5
Ceylon	Rupee	4.76	5.928	5.928
Korea (South)	Won	500.0	274.0	304.0
Japan	Yen	359.7	361.9	357.8

Sources: International Monetary Fund, International
Financial Statistics, Country pages, and
United Nations, Monthly Bulletin of Statistics,
Exchange rates, relevant numbers for both.

in Malaysia, the Philippines, Singapore and Thailand where
the contribution of the industrial sector to total output
varied from around twenty per cent in 1967 for Malaysia
to well over fifty per cent in Singapore.   This expansion was reflected in the composition of both exports
and imports, aspects of which are studied in the next
chapter.

The Lower Mekong River Basin Project

Foremost among development projects in Southeast Asia is the irrigation network based on the Lower

Mekong River which is to provide means of irrigation,
flood control, hydro-electric power and navigation.
One of the longest rivers in the world, the Mekong flows
2,600 miles, from its source in the Himalaya mountains
in Tibet to its mouth in South Vietnam.   It flows south
through Yunan province in mainland China, reaches Indochina and its lower basin at the common boundary of
China, Burma, and Laos, constituting the boundary between
the last two countries for over a distance of 130 miles.
Then, it alternates as a boundary between Laos and
Thailand and flowing within Laos, crosses Cambodia and
then South Vietnam from which it flows in the South China
sea, near Saigon.   Thus, the Lower Mekong which is the
object of the development program, has four riparian
states, Laos, Thailand, Cambodia and South Vietnam who
are the beneficiaries from the project.[2]   These countries are giving close collaboration and financial support to the United Nations Commission for Asia and the
Far East (ECAFE) who is the agency responsible for the
program.   At the same time, the project's great long-
term potential has attracted widespread international
interest and support: twenty-five countries including
the United States, and twelve international agencies had,
already in 1965, contributed or pledged an amount of over
$105 million of which about $38 million for the pre-
investment or feasibility study phase, and $67 million
for the actual investment phase.   By the end of 1969,
the total amount pledged had risen to $197.9 million of
which $142 million for investment in construction.
Table XVII/4 gives details of these contributions.

---

[2] Burma refused to participate in the project and mainland
China did not qualify, not being a member of the United
Nations.

A project of such magnitude requires numerous
and lengthy studies before it can be undertaken: there
was an ECAFE study in 1952, a study by the U.S. Bureau
of Reclamation in 1956, another ECAFE study in 1956, the
report of a United Nations Mission headed by Lt. General
Raymond Wheeler, formerly Chief of the U.S. Corps of
Engineers,[3] and including the best water resources experts available, in 1957, and finally the Ford Mission
in 1961.   Only massive international economic and technical cooperation could get the project started.   The
development of the Lower Mekong Basin includes the construction of a number of dams spanning either the river
itself or any of its tributaries.   The priority project
of the Mekong Committee is the <u>Nam Ngum Hydroelectric
Dam</u>, spanning the Ngum, a tributary of the Mekong, deep
in the Laotian jungle and halfway between Vientiane and
Long Tieng, near where most of the fighting in northern
central Laos has been taking place.   The project was
scheduled to begin supplying electric power early in
1972 with an initial output of 30,000 kilowatts[4] to be
shared by the Vientiane area and northern Thailand.
About half the cost of $30 million was borne by the
United States, of which $3.5 million on the Resources
Atlas of the Mekong River Basin prepared in the United
States.   The project manager, a Japanese engineer, has
been with the project for the ten years that it has taken
to complete; Japanese engineers and supervisors have
given on-the-spot training to Laotian workers, while

---

[3] a wizard who counts to his credit the unblocking of
the Suez Canal in 1957.

[4] to be developed to 120,000 kilowatts.

Table XVII/4

LOWER MEKONG RIVER BASIN PROJECT:

Operational Resources as at Dec. 31st 1969

(in million $'s)

Donor Countries	For Pre-Investment Studies	For Investment in Construction	Total
United States	16.7	16.6	33.4
West Germany	0.002	17.0	17.0
Japan	1.6	13.7	15.3
France	1.7	4.7	6.4
Netherlands	0.6	4.8	5.4
Canada	1.4	4.0	5.4
Australia	1.0	2.7	3.7
United Kingdom	0.3	1.7	2.1
Denmark	0.01	1.3	1.3
Italy	0.05	1.0	1.0
Others	2.9	1.0	3.9
Riparian States			
Cambodia	2.9	9.3	12.2
Laos	2.4	0.9	3.3
Thailand	8.3	52.3	60.6
Vietnam	2.0	11.0	13.0
International Organizations (of which UNDP 11.8)	13.6		13.6
Other Organizations	.2		.2
Grand Total	55.9	142.0	197.9

Source: Mekong Committee, Mekong Monthly Bulletin, vol. 3, Nov. - Dec. 1970.

seven Laotian engineers on the supervisory staff of the project studied in Canada, on scholarships from the

Canadian government.[5]   The project will supply Laos with
cheap power and enable it to industrialize.   It has also
given Laos its first large lake.

The next project to which the United States is
also contributing aid, is the Pa Mong Multipurpose Dam,
located near Vientiane in Laos and Nongkai in Thailand,
south of the Nam Ngum dam.   It is to be completed in
1972.   Still further to the south, the Nam Pong Dam in
Thailand, developed earlier with aid from the Asian Development Bank, provided the first international exchange
of electric power in the Lower Mekong Basin area when
power was transmitted from it to Laos, to help in the
construction of the Nam Ngum.   Thailand is now planning
a pioneer irrigation project for developing a 10,000-
hectare area around the Nam Pong River near Kon Kaen, the
regional center.   This will provide additional farmland
to the economically depressed northeast part of the country.

The Mekong river has been called the "sleeping
giant" because of its great potential.   The objectives
behind the various projects included in the development
program are mainly to increase the land under cultivation
by providing more water for irrigation, and to provide
the framework for industrialization by means of cheap
hydro-electric power.   Generally, then, the purpose was
to improve the standard of living of the more than 60
million people who live in the countries bordering on the
Lower Mekong.   Gradually, the regulation of the water
supply, which is a necessary measure of any well organized
irrigation project, will affect the methods of cultivation
of the farmers.   The ancillary projects connected with

[5] N.Y. Times, March 28th 1971, p. 19.

the scheme will provide employment and widen the market
for the products of the small village industries which
will then be created and these developments will also
bring changes in institutions and customs in the normal
transition from a subsistence agrarian society to a semi-
industrialized and commercialized one. Thus, the scheme
will come to be viewed in its broader context as a means
of realizing social and economic change. For a program of
this magnitude which has spurred international interest
and cooperation on such a large scale, the results are
expected to be in keeping with the bigness of the effort.

The Green Revolution

        The expansion in agriculture which is the
result of new intensive farming techniques combined with
the use of special hybrid seeds for the production of
corn, wheat and rice, has manifested itself in Southeast
Asia in the form of what is called "miracle rice."
This sudden abundance has had its drawbacks: it did
bring about a rapid expansion of rice production in countries, such as Laos, which depended heavily in the past
on rice imports, but it has also forced traditional rice
exporters such as Burma and Thailand, to effect major re-
adjustments in the structure of their economies. In its
report on Southeast Asia's economy in the 1970's, the
Asian Development Bank warns that the benefits from the
Green Revolution will be negated if the new techniques
are merely used to attain self-sufficiency in rice.
Moreover, the expanded output is coming from large farms
thus increasing their economic power; they buy up the
smaller holdings whose owners then go to swell the ranks
of the unemployed. In Malaysia, the government asked
the farmers to cut down on rice production so that only

90 per cent of the country's needs is raised locally;
the rest will be imported. The report suggests that
these techniques be used instead in raising agricultural
productivity by growing a succession of different crops;
thus, not only would the cost of rice production be
lowered, but the choice and availability of other foodstuffs would lower the cost of living and lead toward
diversification in production. Some of the new agricultural products could also be used as raw materials for
the planned small industries such as food processing,
textiles, etc... resulting in the addition of semi-
industrial commodities to total output.[6]

Offshore Oil

Next in the patterns of development, should be
mentioned the accelerated search for oil in Asian waters,
which started in the late 1960's. The range of the
search extends over the whole continental shelf of Asia,
running from the waters offshore Burma to the seas between China and Japan; it is carried out by more than
fifty oil companies who either hold concessions or are
still in the geological study stage. Australia and
Indonesia are the major oil producers in the area; the
latter which has the larger output, hopes to raise its
1970 production of about 900,000 barrels a day which was
mainly from inland wells, to more than a million barrels
a day with the added output to be obtained from offshore
wells.

---

[6] ASDB, Southeast Asia's Economy in the 1970's, Oct.
1, 1970 and Press Release, December 18, 1970, Manila.

Preliminary studies of the Vietnam offshore area have shown it to be a "good risk" and the Saigon government is trying to attract foreign oil firms to invest in more prospection. The waters offshore Burma, Malaysia, Thailand and Cambodia are still at the preliminary testing stage. China has invited foreign oil producers to explore its offshore waters, allowing a renewable period of four years for the survey and a renewable period of twenty years for oil tapping; exemptions from taxes on imports of equipment and on income are also offered. Firms are asked to either join the state in actual production, or on a contract basis. Output from inland wells in Burma has increased from 78 million gallons in 1962, before nationalization, to 186 million gallons in 1969. A new oil refinery was built in addition to the existing one; in 1970 it was still working at half capacity but it is hoped that the increased output will fill the gap.

REFERENCES

1. Allen, George C., Western Enterprise in Indonesia and Malaya: a study in economic development. London: G. Allen and Unwin, 1957.

2. Berrill, Kenneth, ed., Economic Development with Special Reference to East Asia. Proceedings of a conference of the International Economic Association. London: MacMillan, 1965.

3. Black, Eugene, Alternatives in Southeast Asia. New York: Praeger, 1969 - foreword by L.B.J.

4. Carnegie Endowment for International Peace, "The Lower Mekong," International Conciliation, May 1966, no. 558.

5. Cowan, Ch. D., ed., The Economic Development of Southeast Asia. New York: Praeger, 1964.

6. Higgins, B., *Indonesia: the crisis of the millstones*. Princeton, N.J.: Van Nostrand, 1963.

7. Ho, Alfred K., *The Far East in World Trade*. New York: Praeger, 1967.

8. Huh, Kyung-Mo, *Japan's trade in Asia: developments since 1926, prospects for 1970*. N.Y.: Praeger, 1966.

9. Karnow, Stanley, *Southeast Asia*. Time Inc., 1967.

10. Mills, Lennox A., *The New World of Southeast Asia*. University of Minnesota Press, 1949.

11. Morgan, Th. ed., *Economic Interdependence in Southeast Asia*. University of Wisconsin Press, 1969.

12. Onslow, Crawley, ed., *Asian Economic Development*. N.Y.C.: Praeger, 1965.

13. Paauw, Douglas S., *Planning Capital Inflows for Southeast Asia*. Washington, D.C.: National Planning Association, 1966.

14. Royal Institute of International Affairs, Far Eastern Dept., *Indochina 1945-1954*. London, 1954.

15. Schaaf, C. Hart, *The Lower Mekong: Challenge to Cooperation in Southeast Asia*. Princeton, N.J.: Van Nostrand, 1963.

16. *Underdevelopment and Economic Nationalism in Southeast Asia*, ed. by Frank H. Golay and others. Ithaca: Cornell University Press, 1969.

17. U.S. Library of Congress, Ref. Dept.: *Indochina: A Bibliography of the Land and People*. Washington, D.C., 1950.

CHAPTER XVIII

TRADE AND AID IN SOUTHEAST ASIA

The trend in the expansion of exports from the developing countries of Asia, over the two decades of the 1950's and the 1960's followed a pattern similar to that of other developing countries, i.e. their exports, which were mainly primary commodities, grew at a lower rate than the rate of growth in world trade which was about ten per cent. The reasons for the lag were the same also as for other developing countries: technological change was reducing the need for raw materials; synthetic products had in many instances displaced natural ones such as cotton, wool and rubber; the demand for foodstuffs was relatively inelastic in the richer countries, etc... However, there were exceptions to this trend: the most notable among them was Taiwan and also South Korea and Malaysia which registered high rates of growth in exports, and to a lesser extent, the Philippines and Thailand. Laos, which had started at a very low level, also greatly expanded its exports. The reasons behind the higher growth rates are connected with the choice these countries had to make between either export diversification or import substitution.

As seen later in this chapter, industrial expansion which is the prerequisite for both the above policies, became actually possible with the creation of the Asian Development Bank and more generally the availability of technical assistance and credit from foreign sources. The flow of external resources into Southeast Asia since the end of World War II came under either one or more of several forms: export earnings, credit from

suppliers, portfolio investment, direct private foreign
investment, official grants and loans, and technical
assistance and other aid extended by multilateral agencies and non-profit organizations. This chapter will
cover export trends in the countries studied and the
evolution of their international reserves positions.

Export Performance

Table XVIII/1 gives foreign trade data for the
countries of Southeast Asia and table XVIII/2 shows the
trend of these countries' exports over the period between
1955 and 1969. For purposes of comparison, data on
Japan's foreign trade have been added to these tables;
although Japan can hardly now be considered a developing
country, the policies it has adopted to expand its exports could probably serve as a model to be followed by
its neighbors. From table XVIII/1 it can be seen that
Taiwan expanded its exports at an annual rate of 52 per
cent between 1958 and 1969 and that South Korea's rate
for the same period was 35 per cent, compared with
Japan's rate of 41.5 per cent. Looking at table XVIII/2,
we see that these three countries have increased their
exports many times over since 1955, that Cambodia, Laos,
the Philippines and Thailand, have doubled the value of
their exports during the same period, while Malaysia and
Singapore do not show such a spectacular performance,
only because the level of their export sales was much
higher than that of the others in the base period. In
contrast, the level of exports from Burma, Ceylon,
Indonesia and South Vietnam, declined during the period
under review, the worst negative performance being that
of South Vietnam as a result of the war. Burma's exports
grew between 1950 and 1955, remained somewhat stationary

Table XVIII/1

SOUTHEAST ASIA: FOREIGN TRADE

(million dollars)

Country	Exports fob 1958	Exports fob 1969	Imports cif 1958	Imports cif 1969	Surplus or Deficit 1958	Surplus or Deficit 1969	Export Growth % p.a.
Burma	194	111[a]	204	112[a]	-10	- 1	-0.27
Cambodia	56	89[a]	76	116[a]	-20	-27	5.3
China (Taiwan)	156	1,050	226	1,213	-70	163	52.0
Indonesia	791	831	544	697	247	134	0.45
Laos	1.4	4	27	59	-25.6	-55	16.0
Malaysia[b]	616	1,651	542	1,175	74	476	15.0
Philippines	493	855	659	1,254	-166	-399	6.6
Singapore	1,026	1,549	1,222	2,040	-196	-491	4.5
Thailand	309	711	393	1,238	-84	-527	5.1
South Vietnam	55	12	232	668	-177	-656	-7.1
Ceylon	359	322	360	427	- 1	-105	-0.9
Korea	16	622	378	1,825	-362	-1203	35.0
Japan	2,877	16,043	3,034	15,026	-157	1017	41.5

Sources: International Monetary Fund, International Financial Statistics, Trade pages, and Direction of Trade, Country pages.

[a] 1968.   [b] includes east and west Malaysia.

up to 1960 when they started declining.   Indonesia's setback was mainly the outcome of inadequate domestic policies and inflationary conditions.   Ceylon's experience is studied below.

Diversification

It should be noted that the remarkable performance of Korea and Taiwan was almost entirely due to the

development of new export products. For instance, in
1969 Korea's traditional exports of rice and other
staples constituted only 25 per cent of the total, while
such manufactured goods as clothing, cotton fabrics, iron
concentrates and fish preparations made up the balance.
These were new items exported for the purpose of diversification. The case of Taiwan is very similar: while
seventy per cent of its exports consisted of sugar and
rice in 1958, these two commodities accounted for only
four per cent of the total value of its exports in 1969;
the balance was made up of such products as bananas,
canned mushrooms, canned pineapples, plywood, cotton
fabrics, and others. They reflect the creation or the
expansion of light domestic industries to produce for
export. Thus, these two countries are good examples
of how diversification of commodities exported can increase both the volume and the value of exports.

The case of Thailand is slightly different;
the proceeds from its exports which increased by a yearly
average of just over six per cent since 1960, included
traditional exports which are mainly rice, tin and rubber
as well as new agricultural products such as corn, kenaf
and tapioca products which accounted for about 20 per
cent of proceeds from export in 1969. The new products
offset to some extent the 50 per cent fall in the price
of rubber since 1960.

Malaysia avoided more than half the loss it
would have incurred from the fall in the price of its
rubber exports by increasing their volume. Timber and
iron ore are two products which were developed for export to make up the loss in rubber prices and register a
modest yearly increase in proceeds from exports during

the 1960's following a more sizable increase during the
1950's.

Import Substitution

On the advice of ECAFE, Ceylon planned to
replace as much as possible goods imported by domestic
production: it allocated 26 per cent of total funds for
development to industrial expansion and only 9 per cent
to its main export crops, thus overlooking the principle
of comparative advantage in order to change its production and exports patterns. The new manufactured goods
were to provide a surplus for export in the long-run
after replacing imports. This was planned in the belief
that exports would keep growing at at least the same rate
as during the 1950's, when their growth had averaged
about 1.6 per cent a year. The results were a disastrous
setback: exports declined during the 1960's instead of
expanding and this decline hurt the development of the
new import substitution industries for most of which raw
materials had to be imported. A look at table XVIII/3
giving international reserve positions will show that
Ceylon's international reserves took a plunge downward
which precluded imports of intermediate and equipment
goods to sustain the program of import substitution.
The result was a fall in domestic output because of restrictions on the import of the raw materials needed for
the new industries.

Viewed as a whole, industrialization progress
for the countries of Southeast Asia reflects various degrees of structural change and includes a wide spectrum
of activities, from the traditional mining, rice and timber processing to the large-scale modern enterprises,
passing by a large number of small cottage industries.

Table XVIII/2

TRENDS IN ASIAN EXPORTS: SELECTED COUNTRIES

(million dollars)

Country	1955	1958	1960	1969	% Change in Period Shown 1969 1955	1969 1958	1969 1960
Burma	227	194	226	111[a]	-51	-43	-51
Cambodia	42	56	70	89[a]	112	59	27
China (Taiwan)	123	156	164	1,050	552	414	389
Indonesia	946	791	840	831	-27	- 9	-18
Laos	1	1.4	1	4	300	185	
Malaysia[b]	1,964	616	1,189	1,651	39	66	13
Philippines	401	493	560	855	112	72	51
Singapore	1,101	1,026	1,136	1,549	15	24	12
Thailand	335	309	408	711	97	114	62
Vietnam (South)	69	55	86	12	-83	-78	-86
Ceylon	407	359	385	322	-16	- 5	-11
Korea	18	16	33	622	2,428	2,744	1,279
Japan	2,011	2,877	4,055	12,973	545	351	220

Source: I.M.F., International Financial Statistics and
Direction of Trade, relevant pages.

[a]1968.   [b]includes east and west Malaysia.

They all have development plans which have been more or
less efficiently formulated and implemented; they all
have been trying recently to give priority to national
ventures and to reduce, or restrict foreign investment -
or at least its hold over their economies. Finally, they
all have shown repercussions of developments in their
highly industrialized neighbor, Japan, more particularly
in the high increase in industrial activity registered
during the post-World War II years.

The data given in table XVIII/3 show each country's total holdings of gold, Special Drawing Rights (SDR's), reserve position with the International Monetary Fund and foreign exchange; they are given for selected years, starting with 1951 (the year of the boom created by the war in Korea) and reflect changes in the respective countries' fortunes during the intervening years up to 1969. Taiwan, Malaysia and Thailand, as well as Japan and South Korea seem to have greatly increased their international reserves, Burma and the Philippines are still below the 1951 level, while Indonesia and Ceylon have used up their reserves almost entirely. South Vietnam shows a sizable increase (80 per cent) in its reserves; however, considering its poor performance as regards exports, it could be surmised that this increase is mainly the result of United States expenditure in that country.

Sources of Funds for Development

Private foreign investments, public and multilateral loans and grants, and proceeds from exports have contributed a large share of the funds for financing development in Southeast Asia. As the new industrial projects started bringing in returns, an increasingly larger proportion of national income could be saved and invested, at least in some of the countries being studied. Of the other sources, there has been a definite shift from the period prior to World War II when private investments by nationals of the colonial powers were fairly substantial, to post World War II when the main contributions came from the World Bank group and more recently from the Asian Development Bank which is affiliated with the World Bank. A still more recent development - i.e. 1970-71 - is the large increase in Japan's contribution in both aid,

Table XVIII/3

SOUTHEAST ASIA: INTERNATIONAL RESERVE POSITIONS[a]

(million $'s)

Country	1951	1955	1958	1961	1965	1969
Burma	159	92	119	95	177	129
China (Taiwan)	49	79	137	136	300	443
Indonesia	511	307	217		21	6[b]
Malaysia	400	473	502	349	470	680
Philippines	247	155	92	54	193	121
Singapore					203	244
Thailand	358	301	306	454	739	985
S. Vietnam		125	159	175	178	227
Ceylon	217	211	172	90	73	40
Japan		769	861	1,666	2,152	3,654
S. Korea	38	96	146	207	146	553

Source: I.M.F., International Financial Statistics,
relevant numbers.

[a]The international reserve position, or international
liquidity, is a total of each country's holdings of gold,
Special Drawing Rights (SDR's as from 1970), Reserve
Positions in the Fund and foreign exchange.
[b]1967.

through multilateral agencies, and private investment to
its neighboring countries.

A rough estimate of the total amount of private
foreign investment in Southeast Asia before World War II,
was about $2.7 billion.[1] The largest outlay by a single
nation was made by the Dutch in the Dutch East Indies;
the British came next, with investments mainly in Burma,
what was then Malaya, and Thailand. Most of the American

[1]Mills, L.A., The New World of Southeast Asia, 1949,p.229.

investment was in the Philippines and that of the French
in Indochina.   Most of these outlays were invested in
the production of raw materials and food.

Since 1945, more than half of Western capital
investment has come from ploughed-back profits, not new
capital which has now a tendency to be risk-shy.   Also,
a greater share of new investment goes into manufacturing
projects.   Public loans and grants have come mainly from
the United States, Japan, as well as the other nations of
the Organization for Economic Cooperation and Development
(OECD).   Japan's aid channelled through multilateral
agencies was about 25 per cent of its total aid of $1.8
billion in 1970, and that was 44 per cent higher than in
1969.   The remaining 75 per cent went into export credits
and loans to finance development of natural resources.[2]

The main increase, however, has been in private
Japanese investments;   these reflect a complete change in
Japanese outlook which formerly concentrated on domestic
industries and invested abroad only in needed raw materials.   Thus, of the $3 billion worth of outlays by Jap-
anese firms outside their shores since the end of World
War II, $1.2 billion were invested during 1969 and 1970,
and most of these are in goods for export.   To prepare
the market for Japanese output most of the war reparations
(about $1.5 billion during the 1950's) were sent in goods
and services, not cash: bulldozers for the Philippine
jungles, a dam for South Vietnam, a hotel in Indonesia,
locomotives for Thailand, and even transistor radios and
television sets.   This naturally created a market for
spare parts and servicing firms, as well as the taste for

---

[2]I.M.F., International Financial News Survey, Vol. XXIII,
p. 151, May 1971.

more such articles.[3]

　　　Multilateral aid came from the World Bank group
of which the International Development Association (IDA)
plays a big role in Asia, and from the Asian Development
Bank (AsDB).　The latter was inaugurated at a meeting
held in Tokyo in November 1966;　the Finance Minister of
Japan was elected as its first President with a five-year
tenure.　Total subscriptions to the Bank added up to
$964 million from members as well as countries outside the
area.　The two largest contributors, of $200 million
each, were the United States and Japan.　The authorized
capital of the Bank was then set at $1,100 million.[4]　In
January 1967, at a meeting of a nine-nation Conference
for Agricultural Development in Southeast Asia, the
Special Agricultural Fund was created within the Asian
Development Bank;　it is in the nature of a trust fund
for soft loans to promote agricultural development.
Japan promised to contribute $100 million to this fund if
this amount was matched by contributions by the other industrialized countries.　In January 1969, Japan paid $20
million as its 1968 quota out of this amount, and total
amounts contributed to this fund added up to approximately
$125 million by the end of 1969.　Otherwise, the AsDB
raises the funds for its working capital by the sale of
bonds in various money markets and charges from 6 7/8 to
7 1/2 per cent on its loans.

　　　Such examples of projects to which the AsDB has
contributed loans include power transmission and distribution in Taiwan:　19-year loan at 7 1/2 per cent of

---

[3]The Wall Street Journal, May 5, 1971, p. 1.

[4]I.M.F., International Financial News Survey, Vol. XVIII,
No. 48, Dec. 2, 1966.

$12.88 million; rehabilitation of the irrigation system in Central Java, Indonesia: 25-year, 2 1/2 per cent loan of $2.7 million; technical assistance for the Nong Khai-Vientiane Bridge in Laos; a water distribution system in Singapore: 20-year loan at 7 1/2 per cent for $8.3 million; expansion of the port of Silx in Sarawak, Malaysia: 25-year loan at 7 1/2 per cent for $3.5 million; road construction and improvement in Mindanao, Philippines: 25-year loan at 7 1/2 per cent.

SOUTHEAST ASIA

Topics for Reading and Research

1. Agriculture: the advantages and limitations of the Green Revolution in Southeast Asia.

2. Development: the Lower Mekong River Basin as a multi-purpose project shared jointly by four states and financed internationally.

3. Economic structure: a comparison of the levels of per capita income between the various countries of Southeast Asia.

4. Industrialization: the results of import substitution industries compared with export diversification.

5. Foreign trade: composition, value and direction of foreign trade.

353

I N D E X